ETHICS IN ECONOMICS

ETHICS IN ECONOMICS

AN INTRODUCTION TO MORAL FRAMEWORKS

Jonathan B. Wight

STANFORD ECONOMICS AND FINANCE
An Imprint of Stanford University Press
Stanford, California

Stanford University Press
Stanford, California

Special discounts for bulk quantities of titles in the Stanford
Economics and Finance imprint are available to corporations,
professional associations, and other organizations. For details and
discount information, contact the special sales department of Stanford
University Press. Tel: (650) 736-1782, Fax: (650) 736-1784

Printed in the United States of America on acid-free,
archival-quality paper

Library of Congress Cataloging-in-Publication Data

Wight, Jonathan B., author.
Ethics in economics : an introduction to moral frameworks /
Jonathan B. Wight.
    pages cm
Includes bibliographical references and index.
ISBN 978-0-8047-9328-5 (cloth : alk. paper) —
ISBN 978-0-8047-9453-4 (pbk. : alk. paper)
1. Economics—Moral and ethical aspects. I. Title.
HB72.W537 2015
174'.4—dc23
2014036162
ISBN 978-0-8047-9456-5 (electronic)

Typeset by Thompson Type in 10/15 Sabon

To John *"Mort"* Morton
"Dum inter homines sumus, colamus humanitatem."
"As long as we are among humans, let us be humane."
—SENECA

Contents

Figures

Acknowledgments

MY EARLY INTEREST IN ETHICS IN ECONOMICS was aroused by experiences growing up in Africa and Latin America. Economic matters were enveloped in concerns about justice and human rights, and I quickly learned what Douglass North, Ronald Coase, and others have since proposed, that the *thoughtful* practice of economics and public policy cannot be isolated from institutions, history, culture, and path dependency. One important institution is the ethical framework within which economic life unfolds.

As a student, I had the good fortune of working for Rendigs Fels, who exposed me to pluralist ethics in economics. Fels and Stephen Buckles were the authors of *Casebook of Economic Problems and Policies: Practice in Thinking*, 5th edition (St. Paul, MN: West Publishing, 1981). This book influenced me because of the careful way it focused on the multiple values that should always be analyzed in considering public policies. My book goes further in giving recognition to pluralist principles in addition to values.

The idea for this book originated in a grant that John "Mort" Morton and I received from the John Templeton Foundation in 2005, via the National Council on Economic Education (today the Council for Economic Education). The grant allowed a group of scholars to gather for a conversation about what economics teachers should know about ethics. One of the things we discovered is the paucity of resources for teachers on this subject. We subsequently put together a book of lesson plans called *Teaching the Ethical Foundations of Economics* (2007). A large debt is owed to those authors, to the Templeton Foundation, and to the teachers who tested and used the plans in the classroom. A particularly strong acknowledgment is owed to Mort Morton, to whom this book is dedicated, for his inspiration, leadership, and support over many years.

Although teachers now had a resource, a problem remained in that few textbooks were of the length and style to appeal to undergraduates. Charles Wilber (formerly of Notre Dame) and I decided to tackle that problem by cowriting a book. We eventually headed our separate ways as authors, but Chuck's vision and principles remain an important part of my commitment to this project.

My department chairs, Bob Schmidt and Dean Croushore, generously provided me the opportunity to teach a dedicated class every fall on Ethics and Economics. Most of the chapters in this book received insights and criticisms from students going back to 2006, and several deserve particular mention: Devin Ralston, Justin Weiss, Flemming Schneider, Vance Pilkington, and Nabila Rahman. Coinstructing my first teaching of this subject with colleague Douglas Hicks also made it easier. Some chapters were presented at conferences and workshops, and I am grateful to The Association for Social Economics for providing an exciting and invigorating group in which to test out ideas. The Association for Private Enterprise Education likewise offered a productive atmosphere for thinking about ethics in economics.

Many chapters in this book draw on ideas from Adam Smith. The Liberty Fund played an important role in enhancing my understanding of Smith through its seminar programs and its publications in print and on-line; this support led to a prior book, *Saving Adam Smith: A Tale of Wealth, Transformation, and Virtue* (2002). A market without morals makes little sense to the man whose major work, *The Theory of Moral Sentiments* (1759), was to understand the instinctive bonds of social cooperation.

In 2009 the University of Richmond provided funds for a "Symposium on Emotions, Natural Selection and Rationality" (co-organized with Elias Khalil), which provided insights used in Chapters 8 and 9. I am indebted to Khalil, Paul Zak, and others for that experience. In 2010 the University of Richmond launched a major in Philosophy, Politics, Economics and Law (PPEL). I have benefited greatly from its faculty and its first director, philosopher David Lefkowitz.

A number of colleagues and friends added immensely to my understanding of ethics and economics. George DeMartino published *The*

Economist's Oath: On the Need for and Content of Professional Economic Ethics (2011), which bolstered my conviction that the market was ready for the contents of this book. For fourteen years, Sandra Peart and David Levy have provided a yearly Summer Institute on the History of Economic Thought. Here we heard from James Buchanan about his longstanding interest in ethical issues. Vernon Smith also came to campus and has been a source of inspiration and support. Deirdre McCloskey, long a champion of Adam Smith and virtue ethics, provided continued sustenance at conferences. David Colander has likewise been generous with his time and ideas. David Warsh, the economic journalist (www.economicprincipals.com/), has kept ethics in economics in his crosshairs.

Scott Davis helped lead a cross-disciplinary campus reading of Smith's *The Theory of Moral Sentiments* (along with the late Clarence Jung) way back in 1995–1996. He also graciously read this manuscript and made many useful suggestions. Mark White, at the College of Staten Island, read the manuscript and particularly helped refine my treatment of Kantian ethics. He is also the co-founder of the blog, "Economics and Ethics" (www.economicsandethics.org/). Jonathan Anomaly read the entire manuscript with a fine editing eye and made numerous valuable suggestions. David George and Jonas Feit also read the entire manuscript and added helpful suggestions. Erik Craft read several chapters with a keen eye and insightful comments.

I am grateful to the following additional colleagues and friends who assisted on parts of the project, with the usual disclaimer of liability: Al Barrera, Jason Brennan, Marty Calkins, Joanne Ciulla, Richard Dagger, Rob Dolan, Tricia Fanney, Jack Fiedler, Rob Garnett, Jim Hall, Tim Hamilton, Robert Hetzel, Dan Hausman, Rob James, Linda MacCammon, Tim Madigan, Shakun Mago, KimMarie McGoldrick, Julie Nelson, Rob Phillips, Terry Price, Mason Schreck, Clair Smith, and Jean McNall Wight.

Finally, I want to thank my editor at Stanford University Press, Margo Beth Fleming, for her wonderful support, James Holt for able editorial assistance, and Margaret Pinette for valuable manuscript editing.

Preface

TWO IDEAS MOTIVATE THE WRITING OF THIS BOOK. First, critical thinking is enhanced when economists understand how moral norms can help address potential market failure in the presence of moral hazards. If people in a variety of settings are motivated by principles other than satisfying their own preferences, exploring these behaviors can enhance the standard economic model. Second, economists regularly engage in public policy discussions using normative concepts like welfare and efficiency. Many are unaware that these practices involve a particular form of ethical analysis, one that has evolved in a controversial way. As a result, policy advice about economic efficiency becomes questionable in some settings.

If economics is to have validity, the nature of underlying institutional frameworks (including ethical norms) must be uncovered. Although many questions in economics are purely scientific, most policy analyses rely on a conscious or unconscious adoption of an ethical framework and related value judgments. This book intends to make those connections more visible and explicit. Exploring ethics in economics offers the hope of enhancing critical thinking and better preparing readers for a complex world.

Alfred Marshall, whose *Principles of Economics* textbook set the stage for twentieth-century economics, wrote this in the preface to the first edition:

> . . . ethical forces are among those of which the economist has to take account. Attempts have indeed been made to construct an abstract science with regard to the actions of an "economic man," who is under no ethical influences and who pursues pecuniary gain warily and energetically, but mechanically and selfishly. But they have not been successful.[1]

Marshall wrote those words in 1890, and in the next hundred years economists attempted to extricate ethical reasoning from the field. The "economic way of thinking" became purportedly purely scientific. George

Stigler, who won the Nobel Prize in 1982, opined, "The basic role of the *scientist* in public policy, therefore, is that of establishing the costs and benefits of alternative institutional arrangements."[2] In this statement Stigler adopts a particular moral *framework* (that only consequences matter) and a particular moral *value* for evaluating consequences (dollar costs and benefits as a proxy for welfare). "Economics is finally at the threshold of its golden age," Stigler wrote in 1965.[3]

Stigler's pronouncement was prophetic, and the methods of economists soon overran the fields of political science and sociology and made significant inroads into law and other fields. But, in a larger sense, as economics spread to other subjects, the discipline also drew inward in terms of the questions, methods, and goals pursued. Modern economists became less active in liberal education because, unlike their forebears, they rarely examined, or debated, the moral foundations of their own activities.[4]

A liberal education requires stretching one's critical thinking skills in ways that are only partially addressed by traditional methods in economics.[5] Public policy problems cross disciplinary boundaries and raise substantial normative questions. Indeed, if economists maintain that they do not rely on ethics at all, this is troublesome. If efficiency is viewed simply as a "fact," instead of as an evaluative construct, for which alternatives exist, it creates intellectual blinders for anyone doing public policy work. Implicit moral judgments in economics should be subject to scrutiny. We should unpack and examine the ethical framework that informs the standard economic approach and consider its alternatives.

Adam Smith, in the eighteenth-century Enlightenment, saw economics as a branch of moral philosophy. Over the last few decades, economists have again engaged in fruitful dialogue with philosophers. The result of ignoring these linkages, in the words of Nobel laureate Amartya Sen, is that "modern economics has been substantially impoverished by the distance that has grown between economics and ethics."[6] As Marshall predicted, the effort to eliminate ethics would fail. It failed because examining ethical frameworks enhances understanding and prediction, and it failed because policy analysis cannot be done in isolation from ethical choices. Hence, "a well-trained economist should be able to scrutinize the moral underpinnings of a policy statement."[7]

Not all economists would agree. Some would no doubt insist that it is "folly" to suppose that "devotion to moral principles offers the solution of social problems."[8] This statement reveals a semantic problem. Morality in some contexts is conflated with subservience to religious dogmas or socialist ideals about altruism; experience shows that the resulting policies can produce horrific outcomes. Modern economics is a science that offers hope for progress and freedom. Standard economics is a powerful tool for both understanding and changing the world for the better. Yet economists cannot be blind to the possibility that looking beyond preference satisfaction and efficiency can offer coherent and rational arguments for enhancing the world also. Defining and explaining a pluralist approach to ethics is the first task. In the opinion of Sen, who pioneered the resurgence of interest in ethics in economics, "An economic analyst ultimately has to juggle many balls, even if a little clumsily, rather than giving a superb display of virtuosity with one little ball [for example, efficiency]."[9]

Part I defends the idea that ethical inquiry is an essential component of critical thinking in economics and identifies three commonly used approaches. Part II investigates the economic welfare model, which relies on a particular version of outcome-oriented ethics, and explores why it is both powerful and controversial. (Chapter 4 is a review of microeconomics and may be omitted by advanced readers.) Part III explores the ways in which market and political processes rely on more than just efficiency-based ethics. One conclusion is that economists should be careful about what we think we know, and even more careful in recommending policies, when the ethical analysis is narrowly focused or unexamined.

PART I

Moral Frameworks

CHAPTER I

Why Ethics Matters

Economics is thought to rely on the hardheaded calculation of rational self-interest; ethics is often portrayed as mushy do-goodism. Is there any useful connection between these subjects? This chapter makes the central bonds between these topics clearer and shows why critical thinking in economics can sometimes rely on a pluralist understanding of ethics. In addition to concern for an efficient outcome, people are motivated by considerations of justice and principles of duty and virtue. Different ethical frameworks offer complementary insights for positive and normative economic analyses.

THE MORAL ECOSYSTEM

O. J. Simpson—a flamboyant former professional football star and actor—was acquitted of double homicide in one of the twentieth century's most contentious jury trials. In 2006, publisher Rupert Murdoch planned to release Simpson's quasi-autobiographical account, *If I Did It*, of how he "might" have killed his ex-wife Nicole and Ronald Goldman. The public reacted to this news with outrage, and the book and a related television show were ultimately canceled amid widespread mockery.[1]

But why should there be outrage? Many people wanted to read the book! Those who did not would not be forced to buy it. Standard economic logic would say that efficiency is enhanced when consumers get to buy the products they desire. So what was the problem? Clearly, a majority of citizens were repulsed by the notion that Simpson and his publisher were attempting to cash in on his notoriety as a potential murderer. Simpson's flirtation with a blockbuster confession was morally repugnant because *moral norms were being violated.*

In 2014 another celebrity, billionaire Donald Sterling, owner of the Los Angeles Clippers basketball team, was caught on tape making derogatory comments about his African American players and fans. The comments went viral over the Internet, causing widespread condemnation. Within days, major corporations withdrew their endorsements, and the National Basketball Association imposed a lifetime ban on Sterling. Violating moral norms (not showing proper respect for others) can have profound impacts in the marketplace.

Moral norms change, of course, so what was considered outrageous fifty years ago (selling on Sundays) is now widely acceptable in the United States. And an action that was considered by many to be proper three centuries ago (selling other human beings) is now considered abhorrent. Markets operate within a moral ecosystem—but that environment is not well understood by economists. The incorporation of ethical reasoning is as essential for economists as it is for anyone else seeking a liberal education—that is, as a preparation for tackling complex, diverse, and changing problems in real-world settings.

Ethics Defined

There are many ways to define what is meant by ethics. One working definition is:

Ethics is the study of one's proper interactions with others: It is the analysis of right and wrong.[2]

Ethical beliefs and practices constitute a vast and unseen institutional force. A famous example is the generous tip that a satisfied traveler leaves at a highway restaurant—an eatery to which she never intends to return. Why would anyone leave a tip when there is no expectation of future reward? The typical diner shrugs and says it is *customary* to show generosity for good service; giving a tip is simply the "right thing to do." However, we can imagine deeper answers than this. Economic actors may leave a gratuity because they are *altruistic*; or diners may not want to incur the social *stigma* of not tipping; or they may believe that they have a *duty* to act in certain ways; or they self-consciously act in ways thought to be *virtuous*. A pluralist account of why we tip captures the complexity of ethical motivation. Of course, not everyone tips, so the simplistic account of the consumer as a selfish miser—*Homo economicus* or *economic man*—is correct much of the time. But the selfish actor model cannot fully explain highway tips or help us fully understand why O. J. Simpson's book was booed out of the market before production.

Enlightened Self-Interest

Human nature is thus complex and contradictory: sometimes selfish, sometimes altruistic, and sometimes just.[3] Ethical egoism—the norm of doing best by "looking out for number one"—should never be underestimated. George Washington, camped at Valley Forge, Pennsylvania, during the harsh winter of 1778, learned this the hard way. Washington inspired his officers and troops to great personal sacrifices under the patriotic banner of independence.[4] He called on them to fulfill their duties. At the same time, the Pennsylvania legislature adopted price controls on food that caused widespread shortages. Many farmers reacted to the law by selling their grain on the black market at higher prices to the rival British army while Washington's troops starved. Washington stoically observed:

We must take the passions of men as nature has given them, and those principles as a guide, which are generally the rule of action. I do not mean to exclude altogether the idea of patriotism. I know it exists, and I know it has done much in the present contest. But I will venture to assert, that a great and lasting war can never be supported on this principle alone. It must be aided by a prospect of interest, or some reward.[5]

Washington, an astute observer, notes that different men, at different times, are moved by different motivations. No one size fits all, and in marshaling an army he had to understand these differing motives and instincts. Stereotypes of the greedy banker or the completely selfless saint do not help much because few people operate at these extremes. Most people, according to one recent theory, are "strong reciprocators" who are predisposed to cooperate and willing to incur costs on themselves to punish those who violate moral norms, even when it is difficult to conceive that such investments will recoup in the future.[6] To some extent, people are pliable, and customs or rituals that evoke and bolster public-spirited motives can sway individual preferences toward prosocial aims.

Economists do not assume that people are always selfish because people may have preferences that are other-regarding. Being self-interested is not the same as being selfish (as elaborated in Chapters 8 and 9). Adam Smith's great work, *The Wealth of Nations* (1776), explores the workings of markets under the assumption that people are motived by self-interest. He notes:

... man has almost constant occasion for the help of his brethren, and it is in vain for him to expect it from their benevolence only. . . . . It is not from the benevolence of the butcher, the brewer, or the baker, that we expect our dinner, but from their regard to their own interest. We address ourselves, not to their humanity but to their self-love, and never talk to them of our own necessities but of their advantage.[7]

Looking after oneself is instinctual, Smith observes, and following this instinct under the right circumstances can be virtuous in terms of one's own responsibilities and can also produce desirable outcomes for society as a whole.

The mistake some people make is to think that Smith thereby adopts the moral lens of ethical egoism. As discussed more fully in Chapters 8 and 9, Smith denounces egoistic behaviors. His first book, *The Theory of Moral Sentiments* (1759), shows how moral norms would arise to constrain selfish instincts. Far from being anonymous and autonomous agents, people are social creatures with strong instincts for sociability. Even the "greatest ruffian, the most hardened violator of the laws of society" is not altogether without social feelings.[8] Feelings, rather than rational calculations, are the mechanism through which nature adapts humans for successful cooperation in society, according to Smith.

The Social Ethical Lens

Reaching emotional equilibrium with our peers is one of our strongest passions. This forms the basis for the development of ethical norms that lower the transactions cost in trade. Using Smith's model, Charles Darwin observes that the greatest distinction between humans and other animals is not our rational minds but our moral capabilities, which undergird our widespread cooperation. These capabilities are honed instinctual responses. In his conclusion to *The Descent of Man* (1871), Darwin notes, "Any instinct, permanently stronger or more enduring than another, gives rise to a feeling which we express by saying that it ought to be obeyed."[9]

The social instincts work initially through the human capacity to sympathize with others but are strengthened by instruction, exercise, and habit. Ethical beliefs and practices make up the formal and informal rules that generate trust, promote interdependencies, and spur work productivity in a myriad of ways. In everyday economic life there is a vast arena in which economic behavior is shaped by social instincts and ethical mores (as elaborated in Chapters 7 to 12).

In 1943 Norman Rockwell painted a famous illustration for the *Saturday Evening Post* entitled, "Freedom from Want."[10] It depicts an extended family crowding around the dining room table, eagerly awaiting the arrival of a plump roasted turkey. The painting highlights the desire for material outcomes (the turkey), and the individuals, whose stomachs are no doubt growling, hope that they will receive a large serving of the bird for their own personal enjoyment. Yet the painting also demonstrates commitment to concepts beyond the individual, in the sharing of sympathies and mutual sacrifice. The country at that time was pulling out of the Great Depression and fighting wars on two fronts. Although economic behavior is surely in part about self-interest and material enrichment, Nancy Folbre astutely observes, "Markets cannot function effectively outside the framework of families and communities built on values of love, obligation, and reciprocity."[11]

Families are more than collections of atomistic economic agents; members specialize and make investments with a larger focus than the self. Women in particular take on roles of caregiving that are poorly acknowledged or modeled by standard economic theory. Authentic emotional commitment, as opposed to utility maximization, is often a significant decision driver and determination of quality.[12] Everyone who eats at Rockwell's dinner table implicitly (and often unconsciously) accepts the basic ethical norms of the social group, which extends beyond the family to considerations of civic and national duties. People are bound together in a shared endeavor and celebrate togetherness in ritual feasts like Thanksgiving. Although people may be selfish, they restrain themselves because of ethical commitments that do not fully rely on a calculation of gains and losses. Building on this notion, Kenneth Boulding entitled his presidential address to the American Economic Association in 1968, "Economics as a

Moral Science." It advances the idea that traditions and motives beyond enlightened self-interest are at work in economic life:

> In facing decisions, especially those which involve other people, as virtually all decisions do, we are faced with two very different frameworks of judgment. The first of these is the economic ethic of total cost–benefit analysis. . . . It is an ethic of calculation. . . . This type of decision-making, however, does not exhaust the immense complexities of the human organism, and we have to recognize that there is in the world another type of decision-making, in which the decision-maker elects something, not because of the effects that it will have, but because of what he "is," that is, how he perceives his own identity.[13]

If standard economics relies on the winds of self-interest, ethics in economics offers a complementary understanding of hidden currents and tides that move actors on the commercial stage—workers, suppliers, managers, and customers. Ethics provides the institutional framework within which economic activity unfolds, intertwined with concepts of personal meaning, duties, virtues, and social feelings of moral equilibrium.

Positive and Normative Ethics

The study of how people actually reach ethical decisions is called **positive ethics**. Proposing a preferred method of how people *ought* to make ethical decisions is called **normative ethics**. A good theory of normative ethics would likely contain an implicit notion of how people actually can make ethical judgments (positive ethics). When Adam Smith argues that humans learn to moderate their selfishness through aligning moral sentiments, he is making claims about both how people *can* make ethical decisions and how a properly socialized person *ought* to make ethical decisions. Knowing something about human capabilities, both biological and psychological, plays a part in the evaluation of a moral theory: *Ought* implies *can*.

Positive and Normative Economics

Positive economics is the study of the economy, as it currently exists (for example, the discernment of facts). Positive economics can be used to make predictions, based on models of how the world works. Predictive statements take the form, "*If* this happens, then *this* would be the outcome." A thesis of this book is that economists can better understand and predict when they consider ethical beliefs and commitments (for example, when they better understand positive ethics).

Normative economics entails a judgment about the kinds of actions that *ought* to be taken. A second thesis of this book is that economists can provide sounder policy advice when they consider a broader ethical landscape (for example, when they better understand normative ethics). The division between positive and normative economics is not precise. It is not possible to develop a science of facts and objective theories alone because value judgments play a critical role in the selection, collection, and analysis of information. Moreover, the act of carrying out economic research can change the facts, with ethical repercussions. Accordingly, science progresses better when practitioners adhere to ethical norms of truth seeking and honesty, themes developed in Chapter 12.

The following section demonstrates why using economic logic in the absence of complementary ethical frameworks proves to be an expensive lesson for General Motors.

THREE ETHICAL FRAMEWORKS

Economists typically posit that decisions should be made by comparing costs and benefits at the margin. Following this blindly can produce problems unless the wider ethical landscape is considered. To illustrate, this section uses a case study of automobile safety to introduce three different ethical approaches.

The Chevy Malibu Case

In July 1999, a jury assessed $4.9 *billion* in damages against General Motors (GM) for selling the Chevrolet Malibu, a car with a dangerous fuel tank placement that was implicated in a number of fiery crashes. The reason the award was so large is that the jury discovered that GM managers had *known* about the problem and had done nothing to correct it. This case provides an informative window into the world of ethics and economics.

Here are the facts: A GM engineer's secret memorandum calculated that fixing the known fuel-tank problem would cost $8.59 per car. But leaving the car as it was would cost even less, only $2.40 per car (based on settling the product liability lawsuits, with an average expected pay-out of $200,000 per life). Every car *not* fixed earned GM an expected additional profit of $6.19 per car. In considering the costs and benefits for the company, GM managers decided not to fix the fuel tank. Nor did they inform consumers about the issue.[14]

The engineer's memorandum represents a standard way of thinking at the margin about economic costs and benefits. The premise for this viewpoint is that people make voluntary trades that satisfy their own preferences and thus improve their own welfares. Hence, people evaluate what they will gain and what they will lose, and they choose the outcome that maximizes their own individual gain or minimizes their individual loss. In this mind-set it is rational and desirable to take an action as long as the *incremental benefits* of that action exceed the *incremental costs*. It is not only GM engineers who make such economic calculations; consumers do also. Some consumers do not want the safest car possible, because that would make the car prohibitively expensive. Through trial and error, the market discovers the "correct" amount of safety by finding the point at which the marginal private cost (MC) of safety equals the marginal private benefit (MB) of safety.[15]

From the perspective of GM, the $8.59 cost to fix the fuel tank represents the "opportunity cost" to the company of fixing each tank. The value of the lives saved represents the benefit. In wrongful death settlements, courts generally measure the dollar value of a life saved by what the person *would* have earned had he or she remained alive and working for a normal time period.[16] Hence, not all lives are valued the same in legal cases. The economic analysis of whether to fix the fuel tank thus relies on a theory that low-income people would prefer to buy an inexpensive car—even if it is more dangerous—than no car at all. Because there are many cars to choose from, consumers who prefer a safer car can choose that option.

The ethical issues involved in automobile safety can seem overwhelming. Fortunately, there are three standard ways of conceptualizing ethical issues. The three approaches are related, as illustrated in the following schema:[17]

(1) Economic Agent → (2) Action → (3) Outcomes

An economic *agent* takes an *action* that is expected to produce certain *outcomes*. Ethical frameworks differ in their attention to different stages of this progression.

Outcome-Based Ethics (Consequentialism)

The implicit moral framework apparently used by GM managers was outcome-based ethics (Stage 3). More precisely, the particular form of consequentialism used was corporate *ethical egoism*: The right course of action is that expected to produce the best outcome for the corporation. One problem with ethical egoism is that it severely limits the scope of analysis, in this case to the expected outcomes for GM alone. Because one's actions can produce negative consequences for others, many consequentialists would say that actions should be judged not simply by their effects on oneself but by their impacts on others or society at large.

Normative welfare economics also focuses on step (3) but with an important distinction. Economists typically emphasize a different outcome—economic efficiency. Economists try to answer the question: What action or policy would produce the largest net economic value for society *as a whole*, and not simply to one particular company or its shareholders? By considering a wider universe that includes all consumers and producers, standard welfare theory would find that GM's decisions were not efficient. If consumers are misled about the safety of the car (not informed about the faulty fuel tank), the outcome does not maximize the dollar value created because consumers were not allowed to make informed rational judgments as to what to buy. This situation creates a market failure because of **asymmetric information**: One party to the transaction (in this case GM) has relevant information not available to the other side. This creates a **moral hazard** because one party to the transaction has an incentive to do the wrong thing. Hence, even though GM managers used the economic way of thinking (analyzing marginal costs and marginal benefits), their scope of analysis was too narrowly focused to produce an outcome that economists would generally ascribe to as being desirable.

When certain basic conditions are present, however—the existence of competition, no asymmetric information, and no external costs like pollution—a market left to its own devices is said to get close to the outcome of maximizing the net dollar value created for the entire class of consumers and producers in the long run (see Chapters 4 and 5 for elaboration). If these circumstances exist, people can follow their own best interests, and the results will be equivalent to maximizing economic welfare for society at large.

Other consequentialists dispute the notion that human "welfare" can or should be measured by the net economic value produced in markets. The most famous version of consequentialism is Jeremy Bentham's **classical utilitarianism** (Chapter 2). Bentham would agree with economists that welfare should be measured by the calculation of costs and benefits, but these should not be denominated in dollars and cents but in psychological pleasures and pains. Classical utilitarians would say the decision not to fix the Malibu's gas tank did not pass the moral smell test because the slight additional profit from GM's decision ($6.19 per car) would give shareholders a miniscule increase in pleasure. But the cases of death and burns to customers would create enormous physical and emotional pain for the victims and their families that would be likely to far outweigh any pleasure generated for shareholders.

Other consequentialists might argue that the best outcome requires a different metric, such as, which outcome is the most fair? Or, which promotes the greatest freedom? Or, rather than maximizing any one outcome, what *mix* of outcomes produces the best compromise between efficiency and equity or between safety and freedom?

Duty- and Rule-Based Ethics

The second moral framework asks whether the action itself is moral (Stage 2). An action has *intrinsic* value if it is valuable for its own sake and not in regard to the outcomes produced. Stage 2 asks the question, "What action am I duty- or rule-bound to make, either by a commitment to moral principle or allegiance to religious law?" Hence, a different argument against ethical egoism comes from **duty- and rule-based** ethicists. These viewpoints vary, but they derive from the notion that one's decisions ought to reflect one's duty (either to Kant's rational process or to rules given by God). GM's business calculation *not* to fix the gas tank fails the moral test from the duty framework because it shows a disregard for the basic dignity and worth of every human being. By failing to fix the tank, GM managers were essentially using others *only* as a means to their own ends and disregarding basic moral norms of justice (Chapter 3).

One can find a surprising justification for the duty-based view in the writings of Milton Friedman, a Nobel Prize–winning economist who championed the notion that businesses should focus on making profits.[18] Profits are a signal that provides an incentive to allocate resources toward making products most desired by consumers. "Few trends could so thoroughly undermine the very foundations of our free society," Friedman wrote, "as the acceptance by corporate officials of a social responsibility other than to make as much money for their stockholders as possible."[19] Friedman mainly supported capitalism because he thought it is the economic system most compatible with maximizing liberty. At the same time, he also thought it provides the greatest economic value to consumers. Both freedom and economic value are consequentialist outcomes that can be used to justify capitalism. But Friedman did not think that corporate executives could therefore ignore moral rules and duties. On the contrary, the business manager is *duty bound* to carry out the wishes of shareholders who own the company. Friedman's story explicitly relies on managers adhering to nonconsequentialist ethics!

Friedman also inserted an explicit moral caveat. Managers, Friedman asserts, ought to maximize profits "while conforming to the basic rules of the society, both those embodied in law and those embodied in ethical custom."[20] In other words, there is a larger moral universe within which managers operate. The cost–benefit analysis is fine—as long as managers *first* comply with basic moral duties that are nonconsequentialist. Friedman was explicitly presented with this quandary: Suppose a company president learns that his factories are releasing a harmful chemical into the local community. The pollutant is not covered by current environmental regulations. What should the company president do? Friedman's response was unequivocal: The right course of action is to immediately disclose the information to the public.[21] In other words, it is not enough simply to obey the law. Individuals cannot hide behind a corporate shield and must take moral responsibility for their behaviors when others are affected.

So a key complaint against GM managers is that they failed to consider basic ethical duties toward other human beings. The decision not to fix the tank lacked adherence to common norms of treating others with minimal respect as moral equals. A basic moral rule in many religions is, "Do unto others as you would have them do unto you." Basic norms of justice appear to have been abridged, which is perhaps why the jury acted with apparent outrage in assigning such a huge award to the injured parties in the Malibu case.

Virtue-Based (or Character) Ethics

The third approach starts with the *person* in Stage 1 and examines the *motives* for action. It brings to light issues of character that relate to personal growth. It asks, "What way of being is virtuous, and how and why should I become such a virtuous person?" It is fine and well to talk about duties and rules, but why should anyone be ethical in the first place? Virtue ethicists argue that it is important to start by cultivating managers of character who have developed self-control before discussing the duties and rules they are expected to follow.

To virtue ethicists, the GM managers' decision fails the smell test *not* because of the calculated outcomes (pleasure and pain, or profit and loss) and *not* because of rules and duties but simply because of commonplace notions of what a good person should do if confronted with a similar choice. Would a good person be able to sleep at night knowing that she had failed to fix a faulty gas tank for less than $9 per car and then lied about it to the public through silence?

Attention to a wider scope of ethical analysis might have averted personal tragedies for some consumers and ultimately a financial disaster for the company itself. Unfortunately, it does not appear that executives learned from this experience. In 2014 it came to light that GM had also known for more than a decade about a faulty ignition switch on many of its models. When jostled during driving, the switch could shut off, disabling power steering, power brakes, and, most important, airbags. GM's managers decided not to fix the switch, which cost less than $5, nor did it inform the public of this choice.[22]

A WIDER ETHICAL LENS

Public debates about policies, just like jury deliberations about GM's liability, are rarely orderly. That is, arguments come at us from all directions. Although such discussions can appear cacophonous, we can learn to categorize the viewpoints in terms of the moral argument advanced: whether it is about consequences, or duties and rules, or the character of the persons involved. Using a "three-dimensional approach" to frame a discussion may take some time but offers insights not available when we stick within one ethical framework.

Once ingrained, the habit of seeing "the 3-D picture" of ethical frameworks can be helpful in understanding competing points of view. If we asked an average consumer why she does not eat pork, the answer might be, "I don't like the taste." One's preferences and the desire to enhance one's own welfare are good ways to model this behavior. If you asked a devout Muslim or Jew why he does not eat pork, the answer instead might be, "One ought to make decisions in accordance with religious law. Sacred texts forbid eating the flesh of a pig; therefore it is wrong to eat bacon, ham, and other such products." This person's decision is based on a duty to obey a God-given rule, rather than on a particular consequence or outcome.[23] (A different and more widespread philosophical version of duty-ethics arises from the Kantian respect for rationality, covered in Chapter 3.)

Finally, asking vegetarians why they do not eat pork might evoke a third type of response. A vegetarian might say, "I want to live the life of a virtuous person. I ask myself, 'What would Mahatma Gandhi do?' and try to follow that path, regardless of the imposition on me personally." This approach explores the intentions and feelings of someone who is striving to lead a life of transformation and personal growth. It relates to qualities and habits of *character*. The three basic approaches (consequences, duties/rules, and virtues) are not mutually exclusive. In addition to personal growth, a vegetarian might argue that eating fruits and nuts adheres to divine law.[24] Another vegetarian might argue that not eating meat produces a desired environmental outcome (sustaining the planet). Vegetarianism is supported by appeals to all three types of ethical arguments.

Any typology that lumps the diversity of ethical beliefs into three superstructures such as this will encounter problems and fuzzy distinctions. There is substantial overlap. Economists might argue, for example, that duty- and virtue-based ethics are really just variations of the standard economic approach. The devout Muslim, for example, has a "preference" for Islam and is maximizing his own utility by adhering to its laws. Likewise, the environmentally conscious vegetarian has a "preference" for a sustainable ecosystem; her apparent altruism is simply self-interest in trying to save the Earth. According to this view, interpersonal interdependencies can be modeled in utility functions through "other-regarding" preferences.

The problem with trying to cram everything into a utility maximization model is that too much of importance gets distorted or left out entirely. Virtue ethics (at least Smith's version) helps us understand how someone could come to internalize the view that one ought to do the "right" thing, compatible with moral *feelings*, and not because a predicted outcome would follow. One's reasoning process consists in aligning sympathetic convictions, in addition to making calculations of gain or loss. Smith insists that sympathetic reactions "are always felt so instantaneously" that these cannot be part of the calculus of maximizing self-interest.[25] Moreover, the rational calculating model requires too much rationality, and humans are weak at predicting outcomes (see Chapter 8). Other criticisms arise from the new field of behavioral economics, from debates over the meaning of rationality, and from other sources. These discussions are partially addressed in Chapter 6.

Amartya Sen, a modern champion of ethics and economics, won the Nobel Prize in 1998. Sen demonstrates the shortcomings of the utility maximization model with a parable about "rational fools":

"Where is the railway station?" he asks me. "There," I say, pointing at the post office, "and would you please post this letter for me on the way?" "Yes," he says, determined to open the envelope and check whether it contains something valuable.[26]

What is at issue for Sen is not whether people give an honest answer to every question but whether they give self-utility-maximizing answers "often enough to make that the appropriate general assumption for economic theory." Sen argues that commitments, such as to truth telling, are internal moral constraints on maximizing behavior. A commitment can entail a *counter*preferential choice. A worker wants to relax, but she has made a commitment to her boss. Commitments, and the social relations within which they are embedded, are important for workplace loyalty and motivation where it is difficult and expensive for employers to monitor employees. In Smith's moral sentiments model, loyalty can motivate behavior and may derive from considerations beyond promotion or reward.

The rational economic actor model is analytically useful in many situations, but rejecting any consideration other than self-interest "seems to impose a wholly arbitrary limitation on the notion of rationality."[27] Sen argues, "Economic theory has been much preoccupied with this rational fool decked in the glory of his one all-purpose preference ordering. To make room for the different concepts related to his behavior we need a more elaborate structure."[28]

ETHICAL PLURALISM

A more elaborate structure would consider the likelihood that people make choices within a pluralist moral ecosystem, that is, some mix of considering outcomes, conforming actions to principles, and exploring character or virtue as part of meaning and identity. Pluralism can be understood in two ways. One way is *descriptively*, through demonstrating that different moral values or principles are sometimes involved in people's decision making and that these cannot be reduced to a single set such as Bentham's utilitarianism (Chapter 2), Kant's categorical imperative (Chapter 3), or Aristotle's virtue theory (Chapter 3). A second way pluralism operates is *normatively*, through demonstrations that seemingly different principles are at times necessary for the operation of another. For example, we noted earlier that corporate profits, to Friedman, are an instrument for promoting the consequentialist goal of efficient resource allocations; they serve the ultimate interests of consumers. But this consequentialist aim cannot be realized unless business managers are virtuous in adhering to their fiduciary duties to shareholders and to wider duties in society. In this light, the aspects of action that different moral theories focus on do not so much *compete* with each other as *complete* each other.[29] Ethical pluralism is addressed throughout the book and especially in the concluding section in Chapter 3, "Looking Ahead," and in Chapter 12.

This book frequently quotes from Nobel Prize winners in economics.[30] This alerts readers to the fact that ethical discourse is not only how the modern discipline of economics began in the eighteenth century with Adam Smith but also how ethical reasoning has moved to the forefront of many issues that bright minds are working on today. As one example, five Nobel laureates in economics recently pushed for a more nuanced approach to understanding social progress, going beyond a dollar accounting of human welfare.[31] To do this they needed to consider a wider moral universe.

In the 1840s and 1850s Robert Lumpkin operated one of the world's largest auction sites for slaves in Richmond, Virginia. Three hundred thousand African Americans were sold, separated from their families, and marched in shackles over the James River onto ships at the dock, literally "sold down the river."[32] The science of economics can help explain prices in slave markets using supply and demand, and efficiency can be analyzed as maximizing the economic surplus. But that narrow perspective cannot help explain the development and existence of property rights in other human beings. Douglass North won the Nobel Prize in 1993 for highlighting the role played by institutions, the formal and informal "rules of the game." Institutions are humanly devised constraints that determine property rights and structure exchange; they include the moral norms for creating trust and lowering transactions costs. "The central issue of economic history and of economic development," North argues, "is to account for the evolution of political and economic institutions that create an economic environment that induces increasing productivity." Moral sentiments and principles can help us understand why so many Northerners fought so hard to overturn slavery, even though there was a large profit in slave trading. It helps us understand the evolution of norms that enhance efficiency in many ways. The world we live in, and particularly the modification of institutional rules, revolves around the sometimes muddled entreaties of different ethical viewpoints. A liberal education prepares one to discern the moral frameworks that lie beneath the surface of public policy debates. Excavating the history of ethics in economics is one way to start.

A CONVERSATION ON ETHICS IN ECONOMICS

A curious economist engages in dialogue with an interested observer about the issues raised in the first chapter. Let's jump into this debate:

Curious Economist: I'm already covering more topics in my economics class than I have time for. Why should moral inquiry be added to the tool kit?

Observer: The answer is simple: Choices in economics are often enmeshed in social relations, governed by ethical frameworks and expectations. Look at the reaction of Nike's consumers when they discovered that Nike suppliers were operating sweatshops.

Economist: Why can't the standard model of "enlightened self-interest" capture everything I need to know about social relations?

Observer: Economic actors can certainly be portrayed as *Homo economicus*—calculating maximizers—but a significant number of interactions go beyond enlightened self-interest. Human nature also entails *Homo empathicus*—a socially embedded person who engages others. Feelings and principles about right and wrong, rather than calculations of personal gain, are operative in some settings.[33]

Economist: Ethics introduces complexity, but the best models are simple.

Observer: Models need to be as simple as possible but *not too simple*. Adding ethics can enhance the understanding of markets. Such insights make students glad to be studying a discipline connected to the real world!

Economist: Why shouldn't economists let others—philosophers, say— specialize in ethical issues?

Observer: When economists talk about efficiency as maximizing the economic surplus, they are already using a moral framework (consequentialism) and applying a particular version of that framework. That moral framework has evolved substantially over the years and is controversial. Shouldn't students be aware of what's at stake?

Economist: But this is outside my area of competence . . .

Observer: Haven't economists developed new skills over the years? In the 1930s they absorbed Keynesian economics. In the 1940s and 1950s they mastered mathematical modeling. In the 1960s they learned econometrics. In recent decades they adapted to the insights of behavioral economics. Times change, and people have to keep up.

Economist: If ethics is a new field, why don't we wait until all the issues have been sorted out?

Observer: Ethics in economics is actually a well-established field. The frameworks surveyed here go back two centuries or more. Adam Smith, the founder of modern economics, was deeply steeped in ethical analysis. His moral sentiments theory is enormously influential today in fields ranging from political science to biology to experimental economics. Whatever your background, an educated social scientist should know something about Smith's moral sentiments theory. Modern experimental research into ethics is relatively new. But this should not be a barrier for open minds.

Economist: But ethics can be mushy and qualitative. By contrast, economics is quantitative and provides definitive answers.

Observer [laughs]: That's an *engineering view*. It says economics is simply a mathematical puzzle, such as how to design the cheapest bridge across a river. But definitive answers are useless if they give answers to the wrong questions. Critical thinking in economics necessarily involves dealing with ambiguity, uncertainty, and doubt. Lionel Robbins, who strongly pushed for the positive/normative distinction in economics so as to remove ethical dimensions from the *science* side of the discipline, quipped, "The man who can claim for economic science much exactitude is a quack."[34] Robbins, incidentally, did *not* want to remove ethics from applied economics because a broader knowledge of institutions and ethics is needed for policy evaluation.

The "art" of economics involves qualitative dimensions of ethics and other institutions.

Economist: Can you give me an example?

Observer: Sure. Pareto efficiency is often invoked to describe the optimal state of affairs achieved through voluntary trade: Both sides win. But this definition puts economists in a straitjacket: Policy reform always causes harm to someone. A revised approach, called Kaldor-Hicks efficiency, argues that as long as the winners earn more than the losers, it is efficient to implement change, even if the losers are not compensated. It takes only a moment to realize that this version of efficiency involves *compulsory* trade, and the losers are not voluntarily agreeing to it. The only way compulsion can be justified is if we are living in a democratic society with a transparent legal system, good property rights, low transactions costs, and basic human rights. Efficiency in public policy is an uncertain ethical concept in most parts of the world where these preconditions are tenuous (see Chapters 5 and 6). Many economists routinely provide advice to developing countries. If institutional ethics is ignored because it is thought to be irrelevant, advice can go badly awry. Famous examples of this are provided in Chapters 5 and 6. *This* is why economists need to know the philosophical roots of their discipline.

Economist: Okay, you've got me curious enough to keep reading . . .

LOOKING AHEAD

The standard economic way of thinking about costs and benefits is highly productive to our assessment of many policy issues. Yet it is only part of the way of thinking about these issues. Economics operates within a larger moral framework: An economist who ignores larger moral road signs in making policy choices is thinking incompletely and thus failing to think critically about the issue. No single ethical approach can adequately explain the economic world including important concepts of trust, care, obligation, and meaning. Nor can a single framework, by itself, provide adequate guidance as to policy (explored in greater detail in Chapter 12).

This book presents three alternative frameworks of moral analysis (consequences, duties/rules, and virtues) without specifically endorsing any one. Most people probably use all three at various times and in different aspects of their lives. Emerson's popular adage says, "a foolish consistency is the hobgoblin of little minds." Indeed, a theme here is that all three ethical frameworks are needed to explain and evaluate the rich variety of human behavior and political institutions, even if at times they seemingly conflict. The following chapter addresses consequentialist ethics in greater detail.

CHAPTER 2

Outcomes

The previous chapter introduced three ethical frameworks. This chapter explores one of these, the idea that ethics involves producing the best foreseeable outcomes. Purposeful action should be directed toward achieving desired ends.

OUTCOME-BASED ETHICAL SYSTEMS

A famous coaching maxim says, "Winning isn't everything, it's the *only* thing."[1] In this view, having a victorious ending to the game determines the moral significance of the endeavor. Coming in second (having a different outcome) would be worthless. **Consequentialism** is the general name for this approach, wherein it is argued that action ought to be directed toward producing the best foreseeable outcome. Who could oppose making the world the best it can be?

There are some immediate problems with this approach. First, whose interests are being considered in this best of all worlds? Should the only outcomes that count be those that affect me (or my team), or should actions be judged based on the outcomes produced for all? Second, how do we determine which is the *best* outcome or goal? What experiences or states are judged to be the most desirable? To address theory of value one could start by listing all of the good things in life—the most desirable outcomes. Two important *economic* outcomes would be:

1. *Satisfying household preferences.* Standard economics posits that human welfare consists in the preferences that can be satisfied when net economic value is maximized. Creating a larger economic surplus means some people are able to enjoy more of the things that give them satisfaction—more food, better health care, nicer trips, and greater comforts. Hence, one desirable goal of social policy is to satisfy the most preferences possible given current resources (having properly accounted for all costs and benefits).[2] It is important to remember that economic value is *instrumentally* worthy because its benefit derives from other things that money allows one to buy. The economic approach

does not specify what particular things are *intrinsically* worthy for individuals or for society, nor does it say that people should spend money only on themselves; donating to charity also reflects a satisfied preference. The preference satisfaction viewpoint is examined more fully in Chapters 4 through 6.

2. *Economic justice.* Expanding the size of the economic surplus (as in item 1) does not necessarily mean that everyone is better off: Some may be worse off while others are made disproportionately better off. An additional goal of social policy is to ensure a just distribution and/ or process for creating income and wealth in society. Two competing concepts of justice are:

- *Procedural justice:* The *rules* of the game are fair;[3] and
- *Distributive justice:* The *outcomes* of the game are fair.

Satisfying preferences and achieving fairness are two outcomes that many people would rank highly. But trying to achieve both of these objectives may create conflicts and lead to trade-offs between efficiency and equity goals. Economic justice is explored more fully in Chapters 10 and 11.

In addition to these economic outcomes, citizens also value political and other consequences. People are sometimes willing to die for these considerations—as evidenced by the American Revolution and the American Civil War—hence we ought to take them seriously. The following sample list of other values is not exhaustive of all possible desirable outcomes.

3. *National defense and public safety.* Wars and violent conflicts are a constant feature of world history. A critical role of government is to provide public safety by protecting citizens from aggression. Achieving this goal may conflict with other goals because investing in the military may detract from investments that could generate greater economic growth. National defense may also require that some members in society incur physical pain or death while serving in combat.

4. *Freedom.* The self-determination to choose one's religion, one's place of residence, one's occupation, one's friendships, one's political party, and other dimensions of autonomy are important to many citizens.

Freedom is a desirable goal that might be traded off against other desirable goals. Would you be willing to give up some freedoms in exchange for greater national security? Faster economic growth? One
reason China's economic growth rate is higher than other countries
may be because its one-party rule eliminates dissent and allows for
fast-tracking of infrastructure investments like dams, high-speed rail
projects, airports, and so on.[4] Staunch advocates for freedom do not
accept the view that freedom can be traded for other outcomes; they
instead derive arguments for freedom based on a duty or natural
rights perspective (Chapter 3). The right to freedom as stated in the
U.S. Declaration of Independence is "unalienable."

5. *Greatest net pleasure (or happiness).* Humans have a biological instinct for withdrawing a hand from a flame and for seeking physical
   and psychological gratifications that promise to make their lives better. A number of moral theories are based on the premise of "pursuit
   of pleasure"—or avoidance of pain. The familiar economic view in
   item 1 is derived from this principle and suggests that pleasure and
   pain can be measured by dollar votes cast in the market. By contrast,
   classical utilitarianism considers a direct measure of pleasure and pain
   and a wider universe of agents whose interests should be counted. This
   is discussed more fully in the next section.

6. *Intrinsic values.* Concepts such as parenthood, sanctity of life, love,
   truth, and citizenship are matters that to some people are valuable in
   and of themselves. Such *intrinsic* values cannot be bought in a marketplace but may be corrupted in a marketplace (for example, selling
   votes degrades citizenship; selling babies degrades motherhood; and
   selling term papers degrades truth seeking). Promoting intrinsic values in society thus may conflict with promoting market efficiency, a
   topic we'll return to in Chapter 7 when we explore the moral limits
   to markets.

7. *Tradition.* Keeping things as they are is an outcome that some people
   desire. Change is upsetting, and the status quo is often valued for its
   own sake.[5] One's culture is often viewed as an intrinsic value like
   motherhood, and markets can potentially destroy these. Hence, some

people oppose globalization because it creates opportunities and incentives for people to abandon their cultural roots. Friedrich Hayek notes that "it is not certain whether most people want all or even most of the results of progress. For most of them it is an involuntary affair which, while bringing them much they strive for, also forces on them many changes they do not want at all."[6]

By altering the values, opportunities, and incentives of citizens, economic growth can dramatically change culture. Not all such change is viewed negatively: Some economists argue that access to markets can potentially improve the moral climate by breaking down traditions that are unfair or immoral.[7]

Making Decisions Based on Outcomes

In the preceding pages, we listed seven outcomes that matter to people when making decisions (and there are more you can think of). If you are an ethical consequentialist, you would need to decide *whose* outcomes matter, *which* particular outcomes matter most, and *how* to combine and weigh these outcomes across individuals and values.

Let's consider a practical application: Suppose a multinational corporation decides to close its U.S. factory and produce identical products in an overseas factory. This action is expected to increase value to shareholders. The action would produce other positive and negative consequences. In assessing this situation we must first address *whose interests* should be considered. Should we evaluate outcomes only as they affect American stockholders, workers, and consumers, or should we consider everyone's outcomes, including those of overseas citizens? Laying off American workers would increase unemployment at least temporarily in the United States, but it would increase employment overseas. Second, we must consider value theory: What outcomes are most important? Is it profits, employment, or some other measure? Third, because this action produces multiple consequences across a number of values, we must determine a metric by which these outcomes can all be evaluated. What is "good," and how do we assess it?

The Mayflower Compact and the Common Good

An early consequentialist viewpoint was expressed in 1620 by the founders of the first English settlement in New England. The settlers had come on the ship *Mayflower* and were a broody mix of about half religious rebels (called Puritans) and half adventurers seeking fortune. They found themselves thrust ashore at what is now Plymouth, Massachusetts, in late fall. Food was scarce, and they had landed more than 200 miles from their intended destination on the Hudson River. The group was close to disintegrating. To maintain order and promote group survival, the adult male colonists bound themselves together, agreeing to obey a covenant of "just and equal Laws"—those laws thought most fit to produce *"the general good"* of the colony.

What is "the general good," and how shall it be determined? On this point, consequentialists disagree. The *Mayflower* men thought their interests predominated, and women and children were not invited to sign. Classic utilitarians would have explicitly included the interests of these excluded groups (see the discussion on the following pages), as would modern economists, if women and children had funds to participate in markets. Other ethicists would focus on the outcomes of the poor in this group, and still others might emphasize the outcomes of freedom, national security, public safety, the environment, and so on.[8]

Regardless of the differences, consequentialist thinkers proceed by (a) choosing whose interests to count; (b) identifying desired outcomes or values; and (c) evaluating how an action or policy would impact the most important desired value(s) using some metric of comparison. To a consequentialist, the moral worth of downsizing a factory is uncertain until we have carried out these three steps of analysis.

CLASSICAL UTILITARIANISM

The most famous version of consequentialism is classical **utilitarianism.** Classical utilitarians believed that they could construct a scientific foundation for law and public policy based on assessing all different actions using a common value or metric: that of the *net pleasure* produced. Each act produces a certain amount of pleasure and a certain amount of pain that varies in intensity and duration. The action that produces the greatest net pleasure is the moral one.

Jeremy Bentham (1748–1832) was an eighteenth and nineteenth-century legal reformer who clashed with the prevailing orthodoxy of Sir William Blackstone. Blackstone advocated making legal judgments based on the rules of law that came from historical precedents (such as tradition, religious injunctions, human rights, and so on). Bentham, however, reacting to the Declaration of Rights issued during the French Revolution, wrote *"Natural rights* is simple nonsense . . . nonsense upon stilts."[9]

By contrast, Bentham argues that the purpose of government is to promote the general welfare of society by punishing and rewarding different acts. All laws should be evaluated for their usefulness based on the principle of "utility." A law should be deemed good or bad according to whether or not it enhances the overall welfare of the population. Bentham measured welfare in terms of the ability to produce **net pleasure.** Bentham begins his *Introduction to the Principles of Morals and Legislation* (1789) with this insight:

Nature has placed mankind under the guidance of two sovereign masters, *pain* and *pleasure.* It is for them alone to point out what we ought to do, as well as to determine what we shall do. On the one hand the standard of right and wrong, on the other the chain of causes and effects, are fastened to their throne. They govern us in all we do, in all we say, in all we think. . . .

By utility is meant that property in any object, whereby it tends to produce benefit, advantage, pleasure, good, or happiness, (all this in the present case comes to the same thing) or (what comes again to the same thing) to prevent the happening of mischief, pain, evil, or unhappiness to the party whose interest is considered.[10]

Bentham argues that pleasures and pains can be quantified and directly compared between individuals. This is known as the "**hedonistic calculus.**" According to Bentham, there are four direct characteristics of pleasure and pain:

- *Intensity:* how strong the pleasure or pain sensation
- *Duration:* how long the sensation

- *Certainty or uncertainty:* how likely the sensation
- *Propinquity:* how near at hand in time the sensation

Additional considerations include the following:

- *Fecundity:* the probability of whether these pleasures or pains lead to others—in essence, a multiplier effect
- *Purity:* an uncontaminated pleasure is better than pleasure mixed with pain

However, two problems remain: *Whose* pleasure and pain counts? And *how* should these be compared? Bentham knew an obligation factor was needed:

- *Extent:* how many people or feeling animals are considered and how[11]

Bentham says a moral agent must consider the interests of all others, and a moral agent must weight these *equally* with her own, as thus: "Everybody to count for one, nobody for more than one." This principle affirms a moral equality of self with all others—including the women and African slaves that British merchants made such profits from in the eighteenth century. Bentham laments that "the blackness of the skin is no reason why a human being should be abandoned without redress to the caprice of a tormentor." Here's how Bentham's calculation might work: If slavery generated an intense pure pleasure of 300 "utils" for the plantation owner and a pure pain to one slave of 200 "utils" and a pure pain to another slave of 300 "utils," the *net* result in society would be a negative 200 units of utility. Slavery is thus immoral, once a full accounting is taken. Bentham lived at a time when most public policy decisions were made by a small group of elites, and the pleasures and pains of women, slaves, and landless peasants were generally excluded from analysis. In opposition, Bentham argues that the welfare of the masses should be reflected in public policy decisions. This was a revolutionary concept, supporting emancipation and democratic rule.

Bentham also wishes us to consider the pain inflicted on sentient animals that have sense organs for feeling pain:

The day *may* come, when the rest of the animal creation may acquire those rights which never could have been withholden from them but by the hand of tyranny. . . . a full-grown horse or dog is beyond comparison a more rational, as well as a more conversable animal, than an infant of a day, or a week, or even a month, old. . . . The question is not, Can they *reason?* nor, Can they *talk?* but, Can they *suffer?*[12]

Bentham argues that the "best" policy is one that produces the greatest *overall* utility, not one that produces the greatest individual or personal welfare. He goes on to observe that it is impossible to say what the "interest of the community" is without assessing *individual* utility: "It is in vain to talk of the interest of the community, without understanding what is the interest of the individual."[13]

John Stuart Mill (1806–1873) elaborates Bentham's utilitarian approach and for this and other reasons became the most influential British philosopher of the mid-nineteenth century. Critics of Bentham argue that by focusing on bodily sensations of pleasure and pain, utilitarians essentially created a moral doctrine "worthy only of swine."[14] Mill replies, in defense, that the principle of utility can also account for pleasures grounded in "higher" faculties, which include mental, spiritual, aesthetic, and moral pleasures. It is not the utilitarians who have lowered humans to the level of pigs, Mill argues, it is the critics themselves who have too narrow view of pleasure and pain. Mill readily accedes that "some *kinds* of pleasure are more desirable and more valuable than others." Hence, Mill proposes that we consider the moral *quality* of different types of pleasure and pain in addition to their quantities:

Human beings have faculties more elevated than the animal appetites. . . . There is no known Epicurean theory of life which does not assign to the pleasures of the intellect, of the feelings and imagination, and of the moral sentiments, a much higher value as pleasures than to those of mere sensation.[15]

To capture this distinction, Mill proposes the "Greatest Happiness Principle": Utility should be maximized by focusing on the general net happiness in society, calculated according to both quantities and qualities, and recognizing that humans have faculties "more elevated than the animal appetites." In short, "It is better to be a human being dissatisfied than a pig satisfied."[16]

As to how these qualities of pleasure are to be weighted, Mill relies on the preferences of a mature person of experience and good character who has self-consciously examined the issue. Mill can thus be considered a pluralist who does not think any one system, by itself, is sufficient to create a good society. Mill's reformulation relies on virtuous people giving the appropriate weights to higher- and lower-order pleasures to carry out the utilitarian calculus! In his autobiography Mill reflects that a true philosophical system is "something much more complex and many-sided than I had previously had any idea of."[17]

Despite Mill's reformulation (from *pleasure*-seeking to *happiness*-seeking), there is still no scientific way to measure utility—which is now an even more amorphous concept. The previous discussion has focused on **act utilitarianism**, that is, the study of consequences deriving from particular acts. This version of utilitarianism provides no absolute moral standards, aside from maximizing overall utility. The act utilitarian is situational—a different circumstance could give rise to a different moral choice from day to day. This is a desirable feature of a moral system if the world is rapidly changing and if you believe that morality has to do only with producing the best outcomes.

Critiques of Classical Utilitarianism

One immediate problem with utilitarianism concerns its strict version of obligation theory. Is it really ethical to insist that everyone's interests should be weighted *equally* with one's own? The practice of putting ourselves "in someone else's shoes" and experiencing that person's pleasures and pains is an idea developed in Adam Smith's *The Theory of Moral Sentiments* (1759), a work that precedes Bentham by a generation. But, in contrast with Bentham, Smith's focus was on virtue ethics, and it would certainly not be virtuous to say one's obligation to a stranger's child is morally equivalent to the obligation to one's own child. One's intensity of feeling toward one's own children is both desirable and virtuous, and it would be monstrous to argue that in making decisions one should be indifferent between the welfare of one's own child and that of a stranger's child.[18]

Yet many thoughtful utilitarians *do* conclude that right ethical judgment requires that we weigh each other person's interests equally with our own, with no favoritism shown toward Americans or persons of one's own class, creed, race, or gender. One of the foremost modern utilitarians is Peter Singer, who accordingly argues that we have a *global* obligation not simply a national or local one.[19] When Bill and Melinda Gates established their humanitarian foundation (along with Warren Buffett), they found that spending a dollar on health care in developing countries could improve many more lives than spending that same dollar domestically. Accordingly, they devote a significant share of resources toward alleviating suffering in the poorest countries of the world where those funds can have the greatest positive impact.[20] By contrast, many people argue for *partiality*—that is, ascribing greater interest and deference to the needs of people in one's clan, ethnic group, or country over those of other clans, ethnic groups, or countries. In this viewpoint, rules of justice apply to Americans but may not apply to others.

A second critique of utilitarianism is that pleasure and pain cannot be measured directly, at least not in the nineteenth century—which is why economists in that era eventually veered off into counting dollars and cents. Today, economists and psychologists use fMRI brain mapping and hormone studies to get at the underlying physiology of pleasure and pain, so one could argue (controversially) that a scientific measure of pleasure and pain may be possible in the future.[21]

Even if pain and pleasure could be reasonably measured, a third critique asks: *Why* are pleasure and pain the only measure of one's interests? Philosopher Robert Nozick posed this thought experiment: If you could hook yourself up to an "**Experience Machine**" that would impart wonderful pleasure and inflict no pain, would you do it instead of going through real life? Most people would refuse the hookup, Nozick argues, because humans desire to *do* and *be* rather than simply experience: "Plugging into the machine is a kind of suicide."[22] To most people their identities, values, and goals matter, in addition to pleasures and pains.

As noted earlier, John Stuart Mill also worried that utilitarianism could not stand alone as a pleasure machine. In his *Autobiography* Mill recalls finding himself startled by the following question and his own spontaneous answer:

> Suppose that all your objects in life were realized; that all the changes in institutions and policies which you are looking forward to could be effected at this very instant: would this be a great joy and happiness to you? And an irrepressible self-consciousness answered "No!"[23]

Concern for meaning that transcends outcomes is reflected in Mill's cathartic insight. Later, Mill championed the need for character or virtue education as a prerequisite for good policy making. In addition, he argued that the benefits of markets should not be judged on the basis of the greater *common* good produced but on the basis of *individual* good. In other words, Mill stood for the ideals of liberalism.

A fourth critique of utilitarianism is that in establishing overall net pleasure as the single goal to be maximized, utilitarians may unintentionally perpetrate horrendous injustices. We showed earlier that when elites willfully ignored the interests of the masses, as in slave economies, utilitarianism argued that the interests of the masses should be counted. But what if the masses abuse a minority group? Under utilitarianism, a gain to the majority of 200 utils could justify exploiting a minority up to that amount. Persons have no inalienable rights, and "justice" means doing whatever enhances overall utility. More sophisticated versions of utilitarianism can address these concerns but only by moving away from Bentham's strict maximizing to account for other consequences like justice (see rule utilitarianism and rule consequentialism in the following pages).

Finally, a fifth criticism of act utilitarianism is that it is *situational*— the right act varies as circumstances change. If being honest produces the greatest net pleasure in Situation A, then one should be honest—but if not, then lie! "Rule" utilitarians counter this criticism by noting that society can derive general *rules* of conduct that produce the greatest net happiness, and these rules ("Do not lie") would remain fairly stable.

Rule Utilitarianism and Rule Consequentialism

As noted, rule utilitarians focus on general principles or rules that produce the greatest net utility. As with act utilitarians, one's obligation is to weight each person's interests equally. And likewise the value to be maximized is overall utility. But rule utilitarians would argue that the analysis should not be done case by case. Instead, rule utilitarians are the "wholesale" merchants of moral analysis. One can conceive of them as legislators, enacting general rules that are expected to produce the greatest overall utility.[24]

The rule utilitarian approach conforms reasonably well to the moral intuition that commandments like "Do not lie" and "Do not kill" generally produce the best outcomes for society. In this formulation, rule utilitarianism can produce a reasonably absolute moral standard (maximize overall utility) and a reasonably stable set of moral rules.[25] Hence, rule utilitarians can justify the existence and enforcement of human "rights"—and give the appearance of something like a Kantian respect for each person individually—as long as such an institution of rights produced the greatest happiness in society. This approach is adaptable, however, because a radical change in circumstances could provide reasons for a radical restructuring of rules.

It is possible, of course, to be consequentialist but not adopt the same obligation or value theory as utilitarians. **Rule consequentialists** accept the notion that a set of rules can produce the best consequences, but these consequences could include (for example) some measure of fairness in addition to utility. Suppose, for example, that Tax Policy A would increase overall utility by making the majority of middle-class families substantially better off and a minority of poor families worse off. Suppose that an alternative Tax Policy B is "second best": It would lower the overall utility of the middle class only slightly but eliminate the pain to the poor. A strict rule utilitarian would favor the first tax plan because it maximizes utility; a rule consequentialist might prefer Tax Plan B because it considers the *distribution* of utility in society in addition to its total amount.

Rule consequentialism is thus a more flexible theory and more intuitively appealing to some because it allows one to consider the issue of justice or other outcomes. It is a "messier" approach because there are multiple measures of outcomes. In science, Occam's razor asks us to always simplify our models but also be careful not to oversimplify. One supporter of rule consequentialism notes, "[It] seems to be the case [that] the more plausible theory is the messier one."[26]

Summing Up

Earlier we posed this question: Is it ethical for a multinational corporation to close a U.S. factory and send those jobs overseas? This chapter explores one way of trying to answer that, by analyzing the consequences that result from this action. Standard economics is part of consequentialism because efficiency (maximizing net economic value) is said to be the preferred outcome. This is synonymous with the greatest potential satisfaction of consumer and producer preferences, measured by dollar votes cast in a market given the current distribution of income and wealth.[27] Economists going back to David Ricardo in the early nineteenth century have advocated for freer trade based on the notion that efficiency would be enhanced.[28] That is, globalization produces greater economic gains than losses, accruing to those able to participate in the market.

By contrast, classical utilitarians would have a different concept of obligation and of value. It is not sufficient to count the expenditures people are presently willing to make in a market, because not everyone with moral standing has the funds to spend. Instead, utilitarians would say we are obligated to consider how certain acts would affect a wider universe of interests (for example, including people and animals not currently participating in the market). In addition, utilitarians have a different standard of value (utility or happiness), which cannot be accurately measured in the marketplace.

Other consequentialists focus on other outcomes. Some decry the factory move because of its impact on lower-income workers in America. Some worry that foreign factories are located in countries without adequate pollution controls. Some consider the national security concerns when particular factories are outsourced (for example, factories using advanced technologies that might be used by our enemies). Considering a wider array of outcomes beyond efficiency is needed to assess the consequences of the outsourcing of jobs.

LOOKING AHEAD

Although consequentialists of different stripes may disagree about the particulars of whose interests matter and how value should be measured, all consequentialists adhere to the principle of judging right from wrong based on the expected outcomes. Hence, consequentialists are generally considered to be moral relativists: If the situation changes, the morally right thing to do can change. Rule utilitarians offer a defense against this criticism.

The next chapter examines duty theories that reject moral relativism and argue for absolutism based on rules and duties that are unchanging over time. Unlike utilitarianism, Kantian duty ethics will argue that there are a multitude of intrinsic goods and that what is "right" cannot be discerned from maximizing a single fundamental value like pleasure, happiness, or dollars. Virtue ethics, also covered in the next chapter, posits that developing the character of self-control is needed to carry out moral duties.

CHAPTER 3

Duties, Rules, and Virtues

The last chapter addressed how an understanding of outcomes can help
people make decisions about moral action. In this chapter we show that
other ethical frameworks are at times complementary to this approach.
Using more than one ethical framework (pluralism) is sometimes
necessary to create a good and just society.

NONCONSEQUENTIALIST THINKING

For when the One Great Scorer comes, To mark against your name,
He writes—not that you won or lost—But how you played the game.

—Grantland Rice[1]

Is winning the *only* thing that matters? A number of ethical systems
scorn the notion that "being victorious" (achieving a particular outcome)
should be the standard for right conduct. Rather, behaving morally is said
to rely on rules or duties or on one's character. Playing "well" refers to
the process by which one engages others in a sport. Although winning is
desirable, parents struggle to teach their children the importance of trying hard and playing fair.

The 2014 World Cup Soccer Championship in Brazil demonstrates
how both consequentialist and nonconsequentialist approaches can be
operative simultaneously. Every team wants to win, and cost–benefit
calculations determine how the coach picks the players and develops a
strategy within the predetermined match rules. At the same time, there
are unwritten *duties* that most players accept as sacrosanct. When a
player from Team A is down with a serious injury, Team B will deliberately kick the ball out of bounds to stop play. When play resumes, Team
A will voluntarily throw the ball back to Team B. Moral duties (respect
for others) require certain actions, in this case suspending play until an
injured player receives treatment.

Unwritten moral duties are observed in other sports. During the Tour
de France in 2010, a number of riders crashed in icy conditions. Racers
from other teams *slowed down* to let their fallen competitors catch up.

DUTIES, RULES, AND VIRTUES

It is likely that many traditions, rules, or duties for social interaction trace back historically to the desirable outcome that results when *everyone* adopts them. Soccer teams that follow the unwritten injured-player rule may lose an advantage in one game but benefit from it later. Overall, all clubs benefit when injured players get treatment. Hence, rule utilitarians argue that adopting general rules is perfectly compatible with consequentialism, even if we ignore the outcomes in particular instances.

This chapter explores a different reason for why people might adopt duties and rules or virtue ethics. People may come to *internalize* the belief that a duty is the right thing to do *intrinsically*—that is, in and of itself and not for reasons related to outcomes. How do people come to acquire intrinsic beliefs? The answer is found in both duty and virtue ethics.

RULE- OR DUTY-BASED ETHICAL SYSTEMS

Deontology is the study of one's duty, or the constraints to action arising from principled reasoning. Differing versions of deontology exist and sometimes agree or disagree, particularly with regard to public policy; however, they all advance the notion that some actions can be determined to be right or moral because the act has the proper characteristics and not because the act produces the best foreseeable outcomes. Basic moral duties confer rights that are "absolute" or "unalienable" (as in the U.S. Declaration of Independence). These should be respected regardless of other considerations (it is never moral to kill an innocent person for sport, even if this outcome would produce the greatest happiness for the rest of society). In actuality, many deontologists allow for exceptions to the rules, and hence not all deontological theories are absolute.[2] In this section we focus on religious rules and duties arising from Kantian logic.

Religious Rules (Divine Command Theory)

The most familiar moral rules come from religious texts that are said to represent God's commandments. According to Jewish, Christian, and Islamic traditions, commandments from God were given to Moses on two stone tablets. Six of these laws regulate social relationships:

- Honor your mother and father.
- Do not murder.
- Do not commit adultery.
- Do not steal.
- Do not lie.
- Do not yearn for your neighbor's house, spouse, or anything else that isn't yours.

Each God-based rule is succinct. Unlike utilitarianism, these rules are not explicitly derived from an analysis of expected outcomes, nor do they require any calculation. In its simple form, the commandment "Do not lie" is not amenable to equivocation.[3] The metaphor "carved in stone" suggests the finality and absolute nature of these divine laws.

The Catholic pope opposes abortion, for example, because he considers it a violation of God's commandment not to kill. Although benefits might flow to the mother and others from abortion, these outcomes have no bearing on the moral question. There is first an overriding duty to conform one's actions to divine law, and it is morally wrong to consider trading off one goal to achieve another as consequentialists do. The pope and other duty-based thinkers reject cost–benefit calculations used by economists and utilitarians as being a fundamentally flawed approach to moral analysis.

One obvious question is whether religious rules, such as the Ten Commandments, derive from an analysis of long-run consequences, making them a version of rule utilitarianism. If adultery ultimately produces unhappiness for individuals and society, a caring God might invoke a rule against adultery for the utilitarian purpose of preventing pain and suffering. Passages in the Hebrew scriptures (Christian Old Testament) explicitly state that following God's rules will produce desirable outcomes:

If you obey the commandments of the Lord your God that I am commanding you today, by loving the Lord your God . . . observing his commandments, decrees, and ordinances, then you shall live and become numerous, and the Lord your God will bless you in the land that you are entering to possess.[4]

From a biological view, humans might construct religious rules *as if* there were a God because this consciously or unconsciously solves certain commitment problems in society. Religious rules may help solve evolutionary problems of survival and procreation in groups (see Chapter 8). Even if this is true, consequentialist thinking may not be the motive for why someone today follows a duty to religious law.

Although divine command theory offers clear answers on some issues, most Jews, Christians, and Muslims do not blindly adopt public policies simply because they are recorded in the Talmud, the Bible, or the Koran. Reflection and discussion, often lasting centuries, may be required to discern the perceived will of God. Serious scholars, including some economists, concern themselves with these issues.[5] Other ethical frameworks can and do enter the discussion of public policies from a faith-based perspective. For example, the Golden Rule, "Do unto others as you would have them do unto you" can be modified and adopted by those endorsing rule utilitarianism, virtue ethics, or Kantian ethics. We turn now to an exploration of Kantian duties.

Kantian Duties

Immanuel Kant (1724–1804) is one of the key philosophers of the Enlightenment period. Born in German-speaking Prussia, Kant revolutionized moral thinking by addressing the individual as an autonomous, rational person. The Scientific Revolution of the sixteenth and seventeenth centuries had demonstrated that humans could understand, and to some extent control, nature. Enlightenment writers of the eighteenth century sought to apply a similar logic to human society and its institutions. Under attack was the idea that people should simply accept the doctrines of religious or political authorities in conducting one's affairs. Kant argued instead that human reason provides us with the means for discerning moral law. This has become a leading philosophical approach today.

Kant was assuredly *not* a consequentialist. That is, he did not believe that happiness (or some other outcome) could be predicted accurately enough to be of service in deciding action.[6] Even if outcomes could be predicted, there is something unseemly about choosing pleasure or happiness as a moral objective. For example, what if a liar gets pleasure from telling tall tales to listeners who enjoy being misled? A simplistic utilitarian logic might say that such lying is moral because it produces greater net happiness.[7] Kant says lying is unconditionally bad regardless of the happiness or any other outcome produced. Here is Kant's analysis: "When I am in distress, may I make a promise with the intention of not keeping it?"[8] There are short-run advantages to lying, he notes, but the long-run considerations of loss of reputation would likely outweigh these. Hence, it is often better to tell the truth from prudential considerations of consequences. But this is *not* the key part of Kant's story because "to be truthful from duty, however, is something entirely different from being truthful from fear of disadvantageous consequences."[9]

Kant's First Version of the Categorical Imperative

Kant's ethical system uses a decision procedure for ensuring that the principles we act on are moral. The process for discovering our duties is a method of evaluation called the **categorical imperative:**

Act only according to that maxim whereby you can at the same time will that it should become a universal law.[10]

Kant asks us to imagine a world in which everyone makes promises he or she does not intend to keep. Can such a world be rationally construed? If everyone lies, no one would believe anyone else. Universal lying is self-defeating and illogical, and we could not *will* such a world to exist.

Kant would argue that we are all subject to the same moral laws (no exceptions), and the fact that we cannot universalize lying means that our duty is to tell the truth. The categorical imperative is *not*, "Do unto others as they do unto you." Such a formulation yields only tit-for-tat ethics: "If you're honest with me, I'll be honest with you, and if you cheat on me, I'll cheat on you." Kant's formulation is broader: "Do unto others as you would have *everyone* do unto *all* others." In this case the moral agent acts from rational principle, rather than simply mimicking how others react.

A consequentialist might make a counterargument: When Kant argues that we cannot imagine a world in which everyone is a liar, isn't he introducing outcomes through the back door? Kant insists there is a difference. He is arguing that our commitment is to the *process* and applying it to a particular case does indeed require knowledge of the circumstances. Means and ends that are not compatible with the universalizing moral principle must be "abandoned or revised."[11] Kant notes that the only good thing in itself is a "goodwill" that "shines like a jewel for its own sake." A goodwill connotes having the intention to act in accordance with this moral principle, doing those things that your rational mind deduces can be universalized and for no other motive.

Does having a goodwill imply that we should help others? To answer, remember Kant's method of universalizing: Can you imagine a world in which no one ever helped another? This would be a logical contradiction. No one could be born or live through infancy without the aid of a parent. So it is impossible to conceive of, or to will, such a world. One's pure practical reason would dictate a duty to help occasionally. This does not mean one *always* has to help. Imagine that three people line up to assist a person in distress. Which is morally virtuous—is it the Boy Scout who wants to earn a merit badge? Is it the nun who took a vow to God and gets great joy from helping others? Or is it the harried businessman who is running late for a meeting but recognizes his duty to help others on occasion? Although all three helpers might do the same good deed, Kant would say that we are only sure that the last person has the right *motive* for helping: He acts *from* duty even though it goes against his interests and inclinations.

By contrast, acting for the *sake* of duty to family or to God implies that a person lacks independence or freedom. Kant's duties are distinct from "everyday" duties in ordinary life. When a child does her chores *only* out of a sense of obligation to her parents, she is acting for the sake of her duty; this behavior may conform to acceptable behavior but carries no moral worth because it was not done with the intention of obeying the categorical imperative.

Kant's Second Version of the Categorical Imperative

Utilitarians are concerned only with aggregate well-being, and in its cruder versions people are valued only as contributors to the collective good. In contrast, a key feature of Kant's argument is the autonomous nature of the ethical agent who has an independent, distinct value that cannot be summed. A corresponding approach to Kantian ethics asks that we treat others as worthwhile persons for their own sakes. Hence:

Act in such a way that you treat humanity, whether in your own person or in the person of any other, always at the same time as an end and never *merely* as a means.[12]

According to Kantian scholars, both versions of the categorical imperative derive the same laws and duties. Strict duties generally prohibit certain actions: "You should not lie." Wide duties generally involve injunctions to take certain actions: "You should help others on occasion." In summary, Kantian ethics asks of us:

1. Do not make an exception of yourself; you must be able to universalize your actions.
2. Do not treat others as a means only; treat them as valuable intrinsic ends.

Criticisms

What happens when duties conflict? Suppose a murderer arrives at your door and wants to kill your father. Should you tell the truth that your father is in the basement? One has a duty always to tell the truth in Kantian ethics. At the same time, one has a duty to prevent harm to innocent persons if one can. Kant's universalizing maxim may be hard to formulate, and slight variations can produce widely differing conclusions. By contrast, the maxim to treat others as ends in themselves is intuitively appealing and can be said to derive from moral feelings in virtue ethics rather than from pure reason.

In theory, Kantian ethics is absolutist. Once a moral rule is discerned through reason it is unchangeable. Given this, Kantian duties can give rise to irrevocable rights. If Joe has an absolute duty to act a certain way toward Helen, one could also say that Helen has certain unalienable "rights" in relation to Joe. **Rights** are the flip side of duties. For instance, the commandment "do not kill" can be correlated with the "right to life." Similarly, Kant's second categorical imperative can be restated as the "right to be treated with respect." In the last chapter we discussed one critic of natural rights theory, Jeremy Bentham, who called the concept of rights "rhetorical nonsense—nonsense upon stilts."[13] We turn now to a discussion of the origin of rights in a political context.

Natural Law and Natural Rights

Natural law is a doctrine promoted by Greek philosophers and further developed by Catholic theologians, based on the belief that moral laws derive from God's laws of creation. Its theological premise is that all things on Earth have a purpose, and the purpose of all things is to serve humanity. The logic of natural law might proceed like this: Sex serves humankind by reproducing the species. Therefore, sex between a wife and husband for purposes of procreation is moral. Sex for recreation (using condoms or birth control) is therefore immoral.

A problem with this approach is that it assumes that theologians know why something serves humankind. One could argue that sex serves humankind by strengthening the emotional bonds between a husband and wife; if so, then recreational sex would be acceptable. A Kantian, as already noted, might proceed as follows: The statement "I sometimes have sex for recreation with my wife" can easily be made universal as, "Everyone sometimes has sex for recreation with a spouse." The universal statement is logically consistent because the word "sometimes" leaves open the possibility of sex for procreation and reproduction.

Natural rights theory derives from natural law. **John Locke** (1632–1704) strongly opposed an unchecked monarchy, which historically had claimed absolute power as divine right. In his *Two Treatises of Government* (1689), Locke argues that humans, as creatures of God, derive certain individual and inherent rights based solely on the fact that they exist, independent of governmental laws or regulations. God intends and desires human survival, and natural law requires that he provide the means for achieving this, by mandating the right to life, liberty, health, and property.

Locke's writing had an enormous influence on Enlightenment thinkers. Adam Smith, for example, wrote in *The Wealth of Nations* (1776), "The property which every man has in his own labour, as it is the original foundation of all other property, so it is the most sacred and inviolable."[14]

44

Using Locke's approach, Smith also deduced that laws of monopoly were unjust: "To prohibit a great people, however, from making all that they can of every part of their own produce, or from employing their stock and industry in the way that they judge most advantageous to themselves, is a manifest violation of the most sacred rights of mankind."[15]

Thomas Jefferson, in the U.S. Declaration of Independence, restates Locke to argue that the "laws of nature" and the "laws of God" entitle people to govern themselves:

We hold these truths to be self-evident, that all men are created equal, that they are endowed by their Creator with certain unalienable Rights, that among these are Life, Liberty and the pursuit of Happiness.—That to secure these rights, Governments are instituted among Men, deriving their just powers from the consent of the governed.

Natural rights are not bestowed by a benevolent government—they are bestowed by God and cannot be revoked by others. Rights are "trumps," not to be abridged to achieve other values or objectives.[16] Nevertheless, people can come together and voluntarily cede some of their rights to government for purposes of achieving common goals. A constitution is an example of a social compact that is said to derive from natural rights.

The contemporary notion of **human rights** builds on the natural rights doctrine. It serves as the foundation for the Geneva Convention for the Treatment of Prisoners (for example, acceptance of the notion that prisoners have certain unalienable rights). Basic human rights in the workplace might include safety (the right to life), the freedom to withhold work (the right to strike), the freedom of association, and so on. One distinction is vital to this discussion. **"Negative"** rights are those originally intended in the U.S. Constitution, namely one's birthright as a human being is to not have government harm one's self or one's property without just cause. Adhering to this requires that government *refrain* from taking action. Robert Nozick, in *Anarchy, State, and Utopia* (1974), provides a strong defense of this limited rights view. By contrast, the contemporary notion of **"positive"** rights connotes the actions that government is *obliged* to take. The "right to health care" implies that the state has a duty to provide treatment for citizens; health care becomes an entitlement.

Criticisms

In modern times rights deriving from one's nature are giving way to rights based on one's status. Hence there has been an expansion of the concept to include the "rights of the homeless," the "rights of the unemployed," the "rights of people with disabilities," the "rights of veterans," and so on. Whereas natural rights were initially conceived of as limiting the intrusion of government into personal affairs, modern rights have become the obligations of government in personal affairs. Utilitarians argue, in opposition, that if a public policy is proposed (say, building access ramps for those with disabilities), that these should be debated on the merits of costs and benefits, and not by inventing new rights that, by definition, are nonnegotiable, unlimited in nature, and immune to consequential analysis. Despite these criticisms, many people instinctively accept the notion of natural rights. Even if one did not agree that "natural rights" literally were derived from God, one could agree that the discovery or invention of natural rights theory is a useful fiction, similar to the invention of modern money. The only thing backing money is its widespread use and acceptance—and this is perhaps equally true with the natural rights doctrine.[17]

America's founding politicians generally supported a limited rights view. One of the Revolutionary War heroes became the new nation's beloved and revered first president. Although George Washington is no saint, what sets Washington apart to admirers is his exemplary character—his honesty, his bravery, and his dedication to duty in the face of adversity. We conclude this chapter by turning now to an analysis of character and virtue, a subject that has intrigued philosophers over the millennia and is experiencing a resurgence of interest today.

CHARACTER OR VIRTUE-BASED ETHICS

Virtue ethics is both the oldest—and the newest—ethical philosophy. It is the oldest because it can be traced back at least 2,500 years to Aristotle in the West, Confucius in the East, the Buddha in India, and other sages in numerous countries. Excellence of character demonstrates how a virtuous person would strive to live despite many persistent obstacles

46

and temptations. Although different cultures have diverse specific notions of virtue, all cultures embody general notions of what it means to be virtuous. Virtue ethics is also the newest philosophy because it has been "rediscovered" in academic circles in the last few decades (see the subsection on "Modern Revival").

Both utilitarian and Kantian ethics start from the requirement that a moral agent has the goodwill to choose, and the self-control to carry out, actions that conform to their respective ethical moral frameworks. By contrast, virtue ethics starts from the presumption that humans need to be taught, encouraged, inspired, and even cajoled to do the right thing. Humans are not "unencumbered" or "autonomous"; rather they are shaped by families and other social institutions to value certain things. We do not choose the family, culture, or language we are born into, and few people abandon these as they mature. These institutions provide a social and moral context for duties. Our preferences for being a moral agent, like a preference for the English or Chinese language, is to a large extent *learned* behavior.

The Chinese philosopher Confucius (551–478 BCE) extolled the virtues of *ren* (benevolence) and *yi* (righteousness). Personal moral development was the foundation for a good society. Hence:

[Those] who desire to have a clear moral harmony in the world would first order their national life; those who desire to order their national life would first regulate their home life; those who desire to regulate their home life would first cultivate their personal lives; those who desire to cultivate their personal lives would first set their hearts right; those who desire to set their hearts right, would first make their wills sincere; those who desire to make their wills sincere would first arrive at understanding. . . . From the Emperor down to the common man, the cultivation of a personal life is the foundation for all.[18]

In this account, the quality of a country's laws and its constitution do not matter if the individuals within that society lack the moral fiber to uphold them. Character must be widely cultivated and sincerely imbued. Good habits instilled in young people are the means by which good character is formed. Role models are important for revealing life stories that excite the moral imagination and shape the preferences of the community toward the common good.

A further distinction is that some virtue ethicists, like Adam Smith, do not rely on supreme rationality (as in Kant) or on the acquisition of knowledge alone (as in utilitarianism). Imperfect humans with limited rationality must do the best they can, a point also made in more nuanced treatments of Kantian and utilitarian ethics. Adam Smith's view, discussed more fully in Chapter 8, is that social rules of behavior arise initially not from rational calculation but from shared moral feelings. Literature and the arts arouse the moral sentiments more forcefully than a philosopher's tome or the logic of the categorical imperative.

Even John Stuart Mill noted that his wife and intellectual collaborator, Harriet Taylor Mill, operated "not that from a *taught* system of duties, but of a *heart* which thoroughly identified itself with the feelings of others."[19] She is, presumably, the epitome of a virtuous person who would be capable of setting the appropriate weights to higher and lower moral pleasures in Mill's reformulation of utilitarianism. Mill notes that his approach cannot work without virtuous persons: "Utilitarianism, therefore, could only attain its end by the general cultivation of nobleness of character."[20] Moral sentiments alone cannot make a good society, however, and sound reason is needed to translate sentiments into the formulation of good rules.

Aristotle's Human Flourishing

Aristotle believed that great truths come to us by our experiences and that "it is impossible, or not easy, to alter by argument what has long been absorbed by habit."[21] Aristotle's virtue ethics is based on a concept of human flourishing, or *eudaimonia*. This concept is more complex than happiness or pleasure, but it provides the sense of well-being associated with *excellence* in fulfillment. It corresponds with peace of mind. Aristotle would ask, "What kind of people should we want to be?" and "What sorts of lives should we try to pursue?"[22] Habits that support the long-run goal of flourishing over one's lifetime are called virtues; those that defeat this long-run goal are called vices.

The differences between Aristotle's "flourishing" and what economists call "enlightened self-interest" are explored in Chapters 8 and 9. The key distinction is that to virtue ethicists, virtue is *intrinsically* good (good in itself) whereas enlightened self-interest is *instrumentally* good (good only for its consequences). For example, a businessperson could *pretend* to be virtuous to establish profitable partnerships. The calculated approach is contrived, and it produces behavior of a "much inferior order," according to Adam Smith.[23]

Four "cardinal" virtues are considered essential for the proper unfolding of all the other virtues. These are the call to:

- Be temperate (use moderation and self-control over one's impulses for self);
- Be courageous (display fortitude even in a fearful situation);
- Be prudent (use common sense; develop wisdom); and
- Be just (show appropriate regard for others).[24]

In the Middle Ages, Thomas Aquinas (1225–1274) synthesized Aristotelian philosophy with Christian doctrines, revealing the harmony between reason and faith. He added three theological virtues that are considered transcendent—spiritual qualities associated with salvation:[25]

- Be faithful (know thyself: identity comes from knowing, "Who am I?");
- Be hopeful (see the present moment as full of opportunity and purpose); and
- Be charitable (show *agape* love—a disposition of good-will to self and others).

A virtuous person is someone who reflects the seven virtues out of an internal acceptance of the intrinsic goodness of these things—and not for the benefits that might follow from adopting them. Love and respect for virtue itself is the standard. The person who manifests the virtues sincerely is someone of good character.

A vice in Aristotle's world can simply be a virtue taken to extreme. Hence, courage in a soldier means having the proper balance between the excesses of foolhardiness and cowardice; courage is the *golden mean* between these two vices. Likewise, it is important to practice all the virtues together because one alone can become a vice. Virtuous thoughts of love and faith are hollow unless they are grounded in prudent action. As Adam Smith notes, "The most sublime speculation of the contemplative philosopher can scarce compensate the neglect of the smallest active duty."[26]

A metaphor can help discern this point. Imagine that a guitar needs tuning. Each string first needs to be aligned with a pure note, and all strings must be working together in tune to play a song with ideal perfection. A virtue ethicist is not finished when one string is in tune (or one virtue aligned). Life is about making a chord, a combination of notes in harmony; the pursuit of virtue means striving to get oneself in tune to play the song of life.

Thus, an important distinction between virtue ethics and outcome ethics is that the latter may strive to maximize only one thing that is thought to be preeminent—utilitarians seek to maximize net pleasure, neoclassical economists seek to maximize net economic surplus, and libertarians seek to maximize freedom. By contrast, virtue ethicists say maximizing any one thing becomes a vice, because it puts the rest of life out of balance. Virtue ethics means finding the right equilibrium between competing interests and principles. The concept of virtue ethics in business has been growing because it captures the notion of competing frameworks of duties and outcomes.

Character ethics addresses life as a process of becoming. It asks, "Where are you going with your life?" It deals with the need for human identity, which is formed by the pursuit of ideals. Economists have recently rediscovered the importance of this topic.[27] The classic notion of virtue ethics can also be found in many religious traditions. The Koran, for example, following the Judeo-Christian tradition, promotes the virtue of "mindfulness." The traditional meaning of *jihad* before the twentieth century means a "struggle" or striving for self-improvement, a key Islamic duty.[28] Buddhists also see life as a struggle for liberation in which self-transformation is cultivated through a spiritual practice that overcomes dependency and suffering. Whereas the traditional economic view is that happiness is synonymous with maximizing preference satisfactions, the

Buddhist view is that happiness is maximized by *minimizing* wants—that is, through the purification of human character.[29]

The underlying psychological theory of virtue ethics is that human beings are not always accurate at predicting future events (required by utilitarians). Nor are they particularly adept at reasoning (required by Kantianism). Hence, they should be concerned with having the right motives for proper action and the self-discipline to carry them out with consistency. One-time acts of generosity or courage (however laudable) do not constitute virtue; character is not capricious but is reflected in one's normal and customary acts.

Modern Revival

Adam Smith was the last of the European virtue ethics philosophers. By the late eighteenth century the Enlightenment revolution had ushered in two thinkers who quickly supplanted virtue ethics: Bentham and Kant. For much of the nineteenth and twentieth centuries, virtue ethics was considered a dead philosophy, and utilitarians and Kantians dominated ethical discourse. Beginning in the late 1950s, however, virtue ethics began to reemerge as the difficulties and the assumptions of utilitarianism and Kantian ethics became more apparent. In 1981 the philosopher Alasdair MacIntyre published *After Virtue*, a work that placed virtue ethics again within the realm of philosophical debate.

MacIntyre's critique of Enlightenment ethics is this: that Bentham and Kant lacked a fundamental understanding of the ultimate purpose or end of life (*telos*). The goal of a good life is not an outcome like happiness or a dictate like "be rational." To Aristotle and to Adam Smith, the ultimate purpose or goal of life has a proper natural character, and humans need guidance and preparation for understanding and reaching this more complex end. All duties arise from a consideration of the proper or natural ends of humanity and hence from virtue ethics, which involves a balancing of desirable qualities. Maximizing the economic surplus, for example, may achieve a single goal but fail to consider the proper balance between prudence and justice.[30]

The study of virtue ethics is reappearing in leadership, business, and economic realms as social scientists grapple with complex social relations that rely on ethical regularities or habits that no one fully understands and that appear to have far-reaching consequences. Virtue ethics is part of the puzzle of why and how people regularly and reliably cooperate. It is foolish to throw out pieces to this jigsaw puzzle before the picture is complete.

The foremost proponent of virtue ethics from an economic perspective is Deirdre McCloskey (b. 1942). In *The Bourgeois Virtues: Ethics for an Age of Commerce* and other works, McCloskey demonstrates the role that the rise of everyday ("bourgeois") virtue played in the formation of early European markets and the continued operation of competitive markets today.[31] McCloskey champions the idea that Adam Smith was a virtue ethicist, not a utilitarian ethicist.[32] McCloskey is also known for her analysis of the role of rhetoric in economics and the call for ethics in the practice of econometrics.

Criticisms

Critics of virtue ethics note that its proponents cannot agree on what character is, who has it, or even if it is a stable or robust feature of personality. More important, can we predict behavior on the basis of it? One troubling aspect of virtue ethics is that its proponents have sometimes been on the wrong side of history: Thomas Carlyle, a great literary figure of the nineteenth century, argued that slavery was a good thing for Africans, whom he thought lacked the virtues and hence the capacity for freedom (for example, slaves were "indolent" and lacked self-discipline).[33] In Carlyle's view, the institution of slavery is moral because it builds virtuous habits and character in those enslaved. John Stuart Mill led a group of evangelists and economists in denouncing Carlyle's claims about the moral inferiority of Africans. Carlyle labeled economics the "dismal science" for its support of freedom for supposedly inferior peoples.[34] Critics are left to wonder if prejudices like Carlyle's appear as moral principles within virtue ethics—and Mill himself admitted that there is no external measure by which to adjudicate differing claims about virtue.

Two famous experiments in social psychology have also questioned the validity of virtue ethics. In the first, Stanley Milgram instructed subjects to give increasingly large doses of what were believed to be electrical shocks to others. These were confederates of the experimenter and received no actual shocks, although they acted as if they had. Milgram showed that average persons, like Nazi soldiers of World War II, could be pressured by authority figures to do almost anything, even though the actions may be repugnant.[35] In the second experiment, by John Darley and Daniel Batson, divinity students were asked to give a sermon on the "Good Samaritan," a Bible story about a virtuous person who stops to aid a traveler on the road. However, when rushed for time, few of these future ministers bothered to help someone in obvious need.[36]

The implication of both studies is that circumstances—not character—shape action. In other words, cost–benefit calculations or other idiosyncrasies drive actual human behavior even though we may dress up our deeds with flowery rhetoric about character. One researcher calls virtue ethics a "folk psychology": We ascribe our action to virtue, much as prehistoric peoples ascribed thunder to angry gods. However, just because something is widely believed does not mean it is true, or that there is such a thing as "character."[37]

Defenders of virtue ethics counter these criticisms by pointing out three features of the system that may be misunderstood.[38] First, Aristotle thought that the good life of virtue could be attained by only a few elites (whereas Adam Smith was more egalitarian in thinking that the poor had a larger incentive to be well behaved). Either way, few individuals are saints, and many are tempted to do things that they would not do if they had better self-discipline. Virtue ethics is a narrative about personal growth over one's lifetime, with slips and sidesteps of regret along the way. Although virtue ethics can be a guidepost, it is not a straitjacket.

Second, and related, is the notion that ethical character must be consolidated and reinforced. Maintaining friendships with others who support your pursuit of virtue is one way of using social capital to sustain your own sometimes weak individual discipline.[39] Persons join together, as in Alcoholics Anonymous, to bolster each other's courage and self-control. By contrast, hanging out with criminals may corrupt one's character because people's tastes and preferences are malleable.

Third, and perhaps most misunderstood, is that virtue ethics does not require any *particular* behavior that is immune to circumstances. Hence, situations do matter to virtue ethics. Although it is virtuous to help some-one, as in the Good Samaritan story, it is also virtuous to be on time, to be loyal, to be prudent, and so on. Virtue ethics requires a balancing of each virtue and a harmony with other virtues. Whereas in the abstract it is "courageous" of Mary to rush into a burning building to save an anonymous child, if the probability of saving this child is near zero and would seriously endanger Mary who has other children to support, then within this context we would say rushing into the burning building is now "foolhardy" or "reckless"—lacking a proper regard for prudence or practical wisdom.

Virtue ethics remains an important way of conceptualizing several important questions, namely what is "the life that offers the surest chance of being, from the point of view of the person who lives it, a very good life"?[40] This approach is not considered consequentialist because the vir-tuous person pursues virtue for its own sake. A more complete model of Adam Smith's virtue ethics is presented in Chapter 8.

ETHICAL PLURALISM

Categorizing moral theories is fraught with difficulty because the typol-ogy may not provide a perfect fit.[41] Although it is possible to assign labels that compartmentalize the three main ethical frameworks focusing on outcomes, duties or rules, and virtues, it is difficult and perhaps unwise to insist on strict compliance with just one. Most people likely draw on all three to varying degrees, and each foundation draws on aspects of the others. **Ethical pluralism** is a reality of life. As will be elaborated in Chapter 12, *vertical* pluralism means reaching across the three main ethical frameworks to provide a more complete account of ethical be-havior. For example, virtually every moral approach (except perhaps ethical egoism) starts with an obligation to accord some consideration to other persons. This near-universal acknowledgment of a duty to oth-ers is expressed in ancient Divine command theory. In the Christian tradition Jesus is quoted as saying the two greatest commandments are to love God and to "love your neighbor as yourself. All the Law and the Prophets hang on these two commandments."[42] John Stuart Mill noted that the "complete spirit of the ethics of utility" could be found in this passage. A utilitarian thus implicitly relies on an *external* principle that it is ethically necessary to show proper regard to other persons (which begins to sound deontological). Maximizing the good happens, but within a tradition that says that the happiness of a stranger matters *as much as* one's own happiness.

Mill's utilitarian framework also requires that the policy maker be of good virtue, needed to adjudicate between higher and lower pleasures. Act utilitarians are thus required to integrate the pluralist consideration of virtues and duties as part of the process of evaluating good outcomes. Similarly, a rule utilitarian could come to the conclusion that our day-to-day conduct should be carried out in terms of the virtues—those habits or rules that the utilitarian sees will most maximize utility. One can also see evidence of ethical pluralism in the Judaic religion. The Torah, the sacred text of Jews, contains 613 commandments or laws, suggesting that Judaism is a rule-based ethic. At the same time, attention to character development has been an important aspect of this tradition.[43] As noted in Chapter 1, Milton Friedman uses outcomes, duties, and virtues as pieces of the puzzle to understand how markets ought to work to promote freedom and progress.

Horizontal pluralism acknowledges more than one approach within each ethical framework. For example, rather than maximizing a single value like happiness or preference satisfaction, one could be a consequentialist and attempt to achieve multiple outcomes. In mathematics this is equivalent to optimizing with more than one variable. For example, **satisficing** might be adopted as a viable strategy if it achieves *minimum* objectives for both goal X (equity) and goal Y (growth).[44] Deontologists also might arrive at this same conclusion, arguing that one's desires may be subject to prior constraints: Maximizing output is preceded by the deontological principle of doing what is just and cannot be determined by outcomes alone.

Ethical pluralism entails the recognition that human problems are complex and that any simple formula or method is likely to generate problems. A pragmatic approach to ethics in economics draws on different approaches as needed. Thus, John Kay argues that economists need to be eclectic in their approaches:

The subject of economics is not a method of rational choice analysis but a set of problems—the problems that drew students to the subject in the first place. The proper scope of economics is any and all ideas that bear usefully on these topics: just as the proper scope of medicine is any and all therapies that help the patient.[45]

LOOKING AHEAD

Individuals often experience conflicts between their desires for certain outcomes, their commitments or obligations arising from duty, and their conceptions of themselves as moral persons. Attention to all three ethical approaches is desirable and necessary because no one system is likely to work adequately on its own. This topic will reappear throughout the remainder of the book, especially in Chapter 12.

The next chapter provides an introduction to the standard way economists evaluate a mixed-market system and economic policies. From this discussion arises the economist's notion of efficiency, which is ripe with normative elements. *Readers familiar with principles of microeconomics may omit this chapter.*

PART II

Evaluating the Economy

CHAPTER 4

Welfare and Efficiency

In this chapter we explore how economists often judge outcomes
based on the dollar values generated through exchange. In doing so,
economists engage in normative analysis using an ethical framework.
Few realize that economic efficiency is an ethically laden concept.
Advanced readers may omit this chapter.

INTRODUCTION

Economists try to determine how prices and outputs arise depending on
market structure (for example, competition) and other factors. In addition, economists make predictions or forecasts about future prices and
outputs. These activities use positive economics—they attempt to understand the world as it is. Carrying out positive economics entails ethical commitments (such as to be honest) as well as ethical judgments (for
example, how scarce research funds should be allocated). This topic is
explored in Chapter 12.

Economists also routinely examine market outcomes with an eye
toward evaluating whether a particular situation is the most desirable
for society. **Efficiency** is an analysis of the world compared to a desired
"optimal" state. This area of study is necessarily normative because it is
not possible to analyze what is "most desirable" without using a moral
framework. Because economists typically argue that an economic system
should be evaluated on the basis of outcomes, it is part of consequentialist ethical theory.

Peter Drucker, a management expert, once quipped, "There is nothing so useless as doing efficiently that which should not be done at all."[1]
This reminds us that efficiency is not the ultimate goal. Efficiency is the
measure of how well we have achieved some ultimate goal. But which
particular outcome in an economy should be most valued, and how? For
example, is the highest goal of an economy to:

- Promote the greatest amount of freedom?
- Produce the most millionaires?

- Produce the fewest people in poverty?
- Produce the fewest people unemployed?
- Produce the highest life expectancy or other substantive measure of well-being?[2]

Although these and other indicators may be important, this book narrows in on one particular goal that is often cited in standard textbooks. That is the intangible welfare measure of promoting **preference satisfaction**. Future chapters will explore how this view came to dominate the orientation of modern economics. In practice, many economists are more pluralist in considering outcome goals and look beyond this narrow lens. If so, preference satisfaction is a "straw man," easy to tear down but not accurately presenting what every economist does today. Indeed, one popular definition of economics, discussed later, argues that economics is a means of thinking to achieving *any* goal, whatever it may be.

Nevertheless, a standard way of assessing economic efficiency is by determining whether household preferences are being realized. "A chicken in every pot" was the presidential campaign slogan of Herbert Hoover in 1928. But a successful economy would go further than just filling your pot; it would allow you to choose a hot dog or a steak *instead* of a chicken if you preferred it (and were able to afford it). The market economy is celebrated by the slogan, "The consumer is king" because the goal is to satisfy *your* preferences, not a politician's preferences for you.

Because individual preferences themselves cannot be seen or touched, economists infer that people reveal their preferences when they willingly choose. In many contexts people reveal preferences by buying and selling; hence, the capacity to satisfy preferences can be estimated by a proxy variable—the potential net economic value (or economic surplus) created through voluntary trade. Maximizing the economic surplus created through exchange is synonymous with economic efficiency.

We begin, therefore, by addressing these terms and the ethical precepts that lie behind them. Later in this chapter we introduce some complexities. Criticisms appear briefly here and will be dealt with at length in Chapters 5 and 6.

Concern for efficiency and the economic surplus arose in the late nineteenth century with the development of **neoclassical economics**. Whereas classical economists of the eighteenth and early nineteenth centuries concerned themselves with the historical and institutional foundations for long-run growth, a new breed of engineering-trained economists used techniques of calculus to ground the discipline in the mathematics of short-run maximization. In 1920, Arthur Pigou, in *The Economics of Welfare*, laid out a superstructure for studying economic welfare. With modifications, this became the normative economic approach of the mid-twentieth century known as **modern welfare theory**.[3]

Modern economists believe that although utility is not measurable (as utilitarians thought; see Chapter 2), it is still possible to make *inferences* about well-being by observing peoples' behaviors. Consumers are assumed to be rational, meaning that they respond consistently and logically to changes in incentives so as to achieve the best-expected outcomes given their constraints. Hence, economists assume that consumers use money to satisfy their preferences and that satisfied preferences allow people to experience greater well-being. Pigou states that economic welfare is thus "that part of social welfare that can be brought directly or indirectly into relation with the measuring rod of money."[4]

Money is an intermediary and instrumental good that provides consumers with the means to acquire something else that they prefer. Economists today do not try to define or measure what ultimate well-being is or ought to be. "Better off" and "worse off" are simply inferred from the choices in trade and not in reference to any particular state of mind or outcome. Instead of having a precise meaning, economic welfare has come to mean the inferred net gain of taking some action; hence, "utility" has simply come to represent an index of preferences.[5] Modern welfare theory thus focuses on *choice*.

One person could buy an ice cream cone because it induces pleasure in the taste buds; another—who is a masochist—could buy a cold ice cone because it generates pain. Economists make no distinctions because in each case the individuals are assumed to know what enhances their own lives better than anyone else. The neoclassical theory of welfare treats as sacred the subjective (and assumed given) preferences of individuals, treating each as an autonomous person. The modern economic view is that the welfare of society is maximized when the dollar value of individual preferences is maximized today, given the existing resources and the current distribution of income and wealth. This outcome is synonymous with generating the largest potential net economic value in the current time period, after properly accounting for all costs and benefits (including hidden costs like pollution).[6]

As explored in Chapter 5, this measure is "static"—it evaluates only the welfare outcomes of market participants in the current time period. Nor does this formulation imply that the maximum *number* of individuals have had their preferences satisfied, because a few members of society could control a disproportionate share of purchasing power (see Chapters 10 and 11). This approach also does not specify what the preferences of an individual ought to be: Some might be selfish, and others might be altruistic. Nor does this formulation require that everything carry a price tag—because, as Nobel laureate Kenneth Arrow noted, some things are "invaluable goods."[7] Nevertheless, economists do calculate the benefits and costs in market exchange, as discussed in the next sections.

Measuring the Value of Market Exchange

The standard moral analysis of markets might begin like this: In a political election, each citizen rightfully controls only one vote, but in economic decisions each consumer rightfully controls as many votes as he or she has dollars to spend. People who lack income or wealth have no *effective* demand, and their votes should not count. Their preferences thus have no impact on efficiency in the market as measured by economists. Judge Richard A. Posner, an influential proponent of this normative view, notes, "The only kind of preference that counts . . . is thus one that is backed up by money—in other words, that is registered in a market [either an explicit market or a hypothetical one]."[8] Chapter 5 discusses why economists believe that questions of income distribution should be treated separately from questions of efficiency.

Consider the market for hot dogs on a popular beach during the summer. We are studying a trivial case (hot dogs) for the same reason that Adam Smith chose a trivial case for studying economies of scale (pins): If the economic logic is grasped in an insignificant case, it can easily be applied in more complex areas as well.[9] A simple supply and demand framework demonstrates these points, assuming perfect competition, no externalities, and other ideal assumptions. We begin first by addressing the behavior of consumers, adding a *normative* interpretation to actions that then allow us to judge the outcomes.

Demand and the Marginal Benefit of Consumption

Demand means "willingness to buy." As already noted, those who are hungry but have no money do *not* constitute demand because they lack the funds to participate in the market. A **demand curve** shows the various amounts of hot dogs per day that consumers are willing *and* able to buy at different prices, assuming that all other factors besides the price of hot dogs are kept constant.

Let us examine the behavior of specific consumers, using illustrative prices limited to whole numbers. Joseph is a rational, thirty-five-year-old individual who has the necessary resources to be a part of the market system. He knows his own preferences better than anyone else, and, in particular, the *maximum* price Joseph is willingly and able to pay for a hot dog on the beach is $5 (point J in Figure 4.1).[10] Although some might claim hot dogs are an unhealthy food and that Joseph should really lose weight by eating celery sticks instead of hot dogs, economists treat consumers with respect: They assume they are rational individuals who ought to be allowed to make their own choices.

Because Joseph is voluntarily willing to part with $5 in exchange for a hot dog, economists *infer* that he believes he will be better off with the hot dog than with the money. The value Joseph expects to derive from this hot dog is his **marginal benefit** (MB), worth $5. By comparison, if Joseph were willing to pay $8 for a steak, economists would infer that Joseph thinks a steak would make him even better off because the maximum price he would pay for a steak exceeds the maximum price he

FIGURE 4.1. The demand curve.

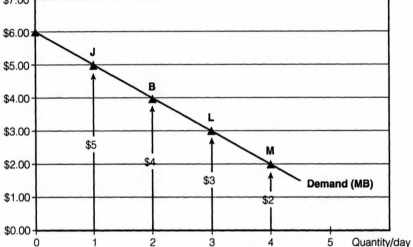

Each point on the demand curve shows the incremental willingness to pay, which is used as a proxy for measuring the marginal benefit (MB) received by each consumer.

would pay for a hot dog. Exactly *how much* better off in psychological terms is impossible to say because economists do not have an absolute scale of reference. What counts is Joseph's *relative ranking* of his satisfactions—his *ordinal* list of states of affairs: Steak is better than $8 → which is better than a hot dog → which is better than $5. Interpersonal comparisons of well-being are impossible when only ordinal rankings are posited, but such interpersonal comparisons are not required in the modern economic formulation.

To recap, the maximum price Joseph is willing and able to pay for a hot dog is his expected marginal benefit of $5 (point J on the graph). We began with Joseph because he signals by his monetary vote that he has the strongest preference for a hot dog, given the current distribution of income and wealth. *Why* Joseph prefers a hot dog at this price is said to be irrelevant to the analysis. Economists infer that willingness to pay can provide a useful *monetary* valuation of the marginal benefit Joseph expects to receive.

Next in monetary order is Brenda, who is willing and able to buy a hot dog if the price drops to $4 (point B); economists infer she is getting a marginal benefit of $4. Lamont would buy a hot dog if the price were $3 (point L), signaling his marginal benefit. And Maria would buy one at $2 (point M), providing her with a marginal benefit of $2. Each customer reveals his or her own preferences by signaling with dollars in the market. Hence, each point on the demand curve can be interpreted as the marginal benefit of consuming that last unit. The inferred marginal benefit gets smaller as we move down the demand curve; only as the price falls will more consumers be willing and able to buy in the market given the lower marginal benefit. This insight is called the law of demand; it explains why demand curves are downward sloping.

The Total Benefit in Consumption

Suppose that the equilibrium price of hot dogs eventually turns out to be $3. In a perfectly competitive market, each consumer ends up paying an *identical* price for the hot dog, regardless of the maximum price he or she is willing to pay.[11] Based on the preceding discussion we know that, if the price is $3, three hot dogs would be bought. Let's consider why: Joseph *prefers* owning a hot dog to owning $5; because the market price turned out to be only $3, Joseph voluntarily makes this trade, and the economy is more efficient for having satisfied his preference. Moving to the next consumer, Brenda *prefers* a hot dog to $4, and the market satisfies her preference when she buys at $3. Lamont is the "last" consumer on the demand curve to buy. The extra benefit to Lamont of the last hot dog just equals its market price of $3. The fourth potential consumer (Maria) would not buy a hot dog, because she values it only at $2 given her financial situation and tastes. Instead, she goes home to make a sandwich, or she goes hungry.

Although each consumer ends up paying the same price, each does not value the hot dog equally. Each consumer has a different *maximum* dollar amount that he or she is willing to pay—Joseph ($5), Brenda ($4), and Lamont ($3). If we add together these maximum marginal benefits, this provides us with a rough approximation of the overall economic benefit

FIGURE 4.2. The total benefit of consuming three hot dogs.

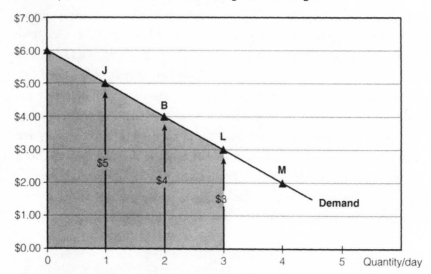

Total benefit is the aggregate of all the incremental benefits. It can be shown as the shaded area under the demand curve up to the quantity bought. Maria's (M) benefit is unrealized because the market price did not get down to $2, her reservation price.

derived from hot dogs in society (see Figure 4.2). However, because the demand curve also includes the value of incremental units, the total economic benefit to consumers is slightly larger: about $13.50.[12] Assuming there are no external benefits to others, the inferred **total economic benefit** produced in this market can be visualized as the shaded area under the demand curve in Figure 4.2.

Total economic benefit is *not* the same thing as economic surplus because society did not get these hot dogs for free. We now turn to the question: What did it cost society to make these three hot dogs?

Supply and the Marginal Cost of Production

Supply means "willingness to sell." A **supply curve** shows the various amounts of hot dogs per day that sellers are willing and able to provide the market at various prices. We assume that all other factors besides the price of hot dogs are unchanged. To derive a supply curve we consider things from the point of view of potential producers. If sellers use their

FIGURE 4.3. The supply curve.

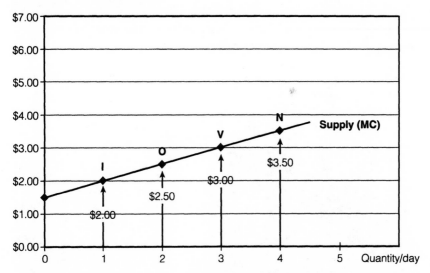

Each point on the supply curve shows the incremental willingness and ability to sell, which is a proxy for the marginal cost (MC) of production.

resources of land, labor, and capital to make hot dogs, then they cannot use them for some other product. Thus, the cost of making a hot dog is determined by its **opportunity cost**—the value of the best thing that had to be foregone to make it.

In this case we assume that the incremental cost of production, called the **marginal cost** (MC), rises as more output is produced. Why might this be? Suppose that the Iowa Meat Company (IMC) has access to the best land for raising pigs and hence for making hot dogs from pork. As a result, IMC has the lowest opportunity costs of production. Consequently, IMC would be willing to sell a hot dog even if the price is as low as $2.00 (point I in Figure 4.3). If the price rose, other producers with resources not quite as productive would find it desirable to enter this market. At the price of $2.50, for example, the Ohio Meat Company, with slightly less desirable land, would find it profitable to now join the market supply (point O). At $3.00, the Virginia Meat Company would enter the market (point V), and at $3.50 the New York Meat Company would start producing (point N).[13]

FIGURE 4.4. The total opportunity cost to make three hot dogs.

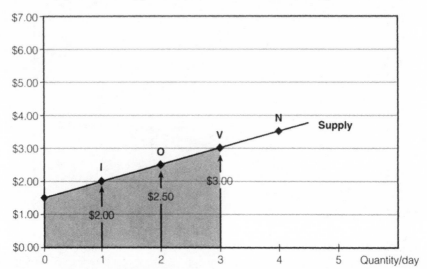

The total opportunity cost of production is the aggregate of all the incremental costs, shown by the shaded area under the supply curve up to the quantity sold. New York Meat Company's (N) cost is unrealized because it did not participate.

The Opportunity Cost of Production

In a competitive market, each seller receives an *identical* price for the product regardless of the marginal cost of production.[14] At the equilibrium price of $3, therefore, only the first three producers would choose to supply the market because $3 covers or exceeds their individual opportunity costs. The New York Meat Company, however, would not be able to cover its opportunity costs and hence would use its resources to make something else. If we add up the marginal costs of making three hot dogs, the **total opportunity cost** to society of making three hot dogs is found by the shaded area under the supply curve, which is about $6.75 (Figure 4.4).[15]

Equilibrium

Putting supply and demand curves together on the same graph allows us to visualize equilibrium in the market (Figure 4.5). The price of $3 "clears" the market: Everyone willing and able to buy at that price gets

FIGURE 4.5. Equilibrium in the hot dog market.

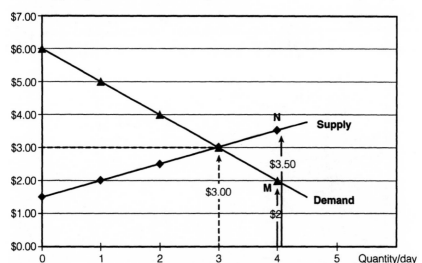

The market clearing price at equilibrium is $3, and three hot dogs are bought. Maria (M) does not buy, and New York Meat Company (N) does not sell. This outcome is efficient because to satisfy demand for the fourth hot dog would use up $3.50 worth of resources yet provide only $2 of value to Maria. The market produces hot dogs only up to the equilibrium quantity. At a price of $3, the incremental benefit of the third hot dog to Lamont just equals the incremental cost of production to the Virginia Meat Company.

to do so, and everyone willing and able to sell at that price gets to do so. If the price were any higher, there would be more sellers than buyers, causing a surplus of hot dogs that would push *down* the price. But if the price were below $3, there would be more buyers than sellers, causing a shortage at that price, and consumers would bid *up* the price. At equilibrium, three hot dogs are bought, and there is no shortage or surplus at that price. Moreover, there is no incentive for the price to change, assuming all else constant.

MAXIMIZING THE ECONOMIC SURPLUS

Given the assumptions of our model, the outcome produced by the market would be efficient because all the preferences that *can* be satisfied *are* satisfied at the equilibrium price of $3. We can demonstrate this by

FIGURE 4.6. The economic surplus.

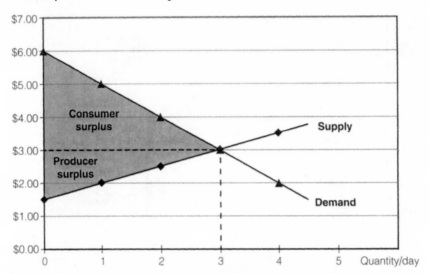

The economic surplus has two parts: one going to consumers and one going to
producers. The consumer surplus is the shaded area below the demand curve
and above the equilibrium price of $3. The producer surplus is the shaded area
above the supply curve and below the equilibrium price of $3.

calculating the value of the economic surplus and showing that its value
would be lower with any other outcome.

Recall that the total economic value created for consumers is shown by
the shaded area under the demand curve in Figure 4.2—which amounts
to $13.50. Also recall that the total opportunity cost incurred by produc-
ers is shown by the shaded area under the supply curve in Figure 4.4—
which amounts to $6.75. The *difference* produces a net economic value
for society created from trade worth $6.75. Visually, the net economic
value is the shaded area between the demand and supply curves up to
the equilibrium amount, as shown in Figure 4.6. This area is called the
economic surplus. The surplus has two parts, one going to consumers
and the other to producers:

• *Consumer surplus:* The **consumer surplus** consists of value received
   but not paid for. Some of the economic surplus goes to Joseph, for
   example, who was willing to pay $5 for a hot dog but didn't have to—
   the equilibrium price turned out to be only $3. Hence, Joseph received

$2 worth of value he didn't pay for (a consumer surplus). Without a market to facilitate trade, Joseph would own his $5 and nothing else. *With* trade, Joseph owns a hot dog that he values at $5 *and* he has $2 left in cash. The market created surplus value through exchange!

- *Calculating the value of the consumer surplus:*[16] The total consumer surplus for all consumers is the triangular area under the demand curve and above the equilibrium price. This area is equal to ½ ($6.00 − 3.00) × 3 = $4.50.

- *Producer surplus:* The **producer surplus** consists of payments received by sellers that exceed the opportunity costs of production. For instance, it cost the Iowa Meat Company only $2 to make the first hot dog. Without market exchange, the Iowa Meat Company would own resources worth $2 and nothing else. *With* exchange, the Iowa Meat Company ends up with $3 in cash instead of $2 in resources—generating a producer surplus of $1. The producer surplus is used to pay for scarce resources in production (like land) whose prices are bid up as the industry expands. Hence, the producer surplus is often referred to as "rent." Note that the producer surplus does not mean "profit." A normal rate of profit is included as part of the opportunity cost (that is, the return to entrepreneurship).

- *Calculating the Producer Surplus*: The total producer surplus for all producers is the shaded triangular area below the equilibrium price and above the supply curve. This area is equal to ½ ($3.00 − 1.50) × 3 = $2.25.

Both consumer and producer surpluses end up in the pockets of households. Households are comprised of consumers who buy the final goods sold in **product markets**. Demand is determined by consumer preferences, and the desire for profit spurs businesses to make the products that consumers demand. Households also own the inputs of production sold to businesses in the **resource markets**. Families supply labor, rent land, furnish capital (by buying shares of stock), and provide entrepreneurship. When a competitive market transaction produces an economic surplus, that surplus ultimately ends up in the hands of households—although not in equal shares (see Chapters 10 and 11).

SATISFYING PREFERENCES

We observe that every consumer who buys at the equilibrium price satisfied his or her preferences. All consumer preferences that *can* be satisfied *have* been satisfied, given the current distribution of income and wealth. For example, Maria choses *not* to buy and is better off using her money for something else she values more highly. The same story applies to sellers. The owners of the Iowa Meat Company prefer to use their resources to make a hot dog that they can sell for $3, rather than use their resources for any alternative transaction. The same is true for all other sellers. At equilibrium, the marginal cost of producing the last unit just equals the market price (hence, P = MC = $3). The Virginia Meat Company is the last company willing to supply at $3 and earns no producer surplus because its marginal cost also equals $3. Recall that normal profit is already included in the opportunity cost; hence, the Virginia Meat Company does not earn a surplus, but it does earn an accounting profit. Hence, every producer who sells at the equilibrium price satisfied his or her preferences. All producer preferences that *can* be satisfied *have* been satisfied, given the current allocation and quality of resources and technology.

The story goes deeper when we consider that the owners of resources used in the hot dog supply chain have *also* maximized the satisfaction of their preferences, given ideal market assumptions. For example, the landowner who rents 500 acres to the Iowa Meat Company is able to satisfy her preferences by doing so; we know this because her decision to rent reveals those preferences. Likewise, the laborer in the slaughterhouse at the Iowa Meat Company reveals his preference for working there over his next best alternative. Although a laborer might wish he were earning more or even working a different job, his *voluntary actions* reveal that given his circumstances he thinks this is his *best* alternative. Stated differently, his preferences are best satisfied when he can realize this transaction.[17]

In Figure 4.5 we noted that, at equilibrium, the last buyer is willing to pay $3 and the last seller is willing to accept $3. Hence, the marginal benefit (MB) of the last unit produced is the same as its marginal cost (MC). It would diminish net economic value to produce either more or less than three hot dogs. Here is why: Maria is unable or unwilling to pay more than $2 for the fourth hot dog. At the same time, the New York Meat Company needs a payment of at least $3.50 to devote its resources to making the fourth hot dog. Because the marginal cost of making the fourth hot dog ($3.50) exceeds its marginal benefit ($2.00), no consumer who had to pay this marginal cost would voluntarily buy. Moreover, society would be poorer if consumers were forced to do this because the economic surplus would *decline* by $1.50 (as a result of using resources valued at $3.50 to make something worth only $2.00). Hence, forcing the market to make four hot dogs would reduce the economic surplus, causing a **deadweight loss** from overproduction.[18]

Let us consider further the consumers and producers who choose not to participate in the market at this price. The fact that a market clears at $3 does *not* mean that all buyers and sellers are satisfied with the outcome. Far from it! Maria would like the price to be $2 or lower so she could buy; and the owners of the New York Meat Company would like the price be at least $3.50 so they can sell. Wishful thinking is not relevant, however: both Maria and the New York Meat Company owners have "ineffective" preferences because they do not have adequate money to buy, or the adequate resources to produce, in this market. Even if the market equilibrium price maximizes the economic surplus, people might argue that the market allocation did not result in the best outcome. Maria, for example, might go hungry and ask for help. Government regulations could set the price of hot dogs at $2 so Maria could now afford to buy (this is called a **price ceiling**—a maximum legal price). But doing this creates unintended and undesirable consequences: Both the Ohio and the Virginia Meat Companies would be forced out of business because their marginal costs of production are higher than $2. With production now limited to one unit and demand now reaching four units at this price, a **shortage** of three units would result.

The New York Meat Company is also dissatisfied with the equilibrium market outcome but for the opposite reason: It thinks the equilibrium price of $3 is too low. If government regulations forced consumers to pay $3.50 for a hot dog, this would allow the New York Meat Company to stay in production. This action would establish a **price floor**—a minimum legal price. Doing this would have unintended and undesirable consequences, because Lamont is now forced out of the market. At a mandated price of $3.50, four units would be produced but only 2.5 units would be bought, resulting in a **surplus** of 1.5 hot dogs that would be unsold at that price.

EVALUATING MARKET OUTCOMES

This chapter shows that under certain ideal circumstances the market equilibrium exhausts all possible voluntary trades that can satisfy the preferences of households, whether for buying or for using their resources in production. The economy is "efficient" at satisfying the most household preferences possible—by producing up to the point at which the marginal benefit of the last unit consumed just equals the marginal cost of the last unit produced. At this point the economic surplus created through exchange is maximized.[19] It is not possible to create a greater economic surplus or to satisfy any additional preferences, given society's current resources and technology.

This idealized outcome happens without anyone being forced to do anything against his or her will. Moreover, in a competitive marketplace, no one can control the final outcome. The activities of many millions of people, making individual choices about how to use their land and labor, and individual choices of how to spend their earnings in the market, result in a spontaneous, self-regulating order reflected in market equilibrium. More important, the market evolves to respond to changes in producer or producer preferences without anyone receiving an order from Washington. In a famous essay entitled "I, Pencil," Leonard Read explores the disaggregated process involved in the production of a simple pencil.[20] No single individual can replicate all the steps involved in making a pencil, because acquiring the graphite is a specialized mining process different from the expertise needed to tap a rubber tree for the eraser in a different part of the world. Similarly, no single person knows how to create the raw materials or to manufacture all the parts to an iPhone. The market, however, can almost magically assemble and coordinate such activity without the guidance of a central planner.

Government regulations such as price floors or ceilings that impede the working of this idealized marketplace impede freedom and would likely reduce the potential gains from voluntary trade, thereby causing a deadweight loss to society. However, actual marketplace conditions can diverge quite noticeably from the ideal. Negative externalities like pollution can impose large costs on third parties, and if so the true marginal costs to society are higher than the market price. And many produced goods like national defense create positive externalities that cannot be fully captured in the market; in such cases, the true marginal benefits to society are higher than is captured by the market price. Hence, free markets tend to overproduce goods with negative externalities and underproduce goods with positive externalities, thus not achieving efficient outcomes. Moreover, market structures are generally not that of perfect competition but rather of monopolistic competition, oligopoly, or monopoly.[21] Cases of price rigging and collusion among sellers are regular staples of nightly news. Chapter 9 explores additional problems arising from information asymmetries that caused moral hazards in financial markets leading up to the 2008 economic crisis. Neoclassical economists are thus well aware that the idealized portrayal of market efficiency in this chapter is a starting point and that government interventions can sometimes (in theory) improve economic welfare.[22]

Understanding the net value to society of economic exchange remains an essential part of a normative tool kit in economics. It can deeply inform many public policies. As should be clear, the evaluation of market outcomes is a *normative* endeavor. Some textbook authors, however, portray efficiency as a "scientific" or mechanistic concept rather than as an ethical concept. This viewpoint may be appropriate in narrow technical training but not in liberal arts learning. The selection of a moral framework and the choice of a goal for the economy are issues too important to be left unexamined as an unopened "black box." Such an ethically blind approach is contrary to critical thinking. The unconscious marriage of economics with preference satisfaction can produce a jarring disconnect, for example when one is attempting to work with policy analysts trained in different fields. Public health students may have a greatly different view of what is meant by "efficiency"—in their minds it may mean achieving the goal of saving the most lives possible—not maximizing the economic surplus in the market (as discussed in Chapter 5). Efficiency is a meaningful concept only when it is properly understood as a particular form of ethical analysis, subject to scrutiny and debate.

LOOKING AHEAD

Modern welfare economists are like other consequentialist ethicists who are interested in answering the question, "Which action produces the best outcome?" Answering this question is not easy, and, even if it were, ethicists using nonefficiency approaches might object. As we show in the next chapter, what economists mean by the "best" outcome has evolved over time. This has particular importance for the practice, interpretation, and evaluation of cost–benefit analysis in public policy making.

CHAPTER 5

Pareto Efficiency and Cost–Benefit Analysis

The standard approach to welfare and efficiency is often portrayed as
uncontroversial in economics textbooks—in fact, it is sometimes thought
to be purely scientific. This chapter shows how a number of ethical
precepts lie at the heart of these topics. When analyzing public policies,
economists today abandon the notion that voluntary trades are the only
basis for enhancing efficiency. A cost–benefit approach relies on a
measure of compulsory action. A wider ethical lens is thus necessary
to judge efficiency in this circumstance.

THE PARETO TEST FOR EFFICIENCY

The last chapter showed that under certain ideal circumstances the market equilibrium exhausts all possible voluntary trades that can satisfy the
preferences of households, whether for buying or for using their resources
in production. In short, the economy is "efficient" at satisfying the most
household preferences as possible—by producing up to the point at which
the marginal benefit of the last unit produced just equals its marginal
cost of production. This is a powerful conclusion and one that needs to
be well understood.

A quick check for efficiency is called the **Pareto test**, named for Vilfredo Pareto (1848–1923). Pareto was an Italian engineer who late in life
turned to the study of economics and sociology. The test he formulated
asks: Are any desirable voluntary exchanges in society still possible?
That is, could one more trade make at least one person better off without
hurting anyone else? If so, the current situation is "inefficient," and it is
possible for society to satisfy *more* preferences today with the existing
resources and technology.

Here's an example of inefficiency coming to light through Pareto's test:
Sam is a college student with plenty of free time. He gets to the airport
early and finds a seat on a plane bound for Rome. Remilda is an attor-
ney who is held up in a meeting and gets to the airport late. By the time
she arrives all spots to Rome are filled (based on seating passengers on a

first-come basis). The shortage of seats will leave Remilda behind. Is this outcome efficient in the economic sense?

If Remilda could communicate with Sam, she might say something like this: "Look, I really need to get to Rome to complete a merger. It's so important that I'd be willing to pay you $500 if you would switch places with me." If Sam could communicate with Remilda, he might say, "Great! I've got more time than money, and I'll catch a later flight." Allowing a voluntary trade in this situation would improve the preference satisfaction of *both* consumers. This is what most airlines routinely do today, asking for a volunteer to switch places in return for an extra free ticket (which the volunteer values more highly than getting to Rome on time). Voluntary trades enhance economic efficiency.

Note that a third passenger also arrives late and urgently seeks a seat on that Rome flight. Cristiano is rushing home to see his dying mother. Unlike Remilda, Christiano cannot afford to pay anyone to switch places with him. Hence, Christiano does not have any preferences that are effective in the market. Hence, an immediate moral objection to economic efficiency comes from those concerned with other consequences besides satisfying the preferences of those with money to spend. Chapter 7 deals with moral limits to markets arising from fairness and duty-based rules for allocation in times of emergency.

In Pareto's view, the economy is efficient only when members of society enjoy the *maximum satisfaction possible* through voluntary trades. Once that peak point is achieved, it is possible to increase the satisfaction of one person only by diminishing the satisfaction of another.[1] The Pareto test is a useful way of summarizing how neoclassical economists evaluate the performance of the economy and can be used to improve some procedures (as in airline overbooking). As discussed in the section later in this chapter on cost—benefit analysis, however, the Pareto test has limited practical value when evaluating most public policy issues.

FUNDAMENTAL WELFARE THEOREMS

The Pareto approach led economists to develop mathematical proofs of what *all* markets would look like in general equilibrium under ideal circumstances—meaning when all markets exhaust all voluntary trades under assumptions of perfect competition, perfect information, no externalities, stable preferences, rationality, and so on. The first fundamental welfare theorem derives from this analysis:

First Fundamental Welfare Theorem. Under ideal assumptions, competitive markets will always lead to an efficient (Pareto optimal) outcome.

The economy produces the right combination of goods in the least expensive manner, and these products end up in the hands of those who get the greatest marginal satisfaction from them (as judged by how much they are willing and able to pay). This is known as the "invisible hand" theorem because it suggests that, in an idealized world, laissez-faire markets (free of government interference) would generate the greatest preference satisfaction in society, even when every participant only concerns him- or herself with satisfying individual preferences.[2] This represents a mythical standard that can never be achieved but remains a lofty goal.

Most economists do not believe that the world actually works this way, because deviations from the ideal assumptions (called "market failures") are not uncommon. For example, economists have developed sophisticated analyses of monopoly, pollution, information asymmetries, and public (or collective) goods like national defense—that may require government regulation or other remedy to generate an efficient outcome. But the abstract contemplation of an "optimal" outcome possible through government intervention ignores the difficulties of how reform works in practice. Government intercession is not a panacea because intervention is costly, and government failure is also a possibility.[3]

Income and Wealth Distribution

Another familiar criticism of markets is that the current endowment of resources—and hence income and wealth—are not "fairly" distributed, an issue evaluated in Chapters 10 and 11. Critics note that in many countries financial capital is disproportionately owned by elites, who perpetuate themselves through manipulating laws and policies.[4] In Latin America, for example, land ownership patterns go back to the colonial era, and two-thirds of the land is still owned by a tiny share of households. Such disproportionate allocations of land and wealth arose from violent conquest, not from an orderly working of voluntary markets. Hence, the poor may look on current market outcomes as reflecting historical injustices.

In 1944 Congress passed the GI Bill, which paid the tuition and living expenses of war veterans so they could attend college. Although economists disagree about the effectiveness of programs that redistribute human capital, any such redistribution would *not* change the allocation efficiency of markets! Redistribution simply changes the mix of products that people are able to buy.

This means that Maria, who in Chapter 4 was left out of the market for hot dogs because she could not afford the equilibrium price, may now be able to buy. If Maria is eligible for the GI Bill—and because of this manages to graduate from college—her lifetime earnings will be substantially higher than otherwise. Maria is now able to acquire a different combination of goods and better compete against others in the market for cars, houses, and hot dogs. Maria's altered consumption results in a different set of final prices and outputs in the economy than otherwise, because companies will now produce more of the things that satisfy Maria's preferences, given her greater wealth, and fewer things for those whose taxes went up to pay for this program. The conclusion of Theorem 1 still holds true: The market will maximize the consumer and producer surpluses given the new distribution of income and wealth.

This insight leads to the second fundamental welfare theorem:

Second Fundamental Welfare Theorem. There will be a different competitive equilibrium for every possible allocation of initial endowments.

Hence, if you are a reformer who is unhappy with the market outcome—because Maria or other poor persons "didn't get enough to eat"—it is possible to reallocate the initial endowment so as to achieve your preferred outcome. Kenneth Arrow notes: "Any complaints about [the competitive market economy's] operation can be reduced to complaints about the distribution of income, which should then be rectified by lump sum transfers."[5] Although theoretically appealing, making cash distributions to the poor is rarely done.

COST–BENEFIT ANALYSIS

The economic view of welfare as preference satisfaction plays an important role in many public policy debates. **Applied welfare economics** is essentially what economists practice when they examine the benefits and costs of public policies. Maximizing the net economic value (benefits minus costs) is synonymous with satisfying the most preferences possible.

Satisfying preferences as a goal is justified on the basis of the Pareto test: It seems incontrovertible that, if two rational adults possessing reasonably good information choose to engage in a market trade, both must expect to be made better off from that transaction. The Pareto test could be used, for example, to illustrate the gains from opening markets to international trade. If Joshua can get a better price for his apples by exporting them to a willing buyer in Japan, wouldn't buyer and seller both gain? And if Christina can get a better car for her money by importing it from a willing seller in Germany, wouldn't both parties again gain? In this imaginary one-on-one trade, there are only winners and no losers. *What's not to like about win-win exchanges?*

The impression that economists can do value-free science when discussing efficiency arises from the belief that there is universal acceptance of Pareto's voluntary trade maxim (that is, the *win-win* scenario). Hence, it is thought to be an "objective" standard of welfare, free of normative elements. In actuality, however, the Pareto approach relies on a series of ethical claims and presumptions, leading one noted scholar to quip, "The idea of value-free welfare economics is simply a contradiction in terms."[6] For example, why should satisfying preferences be the only desirable outcome?

Despite its strong normative appeal, the Pareto test has limited application in the analysis of actual public policy issues. Seldom is it the case that changing policies (for example, removing barriers to trade) will produce only winners and no losers, which is what the Pareto test requires. Because unanimity is virtually impossible in a large democracy, no policy could ever be undertaken if Pareto efficiency were the litmus test. For illustration, suppose 200 million consumers could each save $30 per year from freer trade in dairy products (a total gain of $6 billion). As a consequence, 50,000 farmers would lose their jobs and be forced to find new occupations. After retraining, each farmer would earn $20,000 less per year (a total loss of $1 billion).[7]

The net economic welfare to households could be increased by $5 billion with freer trade, but, regardless of this potential overall benefit, *dairy farmers* would never agree to it. Starting from the existing situation, it is not possible to make consumers better off without harming farmers. Hence, no Pareto improvement is possible. In the 1940s, economists attempted to resolve the Pareto problem by changing the definition of welfare. Under the new **Kaldor-Hicks criterion**, it is not the satisfaction of consumer preferences per se that is the goal; it is the *capacity* to satisfy consumer preferences that is now the normative goal.[8] In the Kaldor-Hicks reformulation, it is no longer necessary to show that everyone gains from a policy change, only that the winners gain more than the losers lose. This subtle redefinition allows for the analysis of public policy using cost–benefit analysis.

In the trade example, consumers gain $6 billion per year from being able to access the world market for milk, cheese, and ice cream; meanwhile, domestic dairy farmers lose $1 billion per year. That produces an overall net gain to society of $5 billion per year from liberalizing trade. This is a *hypothetical* Pareto improvement rather than an actual Pareto improvement. In theory, the winners from freer trade could "bribe" the losers to secure their compliance. Consumers, for example, could pay dairy farmers $1 billion per year, thus making farmers "whole," and consumers would still be ahead by $5 billion per year. Compensating the losers creates an *actual* Pareto improvement. In the Kaldor-Hicks reformulation, however, efficiency is enhanced even if farmers are not compensated for their losses. Money serves as a proxy for the *capacity* to satisfy preferences, and freer trade enhances this capacity (on balance) even though some parties do not agree to the transaction—it is involuntary.

In the next section we discuss why compensation is rarely paid, making the Kaldor-Hicks approach controversial because of its compulsory nature. Under certain circumstances, it also leads to coercion or to inconsistent results.

Social Welfare Functions

An alternative approach to cost-benefit analysis is to model a **social welfare function:** This consists of attempting to aggregate individually ranked preferences into a community ranking that can be used for policy evaluation.[9] A welfare function could be as simple as $W = Y_1 + Y_2 + Y_3$, where social welfare (W) is said to consist of the sum of the incomes (Y) of society's three members. In this example, the distribution of income plays no role in defining social welfare because an extra dollar of income to the richest person (3) raises welfare just as much as an extra dollar going to the poorest (1). Similarly, many social welfare functions simply assume that community welfare increases with *average* per capita income, regardless of its distribution.

At least since the nineteenth century, however, many economists have argued that the value of an extra dollar earned is expected to have a greater positive impact on a poor person than a rich person. Hence, many welfare functions specify that income gains to the poor should be weighted more heavily than income gains to the rich. Macroeconomists often try to simplify the issue of how to aggregate preferences by assuming that all individuals are identical (assumed to have homogenous preferences and interests). Using such a single "representative agent" to stand for all people simplifies the modeling; however, it does not address a key reality in policy analysis—that people, in fact, do have heterogeneous (or varied) preferences and interests, and hence that income distributions matter for welfare and policy making.

Public policies are often vigorously contested in elections and referendums. But voting is no panacea for determining social welfare either. **Arrow's impossibility theorem** shows that, under generally agreed conditions, no voting system can reliably translate individual preferences into outcomes that make everyone better off, as they themselves would judge it.[10] Welfare economics has thus focused on finding a solution to the problem identified by Arrow's theorem. The results demonstrate how science and ethics are intertwined because "Judgment is an essential ingredient in the process of defining social welfare."[11]

In addition, most social welfare models are so abstract that they are of limited practical use in guiding policy. Because of these difficulties, many economists continue to rely on cost–benefit analyses in making policy recommendations. Given the practical problems of compensating losers and the problems of preference aggregation, welfare economics remains in a state of "limbo."[12]

COMPULSION AND COST–BENEFIT ANALYSIS

The justification for Pareto efficiency is that all trades are voluntary and can be inferred to improve the welfare of all concerned parties. Modern welfare theory moves away from this consensus approach by changing the definition of welfare: It is now the *capacity* to satisfy preferences that counts, not the actual satisfaction of preferences. The Kaldor-Hicks reformulation allows for the analysis of policy changes in which harm is done to some parties. As long as winners gain more than losers lose, the outcome is judged to be efficient.

Although compensating losers is theoretically possible, it is usually complicated and expensive to implement. The losers may be politically weak, widely dispersed, and difficult to identify, and the harm may be uncovered only over many years. The transactions costs required to identify and compensate losers could far exceed any potential gains. As a practical result, losers are usually not compensated. Some economists continue to assert mistakenly, however, that obtaining greater efficiency means allowing more voluntary Pareto trades. In actuality, cost–benefit analyses generally rely on implicit force to achieve a desired result. Compulsion can be justified, but its ethical defense is more difficult than voluntary trade.

Nonpecuniary Costs and Benefits

Nobel laureate James Buchanan exposes a methodological problem that also arises when we try to grapple with the involuntary aspect of policy changes. Costs are supposed to be measured by opportunity costs (that is, the highest value of an opportunity foregone). But an outside observer has limited ways of estimating what the lost opportunity costs of individuals (or aggregations of individuals) are:

Cost is that which the decision-taker sacrifices or gives up when he makes a choice. It consists in *his own* evaluation of the enjoyment or utility that he anticipates having to forego as a result of selection among alternative courses of action. . . . Cost cannot be measured by someone other than the decision-maker because there is no way that subjective experience can be directly observed.[13]

The cost–benefit method likely misestimates costs and benefits because nonpecuniary values cannot be observed in involuntary transactions. Let's reexamine the trade policy question presented earlier, in which opening to trade in dairy products could benefit consumers, but at the expense of domestic dairy farmers.

To analyze the harm done to farmers, an economist would ask, "How much would we have to compensate the average farmer (retrained in a new job) to restore her to financial wholeness?" If previously the farmer made $60,000 a year and now earns $40,000 a year, the "cost" to this farmer of changing occupations could be measured by this difference in earnings: $20,000 a year. This is an estimate of the cost to the average farmer. But this hypothetical calculation ignores the involuntary nature of the proposed policy change and the differences that arise because farmers have different preferences. In particular, it disregards the costs to an individual farmer as she *herself* values them. Recall that such differences are what create a producers' surplus in production. Suppose that one farmer enjoys being her own boss and gets psychic benefits from working outdoors. Suppose these nonpecuniary benefits are worth $50,000 a year to her. Hence, a true accounting of the job benefits would be:

Financial benefits:	$ 60,000
Nonfinancial benefits:	$ 50,000
Total benefits:	$110,000

If this were a voluntary transaction, the dairy farmer would only accept a buyout offer of $110,000 or higher to leave her occupation. By typically recording only pecuniary losses and not subjective losses, Buchanan argues that economists often gravely misapply the concept of opportunity cost that is at the heart of economic analysis. At the end of the next section we explore some possible solutions to this measurement issue. The central issue has provoked a raging debate in a famous Supreme Court case about property rights.

The Kelo Eminent Domain Case

The economic approach to legal theory and practice gained enormous traction since the 1960s in a movement known as "law and economics." In its normative version, economists advise judges on the implications of their rulings for efficiency. Instead of deciding court cases on the basis of legal precedents, judges and legislators are now being asked to make decisions on the basis of economic welfare—the potential for maximizing net economic value. One controversial case highlights the issue of duress that is required to reach an efficient outcome.

The city of New London, Connecticut, wanted to gain more tax revenue by tearing down a middle-income neighborhood on the waterfront and allowing a private developer to construct a research facility that was expected to, in turn, attract an upscale hotel, offices, condominiums, and retail establishments. According to the Pareto test for efficiency, if the land is worth more to the developer than to the current residents, and there are low transaction costs, a voluntary private exchange of land for money would make all parties better off, leading to an actual Pareto improvement. But some residents, including nurse Suzette Kelo, did not wish to sell. Kelo's neighborhood was not blighted or causing negative effects on other properties. However, with the goal of maximizing the economic value of the land (and hence its tax base), the city of New London condemned Kelo's property, using powers of eminent domain.

Kelo was offered compensation for her house based on what it would cost to make her financially whole (that is, what it would cost to buy a comparable house in a similar neighborhood). This was lower than the price she would voluntarily accept—because a homeowner may get sentimental value from a particular home arising from childhood memories, proximity to particular neighbors, and other subjective considerations. In addition, some property owners may choose not to sell based on commitments or principles.[14] Also, some sellers might engage in strategic bargaining by misrepresenting their subjective valuations, hoping to extract higher returns by holding out on a potential deal. Essentially, this is the heart of Buchanan's critique against cost−benefit analysis: One cannot distinguish these different reasons for not selling, and hence one cannot calculate the true cost to society of taking someone's land involuntarily.

Determining the costs and benefits under compulsion is a difficult scientific endeavor because economists are not clairvoyant. Viewers of the television show "Antiques Roadshow" often delight to discover what household objects will fetch. Not surprisingly, the market "worth" of an antique is entirely subjective because each buyer and seller will assess the object differently. A set of three antique brass lamps can be reproduced at a cost of (let us say) $2,000. But suppose these *particular* lamps were used to illuminate the wedding of Abraham Lincoln to Mary Todd in 1842. The provenance (or prior history) of an object determines its subjective value and explains why these lamps are appraised between $40,000 and $70,000—more than thirty-five times the material and labor to reproduce.[15] But, without competition to determine a market price, there is no way to know subjective value except by imposing assumptions. This is Buchanan's critique: Cost−benefit calculations typically ignore nonpecuniary subjective considerations, such as how much Suzette Kelo values her own memories and other associations in her family home.

Nevertheless, in *Kelo vs. New London* (2005) the Supreme Court ruled 5–4 that Kelo could be forced off her land by powers of eminent domain, even though the city was simply acting as an agent for a private developer. Although Kelo's preferences were not satisfied, those of potential buyers of her land were satisfied (such as people wanting to buy expensive condos on the waterfront). In this case, satisfying the market preferences for waterfront condos came into direct conflict with two other goals of American life—voluntary trade and the sanctity of private property rights. The endnote to this story is that after the city acquired and relocated Kelo's house and bulldozed the neighborhood, the planned development project never materialized. All the "higher economic valuations" turned out to be a mirage; Kelo's former house lot remains vacant.

Buchanan's critique highlights the subjective nature of cost−benefit analyses. The emphasis on quantification of outcomes, and the conversion of all outcomes into dollar equivalents, can create a false sense of objectivity and technical confidence. This is why some economists maintain that economics is a value-free science. Although economics uses scientific methods, estimates of efficiency gains using the Kaldor-Hicks formulation cannot be falsified by actual voluntary behavior (because losers are compelled to sell). In the rush to calculate, "it is easy to overlook the intangible and prefer to concentrate on the measurable."[16] If these considerations are significant, "any estimate must remain almost wholly arbitrary."[17]

Environmental economists attempt to get around this problem by using econometric estimation techniques and by using surveys to assess "willingness to pay" as a proxy for nonobserved variables like subjective valuations of what a pristine beach is worth. Experimental economists also try to coax this information from participants in controlled laboratory settings. These approaches offer important insights but remain controversial because of the difficulties of replication and the problem of holding all other variables constant. To some extent cost–benefit studies can be definitive in a political sense even if benefits and costs cannot be determined precisely. The use of sensitivity analysis, for example, could suggest that the benefit of some policy is so large, relative to any foreseeable cost, that doubling or tripling the "cost" estimate would not alter the recommended policy.

Lionel Robbins, a key figure in modern neoclassical economics, leveled a criticism against the welfare interpretation of aggregate economic data. In *An Essay on the Nature and Significance of Economic Science*, Robbins notes that prices reflect only relative scarcities; hence monetary aggregates of prices can only provide "arbitrary" meaning. Any major public policy would redistribute income and wealth, thus affecting relative prices.[18] In the previous case, Suzette Kelo's "willingness to accept" an offer for her house depended in part on her current income and wealth. Her willingness to pay for the same house might be quite different after eminent domain is carried out. As demonstrated, it is not possible to make policy recommendations about economic efficiency without grappling with subjective and presumptive aspects of the analysis. This is not a criticism so much as it is a caveat. In a positive light, economic policy making is an art, not a science.

Reply and Rejoinder

Judging outcomes through a cost-benefit approach remains an important part of any tool kit for analyzing public policy. Some supporters of cost–benefit analysis argue that even though compulsion is relied on to reach a more efficient outcome (as in the Kelo case), this can be justified in two ways. First, Thomas Hobbes, in *Leviathan* (1651), provides the groundwork for concluding that people bind together out of necessity and that by staying together they give their consent to having their rights abridged. John Locke noted that consent comes from both the right to exit and from the right to add voice to the democratic process. Citizens may leave the jurisdiction or may stay and voice their views to community representatives, who in turn enact property laws such as eminent domain.[19] If a democratically elected legislature chooses to impose certain costs, taxes, or regulations, it is Kelo's choice to stay and abide by these. By remaining, Kelo implicitly consents to the process by which laws are adopted and her rights impinged by policies such as eminent domain.

Second, if a legislature exceeds its bounds, citizens have the right to seek redress from a jury of peers in an impartial court system. Seen in this light, the compulsion required to reach economic efficiency is not substantially different from that of paying taxes, which the constitution expressly permits for the purpose of enhancing "general welfare" (Article 1, Section 8, on the legislative powers of Congress). Defending cost–benefit analysis in this way draws on a second—and entirely different—type of ethical argument. It is no longer simply the *outcome* of maximizing preference satisfaction that can justify the policy; it is suddenly now the *process* by which we arrive at the outcome that matters! To defend cost–benefit analyses requires assuming the existence and use of institutions for safeguarding basic human rights and liberties through due process. Since rights are the flip side of duties, it is difficult to justify cost–benefit recommendations without relying on duty and other nonconsequentialist ethical considerations.[20]

This insight adds another cloud around the science of cost–benefit analysis. It also raises a red flag of warning about application. Although representative government and an independent judiciary can reasonably be assumed for the one billion people living in high-income countries, three-fourths of the world's people live in societies in which democracy and due process are weak institutions if they exist at all. Welfare theory—and in particular cost–benefit analysis—is devoid of the necessary institutional preconditions when used in these societies. What is *compulsory* in a country with due process laws becomes *coercive* in a state lacking basic safeguards. To construct the world's largest hydroelectric dam at Three River Gorges in China, for example, the communist authorities removed and resettled over one million residents along the Yangtze River. Let us construct an imaginary conversation between a well-meaning economist and a quizzical observer about this project:

> *Well-meaning economist:* The Three Rivers Dam can be justified on the basis of benefit–cost calculations. The peasants produced only a modest economic output of rice on this land. The cost of relocating them is minor compared to the value of hydroelectricity produced. Building the dam generates a larger economic surplus and increases the capacity to satisfy preferences within Chinese households. It is the economically efficient thing to do.
>
> *Quizzical Observer:* How did you calculate the cost to society of relocating the peasants?
>
> *Economist:* In an ideal case, we would offer enough money to get families to move voluntarily. Specifically, we built new peasant villages at another location and paid for their move. There was the cost of concrete, glass, wood, and so on, and the cost of new roads and schools. The residents ended up with bigger and more modern houses than before!
>
> *Observer:* Ah . . . so the peasants *voluntarily* chose to leave and go to the new village with the shiny new houses?
>
> *Economist:* Err . . . not exactly. There were massive protests. Many had to be forced, and those not complying were arrested.
>
> *Observer:* So, some peasants clearly valued their existing plots more than simply as a place for a house and garden? Did your cost calculation include their subjective valuation of the land?

Economist: In some cases we try to measure "willingness to pay" for the scenic views lost. So, yes, we did survey some residents.

Observer: If the goal of being efficient is to satisfy people's preferences, but people are coerced and not allowed to choose what best satisfies their own preferences, how is that compatible with their higher welfare?

Economist: It's simple: The winners from the dam will make more money than the losers will lose. Society as a whole will gain through a higher net economic value created, even though some losers may not be fully compensated for their losses.

Observer: So, it is okay to kill Bob and give his kidneys to Sally and Fred, who are willing to pay a large amount for this to happen?

Economist: No! Clearly not. There are basic human rights to consider. Not all types of compulsory actions are justified. There are moral boundaries.

Observer: So, what you are saying is that the consequentialist theory of cost—benefit analysis requires much more to be a workable theory. It requires certain legal and property rights of citizens, impartial courts to adjudicate, fair and accountable public elections, and probably an independent press to boot.

Economist: I hadn't thought of it. I just assumed that . . .

Observer: You assumed that Western institutions exist worldwide? You assumed *omniscience* on the part of the economic "expert" who would be independent and impartial in carrying out a scientific analysis? But isn't the government paying for these cost—benefit studies? So, cost—benefit also requires a virtuous character on the part of economists and government leaders who design and implement policies, so as to not be corrupted?

Without free speech, political parties, fair courts, or the right to emigrate, citizens in China lack the ability to set the rules for public policy making and to ensure that they are fairly enforced. What is the meaning of "efficiency" in this setting?

Economists trained in the early twentieth century were likely to be attuned to the institutional context for public policy analysis. An example of careful attention to background conditions is given in this 1960 paper:

"It is well to state explicitly at the outset that the society considered in this essay is the sovereign democratic state, that is, a modern Western nation, where law is made and enforced by a responsible government within the context of representative institutions."[21] Economists trained more recently, however, may be oblivious to these problems and continue to see cost–benefit calculations (even involving coercion) as providing a purely scientific answer to policy questions. Larry Summers, a distinguished academic and former chief economist for the World Bank, once distributed a memo recommending that polluting industries in the United States be outsourced to Africa, where both incomes and life expectancies are lower. The memo was written by an aide, Lant Pritchett, and meant to be an ironic critique of welfare theory. Using impeccable cost–benefit logic, the memo deduced that "health-impairing pollution should be done in the country with the lowest cost."[22] The logic is impeccable: Citizens of a poor country indeed might prefer having a polluting industry—even if dangerous—than no industry at all. But when the memo was leaked, most readers did not get the joke. Such a model of Pareto choice *assumes* that villagers have well-enforced human rights in addition to property rights, that citizens enjoy the right to vote in fair elections, that an uncensored press can provide good information about the environmental risks, that violence cannot be used to intimidate workers or voters, and that an independent judicial system can address grievances fairly when citizens are injured by the resulting pollution—in short, it assumes away virtually all the salient characteristics of most poor, developing countries.[23]

For these reasons, the focus on preference-satisfaction as the ideal way to judge an economic system, and on cost–benefit analysis as the mechanism for studying policy recommendations, is problematic in many parts of the world. An economist must at minimum make a normative judgment that the necessary institutions of due process and democracy are in place to justify efficiency enhancements using cost–benefit logic.[24] Even with these judgments, other problems arise for assuming a pure science of welfare economics, adaptable to all countries.

In this chapter we have identified four criticisms of economic welfare analysis (with others covered in the next chapter): one, that it focuses on a narrow measure of subjective individual outcomes (preference satisfaction) and thereby ignores substantive measures of welfare; two, that distributional considerations are generally disregarded; three, that it relies on nonconsequentialist institutions and processes to protect human rights that are often missing; and four, that cost–benefit analyses of efficiency entail intrinsically normative judgments. These criticisms do not mean cost–benefit analysis should be thrown out—because even a flawed approach can be an improvement over no analysis.[25] But it does suggest caution and humility in its application and interpretation. Let us explore this last point further.

EFFICIENCY AS AN ETHICAL CONCEPT

The preference-satisfaction view of welfare has been widely adopted by orthodox economists around the world, ensconced in a tradition over 100 years old. It is now so ingrained that the ethical filters of early utilitarian and neoclassical writers have been mislaid. Hence, many economists posit as uncontroversial the claim that economic efficiency is a *scientific* concept that can be separated from normative or ethical concerns. David Friedman, for example, argues:

As an economist, I have no expertise in good and bad. I can, however, set up a "criterion of goodness" called *efficiency*. . . . One could object that the economist, defining efficiency according to what questions he can answer rather than what questions he is being asked, is like the drunk looking for his wallet under the streetlight because the light is better there than where he lost it. The reply is that an imperfect criterion of desirability is better than none.[26]

As a scientific endeavor, however, this "imperfect" criterion should be subject to thoughtful deliberation and debate. Lionel Robbins, one of the shapers of neoclassical theory, noted that the economic point of view was not meant to stifle ethical discussion. He regarded moral discourse as desirable, even necessary, for public policy analysis: "By itself Economics affords no solution to any of the important problems of life. I agree that for this reason an education which consists of Economics alone is a very imperfect education."[27]

The selling of efficiency as a scientific concept, rather than a moral one, arises from at least three misconceptions, as follows.

1. Settled consensus issue.

The first misconception is that this is a settled issue and requires no defense. The consensus argument is that once a critical mass of economists agree to adopt a particular version of welfare theory, the theory becomes "objective." But consensus simply implies the existence of a shared moral norm, not the absence of moral arguments and normative debate. This is particularly true when the arguments that led to its adoption need periodic updating or reconsideration. A moral norm flying under the radar becomes a dangerous obstacle to thinking: "When economists wax mushy on the virtue of what they call 'efficiency,' it is time to run for the hills, for they are selling a preferred moral doctrine in the guise of science."[28]

In promoting the concept of efficiency economists implicitly are adopting an ethical framework. It is understandable that there might be confusion on this issue. Vilfredo Pareto and Arthur Pigou, two giants in the developing field of neoclassical economics in the early twentieth century, were part of a positivist movement that identified progress with empirical measurement. They strove to find words that sounded scientific rather than value laden.[29] Nevertheless, the attempt failed and "economists claim to be positive scientists yet frequently use normative-sounding words."[30] Kenneth J. Arrow, a Nobel laureate, was acutely aware of the deliberate confusion arising from the choice of the word *efficiency*: "A definition is just a definition, but when the *definiendum* is a word already in common use with highly favorable connotations, it is clear that we are really trying to be persuasive; we are implicitly recommending the achievement of optimal states."[31] Economists use the language of efficiency to *persuade* as well as to describe. Converting all costs and benefits into dollar equivalents imparts the "ring of factual propositions . . . [that] are likely to obscure the evaluations implied."[32]

2. Quantification is value free.

This raises the second misconception, which is the belief that because an economic surplus can be estimated with numbers (for example, using dollar approximations), it is an objective measure of economic performance. However, although the economic surplus can be measured quantitatively, its *interpretation* and *analysis* relies entirely on subjective criteria. The dollar value of the surplus means something only after economists add a normative interpretation—that rational preferences are being satisfied, that satisfying preferences is the goal of an economic system, and that compensating losers is not necessary when assessing public policies. Evaluating the economy requires *both* facts and values.

The criterion of being quantifiable does not confer any special rights: Alternative objective calculations can also be constructed. For example, the next chapter discusses Amartya Sen's Human Development Index (HDI) as a substitute measure of human progress compared to the gross domestic product (GDP). If economists wish to talk about the size of the economic surplus as *one* factor affecting economic welfare, that is certainly quite different from asserting that (by definition) aggregate measures of surplus or income *equate* to economic welfare.

3. Specialization justifies ethical agnosticism.

A final misconception is that economists are skilled in their specialized tasks and have little to say about ethics; economists can ignore the subject, secure that philosophers will cover it. The premise for this belief is false, given the number of Nobel Prize winners in economics who have productively delved into ethical topics.[33] It is more accurate to say that many economists have not yet learned the tools of ethical analysis; this book is intended to help fill that void. Adam Smith, who expounded the advantages of specialization, also noted its chief defect—it promotes ignorance.[34]

Welfare economics remains "essentially an ethical subject" despite attempts to disguise it as science and notwithstanding the lack of awareness of many practitioners as to its moral origins and implications.[35] Ignorance may be bliss, but it is not an aid to critical thinking.

JUSTIFYING THE ECONOMIC VIEWPOINT

If you saw a $100 bill lying on the ground, would you bother to pick it up? Your answer is likely a resounding "Yes!" You probably have unfulfilled desires and an extra $100—manna from heaven—could be used for many worthwhile things or even for frivolous things that would provide satisfaction to you or someone you care about. Economists are loath to leave $100 bills lying on the ground like uncollected leaves. Being efficient means we have picked up all the $100 bills lying uncollected on the grass.

One could say that economists are utilitarians who measure the surplus of pleasure over pain by dollar votes cast in the market. Waste occurs when advantageous trades go unrealized ($100 bills are figuratively left lying on the ground). Waste is considered a bad outcome, whether of resources overused in production, of resources used to make products that are not the highest valued in the market, or of products going to those who do not value them most highly. When consumers and producers fail to complete a desired transaction—because a law prohibits trading or a law fixes the legal price above or below equilibrium—economists say this represents a waste called a deadweight loss: the diminished value to households of the consumer and producer surpluses (see Chapter 4).

Under certain conditions markets can maximize the value of the economic surplus, resulting in efficiency. Laissez-faire markets would not always produce an efficient outcome because sometimes market failures prevent it: the absence of competition, asymmetric information, third-party effects (such as pollution), and public goods (like national defense). Neoclassical economists thus often support government intervention in markets when doing so would enhance the capacity to satisfy consumer preferences.

Preference satisfaction as a measure of human welfare is an important concept that offers a powerful way of understanding markets and government policies. Every economist needs to have this idea in her or his tool kit. At the same time, this chapter has shown that efficiency and related cost–benefit calculations rely on ethical presumptions and arguments. Few textbooks examine the ethical underpinnings of welfare theory, and even fewer address the potentially coercive nature of policy recommendations arising from it.

LOOKING AHEAD

Although the Pareto test relies on voluntary trade and consensus is needed for change, the Kaldor-Hicks reformulation in the late 1930s took the step of asserting that aggregate measures of economic surplus can provide a measure of the welfare gains. As long as the net dollar surplus allows winners to compensate losers *hypothetically*, the overall gain in welfare is asserted regardless of whether the gains go to those most well off and the losses go to those most vulnerable, and regardless of whether compensation is actually paid. This is a huge ethical pill to swallow in the abstract. Amartya Sen, for example, calls the Kaldor-Hicks compensation test "either *unconvincing* or *redundant*." It is unconvincing if no interpersonal utility comparisons assess the *relative* standings of the winners and losers (for example, are the winners all rich and the losers all poor?), and it is redundant if compensation is actually paid.[36] In the eminent domain case of *Kelo v. New London*, discussed earlier, a compulsory trade is shown to enhance economic efficiency in the narrow Kaldor-Hicks sense but does so only by damaging the property rights of homeowner Suzette Kelo.

We turn in the next chapter to additional critiques of the preference satisfaction view of welfare.

CHAPTER 6

Critiques of Welfare as Preference Satisfaction

This chapter explores criticisms of the economic welfare model.
If preference satisfaction is not the Holy Grail of human welfare, this leads
to different accounting measures of success. It could also imply a role for
paternalism in government policies designed to improve direct measures of
well-being. The chapter concludes with an appeal for greater pluralism in
evaluating economic outcomes and processes.

ASKING THE RIGHT QUESTIONS

You chambermaids are used to spying through a keyhole, and so from the tiny
details that you actually see you often draw grand but false conclusions about
the whole thing.

—FRANZ KAFKA[1]

Critics of the neoclassical worldview draw on Kafka's metaphor, arguing
that economists reach "grand but false" conclusions by looking through
a keyhole and drawing a partial or distorted picture of social welfare
that lies behind the door. An ancient Indian legend likewise tells of six
blind men who encounter an elephant; each touches a different part of
the beast (the trunk, the tusks, the tail, the side, and so on) and pontifi-
cates on the whole from this partial impression. The moral of the story
is that "each is partly in the right, and all are in the wrong!"[2] To some
detractors the economic approach of focusing on preference satisfaction
as the only measure of welfare suffers from the same problem: It is at best
incomplete and, in some circumstances, could be morally repugnant. Let
us take a look at these arguments.

It is not possible to assess all the criticisms of neoclassical welfare
theory in this chapter; in-depth reviews are available elsewhere.[3] Chapter 4 notes that the "economic way of thinking" can be used to achieve
ends besides the outcome of preference satisfaction; hence, some confusion
arises when economists talk about efficiency as a broad consequentialist
methodology, as compared to economic efficiency in a narrow technical
sense. In the broader sense, economic metholodology is pluralist, admit-

ting of many possible outcomes. This chapter focuses on the narrow lens of economic efficiency as containing a specific normative value of preference satisfaction; this is the way many students learn to evaluate market outcomes. We begin with a review of normative economics as an instrumental theory of well-being. The following section explores criticisms leveled at preference satisfaction as a means of enhancing welfare. The next section, "When Goals Conflict," demonstrates the trade-offs that exist between efficiency and other goals. The section after that, "Alternative Measures of Welfare," uses these criticisms to develop alternative indicators of economic development. The concluding section explores a pluralist approach as a viable means of evaluating the economy.

Instrumental Well-Being

Instrumental theories of human well-being focus on indirect measures of goodness. Economists tend to focus on monetary values because a medium of exchange serves as an all-purpose measure for things that are important to humans. Money is instrumentally good because it provides Frank with the means to acquire what he truly values—the nutrients to sustain life. Hence, when economists equate a higher GDP per capita with higher well-being, they are using an instrumental or intermediary theory of well-being. Economists take it as self-evident that rational people use money to satisfy their preferences and that satisfying preferences enhances well-being. Economists do not try to define what ultimate well-being is or ought to be. To do so would question the choices made by individuals, who presumably know what enhances their own well-being better than anyone else. The Latin adage, *"de gustibus non est disputandum"* captures this meaning: In matters of preference and taste, there can be no disputes.

To briefly review Chapters 4 and 5: Economists try to address the problem of market evaluation by using an appealing story of individual exchange. If people voluntarily trade with others, it is reasonable to assume that the dollar value created by that exchange—minus the costs involved—will generate a surplus or net benefit that can be calculated and added up across everyone in society. Economists are careful to say that the benefits and costs must be measured whether they are explicit (like a wage) or implicit (like the value of one's time). In addition, it is important to measure costs and benefits that are external to the transaction (like pollution). Once these accounting problems are addressed, the standard economic approach solves the problem of "what" outcome to measure by selecting the highest economic surplus generated by voluntary exchange.

The orthodox economic approach assumes that every dollar value created for one person is equivalent to a dollar value created for anyone else. For example, if one exchange yields $5,000 net value to Bob, and a different transaction yields a $500 net value to Susan, economists think it is acceptable to *add up* these two amounts as equivalent increases to social welfare: The economy has produced an increase in overall value to society of $5,500. Someone might provide additional information by pointing out that Bob is a millionaire and Susan is destitute. Hence, Susan's gain of $500 might actually entail a better outcome for social welfare than Bob's gain of $5,000. However, standard economics gives Bob's gain *ten times* the weight of Susan's in evaluating social welfare. The orthodox approach to efficiency ignores *who* in society gets to enjoy the value produced, and interpersonal comparisons of utility or welfare are eschewed.

In this ethical system "waste" occurs when (a) we use resources without regard for their scarcity, measured by accurate price signals; or (b) when we do not make the correct mix of products that satisfy people's preferences; or (c) when we do not get products into the hands of those who are willing and able to pay the most for them. The Pareto test for the existence of waste asks us to imagine a world in which there are $100 bills lying around on the ground. Being more efficient implies that everyone can be made better off, or at least that *some* can be made better off without hurting others, by allowing people to pick up these $100 bills.

But, as we noted in Chapter 5, this is a questionable metaphor for public policy: It is generally not correct to imply that Melinda can reach out and grab $100 bills that are waiting to be picked up. The reason is that *some* of the $100 bills are already in Katherine's wallet! In other words, most policy changes impose *involuntary* costs on some citizens even if the change generates a net surplus overall. Efficiency cannot mean voluntary exchange when a policy is implemented and compensation to losers is generally ignored. Coercion is sidestepped in the Kaldor-Hicks formulation by assuming that institutions and processes protect basic human and legal rights. These assumptions are not met in many developing countries, even though economists use cost–benefit analysis as if it were scientifically adaptable to any economy.

QUESTIONING PREMISES

The standard welfare model relies on key premises: that individuals are the locus of decision making, that individual preferences are *predetermined* and *stable*, that individuals make *rational* choices to satisfy their preferences, that satisfying individual preferences through *voluntary* trade enhances well-being or *welfare*, and that basic human rights are protected through a justice system and democracy, so that losers, even if not compensated, are protected by procedural fairness.

Chapter 7 explores the moral limits to markets based in part on the alleged involuntary nature of some exchanges. This chapter focuses on whether preferences (as opposed to other substantive measures) should be used as proxies for welfare. The following are six criticisms of the preference satisfaction approach.

1. False Beliefs.

Most preferences are governed by beliefs. People's voluntary choices may not translate into higher welfare if these beliefs turn out to be false. Figure 6.1 shows the connections between beliefs, preferences, behaviors and outcomes.

Suppose Adam is a sixteen-year-old boy who believes that he is perfectly capable of operating a Harley-Davidson motorcycle at 100 mph,

FIGURE 6.1. Beliefs, preferences, and well-being.

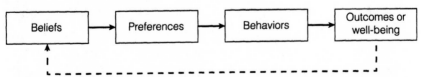

Beliefs about the world are the basis for preferences, which in turn influence behaviors and outcomes. A learning curve (dotted line) shows that beliefs are subject to correction.

because he has done so using computer simulation. Adam's preference to race a motorcycle is based on the false belief that a computer simulation is a good proxy for the real experience. Does it enhance a teenager's welfare to let him act on this belief? Would buying a Harley-Davidson motorcycle enhance Adam's welfare? If you are *libertarian* the answer is unequivocally "yes," because making mistakes is the only way Adam can learn, via the feedback loop between outcomes and beliefs (the dotted line in Figure 6.1). A famous saying in consumer economics is *"caveat emptor"*—let the buyer beware. Experience is often the best teacher.

If you are *paternalistic*, however, the answer to the motorcycle question is "no," because Adam may never get a second chance to learn: Some mistakes are fatal. Teenage death rates from motor vehicle accidents are far higher than for adults. One reliable finding from behavioral economics is that most people (particularly teenagers) consistently overestimate their own abilities. Said differently, they hold false beliefs. Satisfying preferences is a questionable way to enhance welfare if preferences are based on false beliefs.

Richard Thaler and Cass Sunstein argue that false beliefs and irrationality are consistently found in the population and hence that "mild paternalism" is justified in some public policies to "nudge" people to make the right choices for their own welfare.[4] Choice architecture refers to the framing of options in a way that prods the decision maker toward the desired outcome. Special licenses and classes might be required to operate motorcycles, especially by teenagers. In another setting, business firms could automatically enroll employees in savings plans as the "default" option, rather than requiring special action.

2. Preferences for Bad Things.

Melinda may *prefer* a product like heroin even though she *knows* it is bad for her and will reduce her welfare. This suggests a problem arising either from a breakdown in her rationality (inability to choose the right means to her own desired good ends) or a breakdown in her willpower (inability to carry out the right means to her good ends). Satisfying preferences may no longer be justified if it can be shown that Melinda's preferences are destructive of her welfare. For these reasons, as with false beliefs, paternalistic government policies would seek to improve welfare by denying Adam and Melinda the right to buy what they want.

The presumption that a paternalistic government agent could better know one's welfare than oneself is difficult to accept, however. Friedrich Hayek, a fervent supporter of markets, devoted his Nobel Prize lecture to the idea that well-meaning economists delude themselves with the "Pretense of Knowledge."[5] Much government intervention presupposes that bureaucrats know much more than they are capable of knowing. To Hayek, it is arrogant to imagine that policy makers can understand, much less accurately manipulate, the world.

Paternalism may also run afoul of Kantian ethics: Treating Adam and Melinda as children deprives them of the respect owed to each person.[6] Moreover, the value of freedom is enhanced when people can develop through learning from their mistakes. However, the issue is complex because Melinda herself may have a "metapreference"—that is, a preference about her preferences! Melinda's metapreference is that she be free of her heroin addiction, and she may welcome the paternalistic hand that slaps the heroin needle out of her grasp. Is welfare enhanced when Melinda's preference for heroin or her metapreference for no addiction is achieved?

3. Preference Conflicts and Identity Integration.
The previous point raises a key issue: Are we just one person with one set of preferences, or are we multiple selves? Brian has a term paper due on Monday, yet he longs to take Sunday off to watch football games. His preference today is to goof off; but his preference on Monday will be that he had written the paper on Sunday. Which multiple preference set should economists try to satisfy? As Brian's situation illustrates, preferences can be "dynamically inconsistent," reflecting the conflict between our different selves. We are our *past* selves, we are our *present* selves, and we are our *future* selves. To get the paper done, Brian's current self must be *altruistic* toward his future selves by disregarding today's preferences for watching football and substituting Monday's preference that he sacrifice and write the paper today.

We are often confronted with the need to be "altruistic" toward our future selves. Investments in saving more today, exercising, eating right, and so on, require that we suppress our current preferences in favor of promoting the foreseeable enjoyment of our future selves. We are all "trustees of all our possible future selves" and an individual must develop a fiduciary relationship toward that future self based on trust and duty.[7] But why should anyone take painful steps today to satisfy the preferences of some future "selves" that we haven't even met yet? The only way that satisfying preferences in the present will produce future well-being is if personality is integrated among past, present, and future selves. This implies identity, coherence, and deep knowledge of who we are and where ultimate good derives from. In short, this may require a virtue ethics understanding of commitments to our future selves.

The ancient philosophers thought that the virtues were a set of habits necessary for a good life. Prudence means using common sense or reason to discern right action, such as what is the proper duty toward one's future selves. Temperance means moderation of our passion for current pleasure. Both prudence and temperance require the discipline of willpower or self-control, supported by the other virtues—courage, justice, faith, hope, and charity. It takes a village of virtues to overcome the problem of dynamic inconsistency.

4. Endogenous Preferences.

Where do preferences come from? The orthodox model assumes that preferences are innately "given" to autonomous individuals as if by "Immaculate Conception."[8] But what if preferences are not so naturally predetermined? Instead, consider whether preferences are "endogenous"—that is, created by the economic system itself. Frank Knight, one of the great economists of the twentieth century, worried about this problem:

In organizing its value scale, the economic order does far more than select and compare wants for exchangeable goods and services: its activity extends to the formation and radical transformation, if not to the outright creation, of the wants themselves; they as well as the means of their gratification are largely products of the system. An examination of the ethics of the economic system must consider the question of the kind of wants which it tends to generate or nourish as well as its treatment of wants as they exist at a given time.[9]

If preferences are socially constructed, "We cannot afford to neglect the processes by which cultures are created and by which preferences are learned."[10] Billions of dollars are spent on advertising each day, of which only some is informative and the rest intended to persuade. A television commercial shows a beautiful couple smiling as their convertible races along California's mountainous coastal highway. This evocative image intends to sway preferences in favor of luxury and speed and away from prudence and frugality. If preferences are amenable to such propaganda, does that mean the market is simply satisfying unstable *whims*? If so, this might justify paternalistic rules such as a three-day "cooling off" period for returns after a major purchase like a car or house.

The widespread existence of manufactured preferences casts a shadow over the moral justification for markets: It is circular to argue that markets perform a valuable function by satisfying preferences if the market itself creates them. Indeed, a strong critique of capitalism is that markets create desires that previously did not exist—hence people may feel *worse off* after market penetration and saturation advertising. In such a view, preferences are "polluted" by the market.[11]

From a public health perspective, polluted preferences can be harmful if they manipulate medical care treatment. The United States and New Zealand are the only two economically advanced countries that permit direct-to-consumer advertising of prescription drugs.[12] Pharmaceutical advertising was permitted in 1976 by a Supreme Court decision on commercial free speech. Voting against the majority, Justice William Rehnquist cautioned that "the societal interest *against* the promotion of drug use for every ill, real and imaginary, seems to me exceptionally strong."[13]

The paternalistic rationale for banning pharmaceutical advertising is that patients should discuss prescriptions with their doctors who will better know the appropriate medicines to prescribe. Direct advertising may create patient wants before ascertaining patient needs—skewing information because drug companies have no incentive to advertise generic medicines that are cheaper than patented medicines. After the FDA relaxed warning disclosures for electronic ads in 1997, it became possible to advertise prescription drugs on television.

If persuasive advertising is effective, why not alter preferences *directly* as a way of enhancing well-being? Western society is built on a market ethic of maximizing consumption, while Buddhist society in south Asia focuses on minimizing desire. Becoming Buddhist means letting go of one's wants through a process of detachment from one's preferences. Logically, one can feel content even if poor, if one has few desires; or, one can be rich and still feel miserable if many preferences remain unsatisfied. Hence, satisfying preferences is no panacea for achieving a mental state of happiness or peace of mind.[14]

5. Substantive Well-Being.

The view that only preferences matter runs into further critiques from those who administer public policy programs. If preferences alone matter, then the best welfare policy is simply to give qualifying poor people cash payments, with which they can buy whatever they desire.[15] This approach is efficient in an economic sense as discussed in the Second Fundamental Welfare Theorem (Chapter 5). But what about a poor person who uses the cash to satisfy a preference for gambling on horse races? Most taxpayers would insist that government payments should go toward urgent substantive needs, such as housing, food, or health care—even though this approach is "inefficient" in terms of satisfying preferences. The issue of *substantive* welfare versus *preference* welfare plays an important role in evaluating some public policies. We return to the issue of substantive well-being in the section on "Alternative Measures of Welfare."

6. Whose Preferences?

Some preferences may matter even if they are not reflected in market transactions. Suppose Brian buys a plagiarized term paper for $35 rather than writing his own. Although Susan is not in the market to buy a term paper, she cares about this market because she thinks cheating is *intrinsically* unfair, regardless of the consequences to her own or Brian's grades. As with antisocial preferences, satisfying Brian's preference for a bought term paper has a decidedly mixed impact on welfare.[16] Moral limitations of markets arise from such considerations.

An enormous category of people who cannot participate in the market as autonomous agents are those who have not yet been born: future generations. Should an economic system consider only the preferences of current consumers, regardless of its sustainability over time? The welfare-as-preference-satisfaction view to some extent disenfranchises the experiences of everyone not currently in the market.[17] Many times this omission would not seem to matter. If consumer preferences for red cars cause the market to make more red cars today, this seems like a good thing—regardless of whether people who are not yet born like the color red. But a starving child also has no preferences that can be observed in the marketplace. If distributional issues matter for welfare, then satisfying preferences alone will be problematic (see Chapters 10 and 11).

These critiques caution us that preference satisfaction may not be synonymous with maximizing social welfare in all cases. The following section investigates further by examining the potential conflicts between preference satisfaction and other goals.

WHEN GOALS CONFLICT

We began Chapter 2 by listing some of the alternative "good things" that people might want from an economic system, such as freedom, national defense, a social safety net, and so on. Satisfying preferences is certainly one of the important goals, but the question we continue to explore is, "Should preference satisfaction hold a privileged position over other goals?" In broad terms, "efficiency" means being on the frontier of what is currently possible given resources and technology. But *which* goal frontier should we be on? People desire a variety of outcomes in addition to preference satisfaction. Economists walk a slippery slope when they imply that there is an objective and impartial basis for choosing preference satisfaction as *the* goal of the system.

A popular economics textbook illustrates the misconception. The authors carefully note that "efficiency is not the only goal" of society. But they go on to say, as if it were a scientific truth, that "efficiency *should* be the first goal" of social policy. The authors base this claim on the assertion that being economically efficient "enables us to achieve all our other goals to the fullest possible extent."[18] This last statement implies that efficiency is *in fact* the only good outcome because there is some process of alchemy that can magically transform satisfied preferences into any other desirable outcome at no cost. Most economists readily admit that difficult trade-offs exist between efficiency, equity, and other desirable goals such as saving lives or preserving property rights. There are diverse economic problems and a single definition of the economic "goal" is not capable of tackling all of these.[19] The following examples illustrate some immutable trade-offs:

- *Fuel Efficiency:* Your car's fuel efficiency is measured by miles per gallon (mpg). But achieving higher mpg might require making a car lighter, and a lighter car might not be as safe. Hence, achieving greater fuel efficiency might reduce the efficiency in saving lives in car accidents. Although fuel efficiency and savings lives are two stated and objective goals of public policy, neither is actually the desired goal of satisfying preferences. Because consumers may actually desire cars with the attributes of faster speed and greater power, being efficient at satisfying consumer preferences could reduce *both* fuel efficiency and safety.[20]

- *Saving Lives:* A doctor typically strives to achieve the goal of saving the most lives possible. Suppose an emergency room doctor has only two pints of blood on hand and no chance of getting more today. Three patients in critical condition are admitted: Abel and Barb each need *one* pint of blood to survive, and Carlos needs *two* pints of blood to survive.[21] What should the doctor do? If the doctor's goal is to "save the most lives today" then the answer is obvious: He should provide one pint of blood to Abel and one pint to Barb. Carlos would die, but the *most lives possible* were saved given scarce resources. Blood was used "efficiently" to achieve the medical objective today.

    Economic efficiency does not define the goal as "saving the most lives today" but as "satisfying the most preferences today." This means that if Carlos pulls out a wad of cash and offers the highest price for the two pints of blood, economic welfare is maximized when he is allowed to buy the blood. Abel and Barb would both die, but resources (that is, blood) would flow to their "highest" economic use. This outcome creates the largest economic surplus but is not efficient at saving the most lives today. It is not possible to do both!

Medical efficiency and economic efficiency are not complementary in this short-run example.

To summarize, resource allocation cannot be analyzed independently from the normative selection of a goal. Economics in the abstract—"maximizing subject to constraints"—is meaningless until it is applied, and in its application a value judgment is rendered. Saying that economic efficiency "enables us to achieve all our other goals to the fullest possible extent" misses this important distinction.

- *Dynamic (Long-Run) Efficiency:* One could argue that the higher price Carlos paid for blood in the previous example would make it profitable for suppliers to generate more pints of blood today and particularly *in the future.* With a profit motive, the market could eventually save more lives, compared to what would happen if doctors allocated blood solely by medical need and not ability to pay. Markets can thus be justified on the basis of innovation and growth as important economic objectives, in addition to static efficiency (such as satisfying today's preferences).[22] Dynamic efficiency concentrates on achieving the goal of increasing the preference satisfactions in *future* time periods.

There are well-known trade-offs when trying to satisfy current preferences rather than future preferences. For example, monopolies are inefficient in the short run because they reduce outputs and raise prices. However, granting a patent monopoly to an inventor creates an incentive that spurs long-run innovation. Hence, patents promote future inventions but hurt short-run efficiency.[23] Textbook authors routinely glide over the sudden and unexamined switch in goals from static to dynamic efficiency, but the ethical implications are huge. Whose interests should count: those of present or future consumers? By what moral standard do we make such a decision? If the static efficiency view is replaced by dynamic efficiency, what other goals should likewise be reconsidered on moral grounds?

Libertarian economists (who often promote freedom over all else) are suspicious of short-run efficiency as a guide to policy because it could involve heavy government regulations (as in monopoly control). Austrian school economists favor a long-run perspective in which freedom of entry and exit provides a landscape for dynamic innovation. In a famous passage, Joseph Schumpeter outlines this approach:

The fundamental impulse that sets and keeps the capitalist engine in motion comes from the new consumers, goods, the new methods of production or transportation, the new markets, the new forms of industrial organization that capitalist enterprise creates. . . incessantly destroying the old one, incessantly creating a new one. This process of Creative Destruction is the essential fact about capitalism.[24]

Satisfying current preferences is less important to libertarians than providing a legal framework of property rights and markets that encourages freedom and steady innovation over the long run.

To recap, economic efficiency is a measure of whether the preferences of current households are potentially maximized given the existing allocations of income and wealth. It is not the case that economic efficiency will always allow individuals to better achieve their other goals, because trade-offs exist. Hence, a broader discussion is warranted about other desirable outcomes and how public policies can help achieve them.

ALTERNATIVE MEASURES OF WELFARE

Amartya Sen won the Nobel Prize in 1998 for his work understanding poverty and famine around the world. Sen is a notable proponent of the view that economists need to better understand the legitimate role of ethical discourse in the discipline. In *On Ethics and Economics* (1991) Sen argues that economic efficiency is a vacuous standard of evaluation. Although the size of an economic surplus may be an interesting number to calculate, it should not provide the main basis for appraising an economy. Sen observes, "An economy can be optimal in [the Pareto] sense even when some people are rolling in luxury and others are near starvation. . . . In short, a society or an economy can be Pareto-optimal and still be perfectly disgusting."[25] By assessing outcomes only on the basis of dollar votes, economists eschew any substantive account of what makes life worth living. In other words, economists operate in a "barren informational landscape."[26] The value to society of a hot dog (or any other product) is said to be measured only by the amount that someone offers to pay for it. To critics, the value of a hot dog could also be considered in relation to how much substantive benefit it can provide—for example, through calories and nutrients in the diet.

Using a substantive approach, one could make reasoned judgments about the needs of people in society. "Needs" are said to be things required for basic survival; "wants" are everything else. The demand curve we studied in Chapter 4 makes no distinctions about why people buy; it is impossible to say whether Joseph bought a hot dog based on "need" or "want." The difficulty of discerning needs from wants was noted by Adam Smith, who mused that even a common laborer would need a linen shirt to be seen in public without shame. He states, "By necessaries I understand not only the commodities which are indispensably necessary for the support of life, but whatever the custom of the country renders it indecent for creditable people, even of the lowest order, to be without."[27] Hence, "need" can only be defined in light of psychological, social, and ethical norms, and not simply based on biological necessity. A strictly Orthodox Jew offered a pork hot dog may have the nutrients to live, but it may not be a life considered worth living. Moreover, it is impossible for scientists to answer objectively the question, "How many calories per day are needed to sustain life?" To answer this, one would need to define "sustain." Do we mean kept barely alive, or do we mean functioning in peak condition?[28]

Although interpersonal comparisons of utility have been decried in economics since the early 1930s, Sen believes that "rough and ready" interpersonal comparisons can aid decision making and potentially solve Arrow's impossibility problem. Sen's Nobel Prize address is appropriately entitled, "The Possibility of Social Choice."[29] Here is an application of Sen's idea. Suppose that scarce hospital resources can be used for only one operation, and there are two options: One is to perform life-saving surgery on Katrina, a three-year-old orphan; the other is to perform minor cosmetic surgery on Paris Hilton, a wealthy heiress. It defies most people's common sense (and moral intuition) to insist that we cannot distinguish between needs and wants in this situation. Likewise, a Chanel diamond-encrusted handbag sells for $261,000 to a bored socialite;[30] that same money can buy 800 tons of wheat that can feed a village of 4,000 starving Somalis for a year. Most people could agree that we can make distinctions between these purchases, even if economic theory refuses to discern them.

Sen would admit that interpersonal comparisons of mental states—like utility or happiness—are problematical, for the reason that "Utilities may sometimes be very malleable in response to persistent deprivation."[31] For example, a woman living in a gender-discriminating society in which she cannot legally drive may come to accept that deprivation with an altered set of preferences:

She may take whatever pleasure she can from small achievements, and adjust her desires. . . . But her success in such adjustment would not make her deprivation go away. The metric of pleasure or desire may sometimes be quite inadequate in reflecting the extent of a person's substantive deprivation.[32]

Sen notes that there are other sources of information for interpersonal comparisons that can be used for assessing policies that have distributional impacts, as shown in the following section.

GDP as a Measure of Well-Being

The traditional economic approach measures progress as an increase in gross domestic product (GDP) per capita.[33] During the Cold War of the mid-twentieth century the GDP growth rate became a "national virility symbol" not only for rich nations but also for developing countries.[34] However, many emerging nations like Brazil had booming GDPs in the 1960s yet experienced large and rising disparities of income and wealth. Many Brazilian social workers recorded the dire need of starving peasants for food, even though their "preferences" lacked effective buying power in the market. How should Brazil's "economic miracle" be evaluated in this case?

As reported in Chapter 1, in 2009 five Nobel laureates in economics pushed for a more nuanced approach to understanding human welfare.[35] In some circumstances, GDP provides a distorted view of the trends of human progress and provides no indication of sustainability. Well-being is "multidimensional" and requires a multitude of indicators in addition to the aggregate and indirect measure of market activity. The problem of interpretation is acute because of the way GDP growth puts more emphasis on those who already have higher incomes. That is, a 10 percent growth in income of a rich person proportionately counts more than a 10 percent growth in income of a poor person: The share of income provides the weights.

Alternative measures assess social welfare on the basis of whether a rising economic tide is "lifting all boats." Sen notes that "a partial ordering of a complete welfare indicator" is preferable to "a complete ordering of a partial welfare indicator" that omits distributional impacts.[36] For example, much welfare-enhancing domestic production goes unreported because it is carried out in nonmarket settings (for example, caring for family members).[37] To Sen, broadening the base of information deepens our understanding of economic processes and enriches the evaluation of policies. He argues that a better measure of development relates to capabilities. One way this idea has been implemented is through the creation of a Human Development Index (HDI), a hybrid of instrumental and substantive measures of welfare. The HDI is addressed in Chapter 11.

Agency versus Well-being

To continue with Sen's critique, the standard efficiency view is selectively objective: It throws out information that doesn't fit a predetermined normative viewpoint. As in Kafka's *Castle*, economists peer through a keyhole and reach "grand but false conclusions" based on this selective attention. Sen argues economists need to broaden the range of what is considered for evaluation: "We can see the person, in terms of *agency*, recognizing and respecting his or her ability to form goals, commitments, values, etc., and we can also see the person in terms of *well-being*."[38] Suppose Mahira has a preference that candidate X win an upcoming election. But the act of voting imposes costs on Mahira, such as time away from work. Mahira has little expectation of receiving higher well-being from voting because her individual vote is likely irrelevant to the outcome and her candidate has little chance of winning. A calculation of efficiency would suggest that if Mahira votes, her behavior is irrational because it is not expected to satisfy her preferences.

However, Mahira may not be motivated by her expected well-being so much as by her **agency**. Agency is the capacity of a person to act in the world in terms of his or her own values and goals. Agency relates to who we are, not necessarily to our state of well-being (the two concepts, although interdependent, are distinct). For Mahira, voting is *intrinsically* worthwhile and not because of instrumental welfare benefits. A commitment to voting arises from Mahira's motive to do what is right as a citizen, and this commitment often "drives a wedge between personal choice and personal welfare."[39]

Happiness

In recent years some economists and psychologists have also advocated **happiness** as an alternative index to GDP per capita or other measures of well-being.[40] Bhutan, a country in South Asia with a large Buddhist population, has formally adopted gross national happiness (GNH) as its official goal of development policy. In this view, welfare is not the satisfaction of preferences (which, as noted, may rely on bad beliefs and other problems); rather, welfare is synonymous with happiness.

The happiness indicator revives, in some ways, the classical utilitarian viewpoints we explored in Chapter 2. To Jeremy Bentham, happiness meant the hedonistic difference between pleasure and pain. To John Stuart Mill, happiness reflected experiences of a more refined nature, involving moral sentiments and intellectual pleasures. This raises immediate problems with trying to measure human welfare using happiness: What does the term mean? Happiness could mean a judgment or appraisal of how one's life has gone to that point (with anticipation of the future), or happiness could simply mean an affective sentiment, a feeling, a matter of mood at the moment.

There are a variety of ways of asking people about their happiness or life satisfaction, and the answers given would not necessarily be comparable. For example, a five-step scale question asks: "How happy do you feel as you live now? (1) very happy; (2) fairly happy; (3) neither happy nor unhappy; (4) fairly unhappy; or (5) very unhappy." Can any useful interpersonal comparisons be made of the answers? If John rates his happiness as "1" and Johann rates his as "2," do we have confidence that these numbers have any absolute or relative meaning? For example, some cultures socialize people to be modest, and it may appear to be bragging to claim too much happiness. Or someone who is desperately unhappy may have been socialized to put on a "happy face" for strangers who come knocking on the door asking survey questions. Defining, measuring, and interpreting something as fluid as happiness is a huge difficulty.[41]

Nevertheless, researchers have reported that the relationship between per capita income and happiness appears to be positive, but there are diminishing returns as income increases. Hence, a $1,000 increase in income to a poor person has a larger expected impact on happiness than the same dollar increase accruing to a rich person. However, causality may run in both directions: A happier person may earn more *because* happiness is an aid to social capital that produces success in some occupations (such as sales). Overall, differences in income appear to explain only a small proportion of the differences in happiness between persons.

Both the substantive measures of welfare (as in the hybrid HDI) and the self-reported measures of happiness generally show a positive correlation with GDP per capita. However, the distinctions and nuances raised argue in favor of a pluralistic account of welfare that goes beyond income measures alone.

Economics Redefined

One reason people evaluate the economy in different ways is that they have different conceptions of the economic problem. Lionel Robbins provides a commonly used definition:

Economics is the science which studies human behaviour as a relationship between ends and scarce means which have alternative uses.[42]

In proposing the *ends* and *means* definition, Robbins sought to stretch the boundaries of the field beyond the confines of his day (the 1930s), in which economics was limited to explaining only the causes of material welfare. Robbins expands it to include any outcome-directed activity in which there are resource constraints. Hence, modern economists like Gary Becker use the model of preference satisfaction under constraints to understand the choice of family size, the decision to marry or divorce, and crime as a career option.[43]

In light of the additional outcomes and nonconsequentialist approaches considered important by many people, an even broader definition may be warranted:

Economics is the systematic study of the patterns of individual and group behavior used for the provisioning of the socio-cultural-material system.[44]

In addition to satisfying preferences, this definition can encompass rules, duties, commitments, and virtues in economic life, as well as the study of cognitive mechanisms that are not consciously controlled yet likely play some role in some economic activity.[45] It encompasses concerns for procedural justice as well as for outcomes and better captures the dynamics of social interaction in which trust and fairness are crucial aspects of exchange.[46]

SOLUTIONS TO THIS CHAPTER'S CRITIQUE

It is tempting to argue (in a circular fashion) that choices reveal welfare-enhancing preferences and that welfare is whatever is revealed through preference-enhancing choices. By ignoring nonconsequentialist ethical frameworks and insisting that all actions reflect only utility based on preference satisfaction, economists construct "an extremely limited way of assessing social achievement."[47] One Confucian writer playfully notes, "Four thousand years of efficient living would ruin any nation."[48] The problem with efficiency is that it cannot produce all the desirable outcomes (or desirable processes) that society demands of its economic system. Maximizing the economic surplus has numerous desirable features, but it may fail to enhance individual or overall well-being if, as discussed earlier, preferences rely on false beliefs and are polluted, or if income and wealth distribution are highly skewed. Efficiency cannot, to continue the Confucian critique, provide a credible philosophy of living.

In recent years development economists have shifted their focus from instrumental theories of well-being to substantive ones. Rather than relying on income alone as the only measure of economic success, economists are now examining success as a family might around the table. Families discuss literacy, health, life expectancy, freedom, and other components of agency. Substantive measures of well-being directly examine what is "intrinsically good" about human life—that is, what is good for its own sake and not any ulterior purpose.

There are problems with both instrumental and substantive theories of human well-being, and readers should note that the subject is controversial. Some economists see government playing a critical (if paternalistic) role in improving society's well-being across a range of issues. A focus on substantive measures of well-being could lead to stronger government roles in provision of public goods like education and health care. In addition, even if a market system is used to produce goods, some government regulations are proposed to "improve" consumer choice. Since 1998, government rules require that automobile manufacturers install air bags in every new vehicle. The implicit assumption is that, if consumers were given an option, some would prefer not to buy what it is thought to be in their own interest to buy (a safer car). By mandating airbags, paternalists argue that the substantive gain in human lives saved is a more valuable outcome to society than the loss of preference satisfaction and freedom in the market.

On the other side, economists who favor freedom and limited government are more inclined to accept instrumental theories of well-being, in which it is assumed that rational consumers have stable preferences and that money is used to provide for an individual's own best outcomes through the invisible hand. Government intrusion will generally reduce well-being by denying people what they themselves think will make themselves better off. Even if a consumer's preferences are ill-informed or irrational, public policy can still defer to personal choice as the assumed default. In this vein, Kantians object to government intrusions that fail to show proper respect for the autonomy of the individual.

Considering the criticisms of this chapter, what is an economist to do? One possibility for bringing these sides closer is to change the definition of welfare. Some economists propose that well-being is really not the satisfaction of *actual* preferences held (because some might be ill-informed) but of fully rational, fully self-interested, and well-informed metapreferences. This is a step toward a substantive theory of well-being, because it asks us to judge what it is rational for well-informed people to prefer for themselves. This also allows for some modest paternalism that would not be permissible in a libertarian approach. The rational and well-informed preference view cannot be observed directly by watching people's behaviors, unless we argue that all behaviors are rational, self-interested, and well informed.

Daniel Hausman suggests an alternative approach:

A second possibility is for economists to avoid committing themselves to any philosophical theory of welfare and to take preference satisfaction merely as *evidence* of well-being, whatever well-being may be. . . . Knowing that good health, happiness, enjoyment, the respect of others, intimate friends and so forth generally contribute to welfare gives content to talk of welfare without defining the term.[49]

Rather than accept preference satisfaction as *the* indicator of welfare, economists can see preference satisfaction as *an* indicator of welfare. This approach is pluralistic in that it admits that more than one measure is needed to understand human well-being. It is also a more humble approach because it recognizes that the goal of efficiency should always be understood within a wider ethical framework of policy analysis.

One can see an example of the pluralist approach in the work of the Bill and Melinda Gates Foundation, previously noted in Chapter 2. The Gates Foundation motto is, "All lives have equal value." This is a break from neoclassical economics, which values lives differentially based on earning power in the market. The differences in health policy that result are quite startling. In the market view, resources should go toward curing the diseases of those who have the most spending power, because this will generate the largest consumer surplus in dollar terms. But saving one more elderly rich patient with heart disease costs a lot of money compared to saving one impoverished child with dysentery. The Gates Foundation, by valuing all lives equally, allocates resources toward those activities that save the most lives per dollar spent.

The Gates Foundation imposes transparency and effectiveness by insisting on a cost–benefit analysis. It is ethical to insist that resources must be used where they achieve the biggest "bang for the buck," but the *measure* of success is not maximizing consumer surplus but maximizing the number of lives saved—a substantive (rather than an instrumental) goal. The Gates Foundation demonstrates that one can be hardheaded about being efficient, using marginal cost and marginal benefit analysis, without adopting a goal of preference satisfaction.[50]

LOOKING AHEAD

Part II has considered the ways that economic views evolved in terms of how to evaluate the performance of the micro economy. As shown, ethical arguments permeate the economist's conception of efficiency. The concept can be defended, but doing so requires the help of other ethical frameworks and relies on particular institutional arrangements that are conspicuously absent in some parts of the world.

Part III explores the ways in which knowledge of ethical frameworks aids the understanding of markets and the call for public policies that address perceived market failures. The next chapter shows that moral norms can constrain market activities.

Topics in Ethics and Economics

CHAPTER 7

Moral Limits to Markets

This chapter explores why societies restrict or ban particular market transactions. Efficiency is not the only consideration in designing and regulating markets. Considerations of intrinsic value, background circumstances, fairness, duty, and character also arise.

INTRODUCTION

Although economics textbooks analyze market failures arising from losses of efficiency, rarely do they address potential market failures arising from conflicts about inherent social values—a community's desire, for example, for intrinsic moral goods over market goods. A robust literature exists on this topic.[1] The bottom line was summed up by Paul Samuelson more than forty years ago when he quipped: "Do not render unto the market that which is not the market's."[2]

Economists who address market prohibitions often analyze the consumer welfare gains and losses from legalizing a banned product, such as marijuana. As important as this activity is, the economic welfare view provides only a partial consequentialist perspective. A more general analysis of moral theories can enrich the discussion, especially in trying to understand controversies like stem cell research, sweatshop labor, and human organ sales. Critical thinking requires an understanding of arguments arising from other types of outcomes (for example, fairness), from ethical rules and duties (for example, Kantian or religious based) and from ethical character (such as Aristotle and Adam Smith).

Moral limits to markets arise for at least two distinct reasons:

1. A repugnance at selling particular kinds of goods and services that embody beliefs relating to *intrinsic values*; and
2. A rejection of market price as an allocation mechanism in particular *background circumstances* of trade.

Family and community relationships are the glue that binds societies together. People in groups are bound together by "mutual trust, respect, and dignity," but the market "may confront, clash, and destroy" such relationships, according to Vernon Smith, who won the Nobel Prize in Economics in 2002.[3] Using prices to allocate goods may in some cases violate deeply held moral and civic norms. Society tends to use nonprice allocations—rationing, first-come/first-served, favoritism and lottery—to deal with scarcity when community values other than efficiency are paramount. Society also tends to discourage or even ban activities that are thought to degrade important institutions in society. At the same time, markets and market penetration may enhance moral values and the moral imagination, a topic explored more fully in the section later in this chapter on "Markets and Dignity."

INTRINSIC VALUES EMBEDDED IN MORAL GOODS

The selling and consumption of particular goods and services can provoke strong feelings of repugnance and abhorrence when a sale is thought to degrade intrinsic values in a community.[4] Goods possessing these essential qualities are called **moral goods**. Market critics argue that moral goods can be eroded and crowded out by their commodification in markets. Hence, the sale and purchase of sex through prostitution weakens family ties; the sale of course grades demeans the educational system; and a bribe to buy a pardon for a criminal diminishes respect for and allegiance to the rule of law.

The values and abstract ideals of moral goods are culturally determined. For example, Chinese markets sell puppies and kittens as delectable dinner treats; in the United States, cats and dogs are bought for the purpose of acquiring a family pet but not for eating. If pets are family members, and if it is immoral to eat one's family members, then it is immoral to eat one's cat or dog. Horses play a dual role as pets and work animals; there is occasionally moral outrage when it is revealed that a favorite horse was sent to the "glue factory." Even worse is when a California diner wishes to enjoy a horsemeat hamburger.[5]

What constitutes an intrinsic value for a community is open to question, particularly in a multicultural society. Nevertheless, one can try to understand the argument by exploring the ideal of virtue embedded in certain abstract concepts. When one thinks of "motherhood," one imagines the ongoing sacrifices of a parent needed for a child's success and the expectation of a mother's unconditional love for her child. If "motherhood" is put up for sale—through selling babies and through surrogate parenting—this generates complaints based on the argument that these markets corrode the ideal concept of motherhood needed for a good society.

Richard Posner, the distinguished economist-jurist, and Elisabeth Landes have pushed back on this point. They argue that selling babies from poor mothers to rich parents would produce good outcomes for the child.[6] The purchasing parents would likely be richer than the biological parents and provide more human capital investments. "Slippery slope" arguments against buying babies seem to gain some traction here. If buying a newborn is permissible, could not the same arguments be used to argue for buying a one-year-old baby? What about a three-year-old child? Does a parent have property rights that can be used to turn a profit if a child can be sold later to a higher bidder? What impact will a sale price have on the child's future concept of self-worth? If a child can be sold, what about selling photographs of that naked child? Pursuing this slippery slope argument, Jonathan Swift in 1729 satirized the economists of his day, proposing to create a meat market from the surplus children of Ireland:

I have been assured by a very knowing American of my acquaintance in London, that a young healthy child well nursed, is, at a year old, a most delicious nourishing and wholesome food, whether stewed, roasted, baked, or boiled; and I make no doubt that it will equally serve in a fricasie, or a ragoust. . . . the skin of which, artificially dressed, will make admirable gloves for ladies, and summer boots for fine gentlemen.[7]

Buying infants (as suggested by Landes and Posner) is considered wrong by some not so much because the child would be worse off (as in Swift's parody) but because selling one's child degrades the inviolate ideals of motherhood, fatherhood, and more broadly, personhood. Selling photographs of a naked child is reviled because it commodifies and corrupts the ideal of innocence; the role of an adult is to love and nurture, not exploit. These domestic ideals do evolve over time, as documented by artist Sally Mann's museum portraits of her nude children and by new laws legalizing adoption rights for married homosexual partners, who do not fit the stereotypical family model depicted in 1950s television shows.

In older times it was thought acceptable to sell oneself or one's child into slavery; even in the early nineteenth century it was permissible to sell oneself as an indentured laborer for a period of years (which is how many European immigrants managed to pay the high cost of transportation to the United States). Today such sales would be considered morally invalid because the autonomy of a person is an ideal that cannot be sacrificed, even by a willing seller.

Intrinsic Acts and Motivational Crowding Out

In most markets, raising the price of a product increases its quantity supplied, as shown in Figure 4.3, because the higher price compensates producers for their higher opportunity costs. But in contexts in which supply stems from *intrinsic* motivation, money can offend and "crowd out" desirable sources. This is a counterintuitive and counterproductive outcome. Recall from Chapter 3 that duty-based ethics starts from the presumption that acts *in themselves* can be determined to be right or wrong. A person ascribing to virtue and duty ethics focuses on being the kind of person who does the right act for the right reasons. The characteristics of the act, and the motivation of the actor, are what matter in certain realms of life, not the effects or consequences. If people ascribe to such beliefs, and act on them, then the appropriate material incentive is no incentive at all, in those special circumstances.

Richard Titmuss purportedly discovered the most famous early example of this in the 1970s, when he compared altruistic blood donations in England with commercial blood supplied in the United States. Some people donate blood to unknown strangers from a sense of obligation to those in need. Giving blood provides the "gift of life," which is priceless. When a market for blood is introduced, however, blood donors are confronted by the reality that their gift is not priceless after all; a pint of blood is worth only the market-clearing price. Instead of supplementing blood donations by attracting additional suppliers, the commercialization of blood "represses the expression of altruism [and] erodes the sense of community."[8] Commercial blood is also found to be of inferior quality (introducing higher risks) because sellers have an incentive to lie about their health histories. Titmuss's conclusion is that although Britain obtains about the same amount of blood per capita as the United States, the volunteer British system is much less costly overall and more efficient in terms of blood use and quality than the mixed-market system in the United States (with donors and sellers).

Critics note that Titmuss's study does not control for the different historical developments and other issues relating to British and U.S. health situations, and some of the data do not directly compare.[9] Furthermore, it is not correct to suggest that all or most British citizens are altruistic; a relatively small share of the population donates most blood there. As a small island nation, cognizant of past world wars, the spirit of civic mindedness may be particularly high, compared to the heterogeneous U.S. population. In this light, one reason commercial blood collection exists in the United States may be because the altruistic donor pool was inadequate.

A test of Titmuss's conclusion was conducted in Sweden, finding an important gender difference. When payment for blood was introduced, women's willingness to supply decreased from 52 percent to 30 percent; there was a non–statistically significant drop in men's participation.[10] A similar story of crowding out of civic virtue was found in Switzerland.[11] The government identified two communities as being the best locales for a nuclear waste repository (nuclear power accounts for 40 percent of electricity in that country). Researchers surveyed residents in the first community and found that 51 percent of respondents were willing to accept the nuclear waste repository in their community if it were determined by scientific experts to be the best site. This response came even as 80 percent of respondents stated they believed that local residents would suffer serious consequences if there were an accident (such as contaminated groundwater).

Researchers then repeated the question about accepting the waste repository but added monetary incentives ranging from $2,175 to $6,525 per person in the community. In keeping with Titmuss's theory of motivational crowding out, the level of acceptance *fell* from 51 percent to 25 percent. Explicit offers of monetary reward suppressed the supply of a public good, perhaps because some individuals no longer identify acceptance with virtue and duty but have been "informed" by the price offer that this is purely a financial transaction. Hence, money "crowds out" virtue and duty. Repetition of this survey in the second community found similar results.

Except for the negative supply response to price, these respondents behaved according to standard economic theory. Acceptance of the waste depository fell as the perception of risk rose, it fell as the negative economic externalities rose, and it fell for respondents owning their own homes. Respondents were clearly behaving rationally, as defined by economic modeling. But somehow the introduction of a monetary incentive reduced their willingness to sacrifice for other citizens. How people move psychologically among considerations of virtue, duty, and outcomes depends on context, and context is highly influenced by the framing of the issue. The researchers in this study theorize that some people are, to some extent, civic minded, and "where public spirit prevails, using price incentives to muster support for the construction of a socially desirable, but locally unwanted, facility comes at a higher price than suggested by standard economic theory because these incentives tend to crowd out civic duty."[12]

These findings might be explained using standard economic theory. For example, it could be argued that respondents gain social status from signaling their willingness to sacrifice for the community good. This theory, although plausible in many settings, may not fully cover the extent to which people are motivated by feelings and principles. Intrinsic motivation, rather than calculation of external reward, may be at work in some cases. Nobel laureate Elinor Ostrom argues that, instead of automatically assuming a single representative economic agent who is utility maximizing, "a better foundation for explaining human behavior is the assumption that multiple types of individuals exist in most settings . . . who are motivated by both intrinsic preferences and material payoffs."[13] To some people, doing one's duty as a citizen is part of one's identity and may at times require sacrifice.

Incentives that are nonpecuniary can sometimes be effective at stimulating prosocial behaviors that preserve intrinsic values. For example, offering potential blood donors a lottery ticket can increase donations marginally.[14] The expected payout of a typical lottery ticket approaches zero, less valuable than the cost of milk and cookies offered at blood donation banks. Yet it is a way of saying "thank you" and recognizing service to the community without degrading the motives of the participants. Consider why this might be so. Imagine a college student who would like to enjoy sex on Saturday night. At a party he meets a potential mate and flirts with her. Suppose in order to sweeten the deal he pulls out a $100 bill and says, "Here, let me *pay* you." A potential mate may feel repulsed by the offering of cash for sex, because it degrades her own image of herself—by demonstrating what the other person thinks of her character. However, offering to take this person out for an expensive dinner could involve the same amount of money but not convey information that would degrade intrinsic ideals.

Along a similar vein of virtuous ideals, many organizations present prestigious awards to recognize and encourage exemplary service. Police departments, fire departments, and the military bestow awards for bravery and other types of commendable conduct. Although occasionally these awards come with token cash payments, the value of these awards is primarily the social recognition and public approbation. The Medal of Honor is the U.S. military's most distinguished decoration. It is not awarded to the highest bidder but to persons whose actions best reflect the virtues of courage under fire; its conferal reinforces the ideals of commitment to the unit and the country, not to the self. The award's worth comes from its scarcity and the fact that *no one can buy it or sell it.*[15]

Intrinsic values in society are not always well understood or articulated, but they are often ubiquitous and taken for granted. The most precious things in life are often overlooked. Imagine that your ship has run aground on a warm, deserted land. There are no predators. What material substance is *most* necessary to sustain your life here over the next few days?

a) drinkable water
b) edible food
c) other material substance

Most people answer that *water* is the most important material substance, because without it we could not survive but a few days. But this is a trick question. Suppose the "ship" is the *Starship Enterprise* and the new "land" you have discovered is in a far galaxy! The correct answer is now c—*other*. What is most necessary to sustain life is oxygen; without it you would be dead in just a few minutes.

Most people do not think about oxygen because it is invisible and we breathe it unconsciously. Similarly, we unconsciously rely on invisible virtues for much of what makes society function well. When the ideal values embedded in a product are unarticulated, putting the product up for sale generates "disgust" or "revulsion" without reflecting any corresponding intellectual moral argument. Hence, it is premature and perhaps foolish to ignore feelings of revulsion without first understanding the underlying virtues that have promoted these feelings. Heyne, a gifted teacher of economics, wrote eloquently in the moral defense of markets. At the same time, he worried that markets rely on aspects of duty and virtue that derive from other institutions, such as the family and church:

For the market requires moral foundations which cannot be created by market transactions themselves. Moral foundations are nurtured in communities—in families, neighborhoods, religious fellowships, local political associations, and other voluntary groups. By fostering the steady disintegration of these communities, market transactions may tend over time to undermine the moral foundations upon which they rest.[16]

Virtue ethicists thus may not approve of *all* markets, even if the conditions of perfect competition and other qualities could be met. The reason is that some markets are thought to be inherently destructive of moral character. The market for prostitution, for example, satisfies the preferences of customers and sellers to trade sex for cash. It may be "efficient" to allow the equilibrium market transactions (assuming health and other externalities can be reasonably addressed). But to virtue ethicists, not everything that can be sold *should* be sold in a market. One's body, one's vote, and one's identity are sacred. Selling these degrades fundamental values like motherhood, citizenship, and truth seeking. Markets for some goods are simply out of bounds.

One can readily appreciate the moral limit to markets when the product in question concerns national security. From a purely economic view, exporting advanced military hardware to an enemy nation can be profitable for a company and increase the economic surplus as predicted by comparative advantage trade theory. But it is abhorrent because it flaunts the desired virtues of citizenship and loyalty, qualities that require putting the interests of the group ahead of individual interest. Group allegiance is necessary for survival in times of crisis. In 1987, the Toshiba Corporation of Japan was accused of illegally exporting to the Soviet Union the technology for producing ultraquiet submarine propellers—which had provided the U.S. Navy with a huge technological advantage over its Soviet rival during the Cold War. The moral outrage caused by Toshiba's sale led members of Congress to wield sledgehammers and bash Toshiba television sets on the steps of the Capitol. Satisfying preferences is not the only important value in society, and market restrictions are at times imposed so as to uphold intrinsic values like patriotism.

Michael Sandel, a political philosopher at Harvard, is one of the most vocal proponents of the cautionary view toward markets. In *What Money Can't Buy: The Moral Limits of Markets* (2012), Sandel argues that evaluating markets on the basis of preference satisfaction—in which preferences are assumed to be given—ignores the realities of one's engagement in society.[17] Preferences are shaped by the communities and families in which we live and work. Just as we don't choose our parents or our native tongue, neither do we have full conscious control over our choice of preferences, which are formed in the maelstrom of human interaction. To the extent that this is true, "individual" preferences are a misnomer: They are socially shaped. If preferences are shaped by family and community institutions, and if ethical character is molded in early socialization, then market activities that corrupt intrinsic family values and impede proper socialization will be the object of attack by some ethicists.

Vestiges of laws remain on the books that limit activities thought by some to corrupt basic values. Some communities in America are still "dry," meaning they maintain bans against selling alcoholic beverages. The Federal Communications Commission has until recently banned the use of "indecent" content broadcast over television and radio airwaves. In a pluralistic society undergoing rapid change, it is difficult to know what types of market transactions should be prohibited so as to promote a virtuous society. Standards change: In a time not too long ago, it was perfectly acceptable for the rich to hire surrogates to take their places in a draft army. George Washington, considered a paragon of virtue in his time, thought it perfectly acceptable to buy teeth from willing sellers, who ironically presumably lacked money to buy food.[18]

Many U.S. states have a death penalty for murderers. Those states could raise substantial sums of money by auctioning on e-Bay the right to pull the electrocution's lever. Should such a sale be legal? Whereas standard economics considers it out of bounds to question the motives of a buyer, virtue ethics begins with exactly such an examination. Someone who is willing to pay to legally kill another person can have motives of revenge, sadism, or thrill seeking. Advanced democratic societies have laws prohibiting revenge killing, arguing that it is the role of the state to administer justice, not that of individuals. Selling execution rights degrades the concept of the state as having the only legitimate monopoly on violence. An execution sale could suggest that vigilante justice and lynching are broadly acceptable. With regard to the motive of sadism, society has an interest in not feeding this personality preference because there are obvious negative externalities. The motive of thrill seeking is not itself considered a vice and is legally practiced when people parachute out of airplanes and kayak down Class V rapids. But putting a murderer to death is another matter entirely. The modern state has an interest in preserving the execution as a somber time, remembering the victim and reflecting on the vices of the convicted. Justice is not entertainment, and it demeans the concept if it appears as such.[19] An analysis of motives provides the possibility of discovering the ideal virtues that would allegedly be degraded by a market sale and hence that provoke repugnance in many people.

Duties and Rules

The standard economic approach in defense of markets are often questioned from duty or rule-based ethical perspectives. In religious duty, one's actions should conform to rules laid down by spiritual authorities. In both the Bible and the Koran, for example, there are prohibitions against usury (charging excessive interest on a loan), even if this price would clear the market. The Hebrew Scriptures provide a "sunset" clause on loans, wiping the slate clean of debts every seven years. "Blue laws" still exist in some U.S. states that prohibit market transactions on Sundays. The presumption is that people should be in church on the Sabbath and not forced (or tempted) to labor or shop. There are numerous other religiously based market interventions: Sharia law ("the pathway to be followed") restricts consumption during the holy time of Ramadan, prescribes clothing to be worn, and regulates many other aspects of economic life, such as inheritance and divorce. These restrictions on markets may be on the rise in many parts of the Islamic world.

As noted in Chapter 3, Immanuel Kant was generally supportive of markets. But a Kantian objection to markets might arise because the right action is that which can be universalized through a rational process, not that which offers the best outcome (such as maximum preference satisfaction). One should never use another solely as a means to one's own ends. In neoclassical theory, by contrast, workers are often modeled as depersonalized and dehumanized bundles of labor—commodities bought and sold to maximize profits and preferences. In this mind-set one could debate the economic costs and benefits of slavery, as viewed by plantation owners. Even if slavery were shown to produce a net economic benefit, this calculation could be trumped by Kant's appeal to intrinsic rights and dignities of all humans regardless of the economic consequences.

In the debate over the use of human embryo stem cells in research, proponents of experimentation argue that the expected benefits of lives saved and diseases cured outweigh the moral costs. But, to some religious groups, one's duty to preserve life and human dignity cannot be "bought" by an appeal to desirable outcomes. Thus, economists' concern for efficiency is seen as one consequentialist goal, and other moral approaches are shown to appeal to reasoning of a different sort. Communities strive to encourage virtuous behaviors as part of a socialization process and prohibiting some transactions is an effort to limit vices that degrade moral goods.

BACKGROUND CIRCUMSTANCES OF TRADE

In addition to moral goods, some background circumstances of exchange can affect the moral justifiability of markets as allocation mechanisms. Following are some situations in which markets may not be considered appropriate to allocate goods and services, even if it were legal.

Personal Relationships

Family members and close friends have duties and obligations to each other. Benevolence and fairness are voluntarily assumed and reciprocation expected. In these circumstances, scarce goods are generally given, shared, or allocated based on substantive need. Renting love or friendship to the highest bidder debases these concepts. The wise Polonius, in Shakespeare's *Hamlet*, counsels his son thus:

> Neither a borrower nor a lender be.
> For loan oft loses both itself and friend . . .
> (*Hamlet*, Act 1, scene 3, 75–77)

Adam Smith, in his first book on morals (covered in the next chapter), observed that humans "can subsist only in society," and are "fitted by nature to that situation."[20] Smith's account is of the shared moral feelings and duties that arise in close and even distant relationships. Benevolence is a strong motive for action in appropriate circumstances. However, in Smith's next book on trade, he observes that benevolence *alone* as a motive is not the only means of providing assistance to others. This is not a contradictory view. Rather, it suggests that it is important to know when it is appropriate to rely on family and friends for benevolence and when it is better to use a market based on self-interest. In a notable essay on "Love," Samuelson puts it this way:

> . . . family life itself is a form of communism with a small *c*. In the home the doctrine prevails, "From each according to his abilities, to each according to his needs." The good parent does not say, "Because Tiny Tim is lame, he shall get the wing. The go-getters may compete for the drumstick . . ." *The moral is to render unto the market that which the market can handle.*[21]

Kenneth Arrow notes that social institutions like the family can play a key role in reducing insecurity when key aspects of life involve uncertainty. Hence, "The economic importance of personal and especially family relationships, though declining, is by no means trivial in the most advanced economies; it is based on non-market relations that create guarantees of behavior which would otherwise be afflicted with excessive uncertainty."[22]

This point can be explored by considering the background circumstances of friendship. Paul Heyne gives this example: Suppose your neighbor Jack strains his back, and out of friendship and genuine concern for him you mow his lawn. Your motive for acting is to demonstrate fellow feeling and compassion, with the goal of easing his suffering. You might expect Jack's gratitude and thanks in return. Suppose instead he hands you a $20 bill, which is the opportunity cost of your time. Heyne asks:

How would you feel? Probably stunned. Embarrassed as well. Even insulted. Why? Because what you did was done out of friendship and personal concern. It wasn't done for money, and the offer of money asserts that you and Jack are not friends.[23]

The background condition of friendship requires that acts be undertaken with the right motive; helping someone with the expectation of economic gain undermines the friendship. Money is impersonal and hence may fail to convey the feeling of gratitude in a way that enriches that ideal.

However, many gifts do come with strings attached. French sociologist Marcel Mauss wrote *The Gift* (1923) to hypothesize that gift giving is a special type of exchange.[24] A gift exchange creates social cohesion through bonds of solidarity. The recipient of a gift must reciprocate to maintain honor and status. If your neighbor Jack took you out for a beer and pizza costing $20, that social reciprocation is considered entirely appropriate, even though a $20 cash payment for mowing his grass would not be. Giving, receiving, and reciprocating are intricately bound ideas of social behavior. Refusing a gift, or refusing to reciprocate a gift, is considered rude and socially disruptive behavior.

The gift exchange economy may weaken as the boundary of market activity expands: Families are more dispersed, and transportation improvements along with policy changes have globalized the world. Vernon Smith worries that "the rules of the market may confront, clash, and destroy the old connectedness [in society] without making visible the productively superior replacement connections." The trust that individuals once gave to family members and friends must "somehow be transferred to institutions that enable exchange and specialization . . . to vast networks of strangers."[25]

Social Groups

Individuals belong to social or civic groups such as schools, clubs, and places of worship in which identity is conferred by membership; members have duties and obligations to each other. Once someone is selected as a member of the group, he or she is usually accorded equality; fairness is expected. In such contexts people often allocate scarce goods by rationing; lottery; first come, first served; or favoritism.

Social groups play a major role in childhood development using emotional bonds of connection and control. Early socialization in kindergarten consists in sharing songs; the physical act of singing and dancing in unison enhances cooperative behaviors noted in psychological and neuroeconomics experiments.[26] Physical touching (such as hugging one's teammates) releases the bonding hormone oxytocin that promotes trust and cooperation.[27] Cooperation deters **free riding** or shirking—failing to contribute one's share for the common good. In schools, students are subject to the visible hands of parents and paternalistic institutions that condition attitudes toward scarcity and allocation. Socialization usually entails repeated calls for sharing, ensuring that all members of the group receive an equal piece of the dessert pie, and those with special needs may receive even more. Through many such experiences, young people may acquire the view that nonmarket mechanisms of allocation are the normal or most desirable means of handling scarcity.

Accordingly, many people come to expect that valued goods do not always go to the highest bidder. Many schools, for example, rely on non-price allocation mechanisms. Demand for slots at selective universities far outstrips supply, and students learn that (with few exceptions) colleges resolve the shortage through favoritism—merit selection based on grades, SAT scores, athletic ability, leadership, and other attributes.[28] Many financial aid packages make up tuition shortfalls so that the cost is "fairly" adjusted, taking family income into account. This allocation method does not eliminate competition because students will vie for relative status and rankings.

Nonmarket allocations continue after students arrive on campus. If there is excess demand for the best dorm rooms, a lottery rather than price bidding determines who gets them. Seats in the most popular classes fill up first, and registration is typically carried out with some mix of first come, first served and favoritism based on class standing or permission of the instructor. To query students on how they view the market solution to these shortages—by allowing wealthier students to bid up the tuition price in the most popular courses—provokes outrage and disgust. One instructor reports that students nearly came to blows in a classroom experiment over the unequal distribution of a few extra credit points.[29] At almost every step in their academic careers, from kindergarten to college, students have been instilled with the belief that fairness (or some other motive other than economic efficiency) is a guiding virtue for dealing with scarcity in social and institutional settings.

Hence, one key to understanding the moral limit to markets is to recognize that some people unconsciously accept the "fallacy of composition"—the faulty reasoning that a national economy should operate using the same motivational principles as a family. In a survey conducted by Columbia Law School, two-thirds of Americans stated they believed Karl Marx's socialist creed that "from each according to his ability, to each according to his needs" is or could be a guarantee written into the U.S. Constitution. In another study, researchers found that the vast majority of high school students, even those having taken a course in economics, would disallow stadium vendors from raising prices to avoid running out of hot dogs.[30] If a family rations a pizza so that each member gets a slice, why shouldn't the greater society do that as well? In short, there may be the desire for *transference*—adopting and extending the mechanisms of personal and social bonds to that of impersonal markets.

Vulnerability

In some transactions, one participant may be in a weaker bargaining position due to intrinsic circumstances. A young child or a sick person may not have the capability of human agency to exercise proper regard for his interests. Such transactions may be *coercive* or exploitative rather than mutually beneficial. Communities generally uphold a duty to protect the vulnerable, so society often regulates or prohibits market transactions that involve minors or others unable to make informed decisions.

To some market critics, vulnerability also arises because of greatly different economic circumstances. For example, people without financial resources have a difficult time claiming and defending property rights. A peasant farmer who sells his land may be facing intimidation and duress based on the buyer's economic and political standing. Or a destitute young woman in Thailand may have no viable employment options and may enter the sex trade out of desperation. Should such transactions be considered voluntary given these background circumstances? Debra Satz criticizes the market for surrogate pregnancy not because it corrupts the concept of motherhood but because she believes such contracts reinforce the unequal background circumstances of men and women.[31]

Economists might argue that background circumstances of buyers and sellers *always* differ in markets. If they did not, buyers and sellers would have identical situations and no market could exist. Denying people the right to sell their labor in a sweatshop (often depicted as coercive labor) deprives the poor of the opportunity to better their circumstances. Milton Friedman famously noted that his own mother started work at age fourteen in a sweatshop in New York.

Markets are cognizant of vulnerability and bargaining power. Coca-Cola has tested a vending machine that raises prices as the outside temperature rises.[32] Such **price discrimination** is widespread in business. Airlines charge more to customers who book at the last minute, indicating that their schedules are less flexible or their circumstances more desperate. These arrangements allow airlines to become more efficient at allocating seats by maximizing the economic surplus. Many economists likewise encourage **peak-load pricing** as a way to obtain greater efficiency. The City of London charges automobiles a congestion charge of £10 for travel in the restricted zone between 7 am and 6 pm on work days. As with the hypothetical Coca-Cola vending machine, this charges more precisely when demand is its greatest—and the customer most in need. Uber, a ride-share service, raises prices when bad weather raises the demand and reduces the supply. The higher price clears the market, but infuriates many riders.[33]

Although initially viewed with skepticism, peak-load pricing and price discrimination might be more widely accepted if people understood the advantages arising from an efficient system. Economic theory can provide valuable insights on this issue and moral norms about what is acceptable pricing can change over time.

Times of Crisis

During disasters, dangers, or war, people are reminded of their common vulnerabilities and their membership in broader society. Social norms expect and rely on people doing their civic duty to share and sacrifice for the common cause. In emergencies, rationing and favoritism are often employed to allocate scarce goods such as lifeboat spaces on the *Titanic*.

This can explain why laws against price gouging are popular with the American public. The state of Florida prohibits merchants from raising prices on necessities like ice, flashlights, or hotel rooms during hurricanes. Economists argue that these price controls make the disaster worse by creating shortages; unless prices are allowed to rise, entrepreneurs have no financial incentive to brave the elements and bring in increased supplies. Yet the standard economic view may be dangerously incomplete on this public policy issue. The standard assumption is that allowing prices to rise during an emergency would not alter any other behavior that could shift supply or demand. In reality this is not likely the case. During emergencies there may be a natural increase in public generosity and altruism. The supply of rooms available for refugees might naturally shift to the right when people in a community open their homes to help one another, not for the expectation of monetary gain but out of a sense of community identity and obligation. If everyone pitches in, the shortage of rooms during an emergency can be met with voluntary actions. However, if some people take the opportunity to price gouge, and this cannot be justified by a rise in their own marginal costs of production, the moral outrage is widely felt.[34] When prices rise during emergencies simply because a seller takes advantage of market power, the sense of public sacrifice for common good is corrupted. The volunteer spirit is diminished, and the result of less natural altruism is that the supply of donated rooms will diminish, and it will now take a higher market price to clear the market than before.

Just Price Theory

Just price theory is a doctrine that argues it is immoral to take advantage of buyer vulnerability. It attempts to lay out standards of fairness in transactions. With its intellectual roots in ancient Greek philosophy, just price theory was promoted by Thomas Aquinas (1225–1274), an Italian Dominican priest. Aquinas argued that the buyer's background circumstances should not be used to obtain a higher price:

If someone would be greatly helped by something belonging to someone else, and the seller not similarly harmed by losing it, the seller must not sell for a higher price: because the usefulness that goes to the buyer comes not from the seller, but from the buyer's needy condition: no one ought to sell something that doesn't belong to him.[35]

Because the higher value arises from the buyer's needs, rather than the seller's cost, charging a higher price constitutes a form of theft, according to Aquinas.[36] Likewise, lending money involves no creation, and earning interest means gaining money for nothing. Hence, Aquinas argued that interest should be banned.

Just price theory is more than a philosophical abstraction. It was instituted in the Massachusetts Bay Colony of 1639. Just price theory held that sellers could not charge above the "current" price—what someone who knew the worth of a commodity would commonly or usually pay. When a shopkeeper in Boston was caught charging higher prices than his competitors he was hauled into court and fined £200. He later confessed to church inquisitors that he had had a "covetous and corrupt heart" and he had been "misled by some false principles" namely, "That a man might sell as dear as he can, and buy as cheap as he can."[37]

Within a community, "normal" prices set a reference standard (or entitlement) on which the fairness of later prices is judged. The preference for fairness and common sacrifice probably also grows during times of crises—wars, depressions, natural disasters. Community standards thus limit what is deemed acceptable in terms of price increases, even when there is clearly excess demand in the market. Just price theory remains a powerful force in the minds of many who decry market outcomes. It is prominent in the "Living Wage Movements" of San Jose, CA; New York; Washington, D.C.; and elsewhere and in the criticisms leveled at outsourcing of jobs to overseas sweatshops. It also appears to be independently derived in other settings. In traditional Mayan markets, buyers and sellers negotiate a "fair" price based on background circumstances that favor the party most under economic duress. A wealthy family will pay more for a weaving, thus providing charity in a form that preserves the dignity of the receiver.[38]

Discrimination

Group identity is a powerful force leading people to cluster in neighborhoods with others from their own cultural or racial groups. "Fitting in" is a powerful incentive for voluntary segregation. At the same time, overt and covert discrimination historically prohibited blacks and other minorities in America from living where they would have liked.[39] Market-based discrimination is efficient in the sense that landlords' preferences for certain kinds of tenants (say, whites) are being fulfilled. Such behavior can be profit-maximizing if other white tenants strenuously object to blacks being admitted. The Fair Housing Act of 1967 banned discrimination in housing based on race, religion, and national origin, and later acts included gender (1974) and disability (1988). In passing these laws, society created a moral limit to the market—asserting that the preference satisfaction of landlords is not the highest goal in society; rather, treating each individual as an equal and autonomous citizen is a more important end.

Market transactions that would lead to efficiency in the Pareto sense— finding mutually advantageous trade—can sometimes lead to the destruction of moral and political norms when some buyers and sellers are excluded. If a department store has 80 percent white shoppers, and these shoppers are racist, the profit motive could lead that store to ban blacks from its lunch counters, as indeed happened throughout the South. It is also possible that white storeowners were willing to sacrifice profits to maintain their social standing in the community. Some people have a preference for prejudice, and they are willing to pay for it. A key problem with racism is that it can be a self-fulfilling phenomenon. If people believe that Joseph will be a less productive worker because of his race, there will be discrimination in hiring him. Facing lower demand for his services, it is then rational for Joseph to underinvest in his own education because the expected returns will be lower.[40]

In the Jim Crow era (1876–1965), the power of government was used to force markets to segregate and discriminate. Some businesspeople resisted. Streetcar operators in the South wanted to lower their average costs by packing in as many customers as possible, but segregation laws forced them to operate separate cars for blacks. In this case, the profit motive was supportive of equal treatment for blacks. Generally, economists hold that the profit motive can lead to the breakdown of discrimination.[41] If a business fails to hire the most qualified worker, who happens to be black, that company's productivity will suffer compared to the company that does hire her. Jackie Robinson's extraordinary performance once he broke into major league baseball with the Brooklyn Dodgers led other teams to bring on talented black players, eventually breaking down racial segregation in sports. For reasons discussed further in Chapter 11, the profit motive is not sufficient, by itself, to ensure fair treatment, and the Civil Rights Act of 1964 finally banned market segregation and discrimination.

Kantian Ethics and Markets

Kant was a contemporary of Smith, although the two never met or corresponded. Kant did note approvingly of Smith's analysis of the division of labor and other progress-enhancing features of commerce. Kant's best friend was a merchant, and the two companions spent countless hours discussing business and the marketplace. Although Kant himself generally supported competitive markets, Kantian ethics can be used to criticize some aspects of market behavior.

The second version of the categorical imperative (Chapter 3) offers powerful insights into how people should interact in markets. When GM essentially lied to its customers by failing to disclose known defects in its cars (Chapter 1), one could argue that they failed to treat their customers as ends in themselves *in addition to* a means for making a profit. A new business model of "stakeholder" theory thus asserts, using some Kantian logic, that business executives have a duty to their workers, suppliers, and customers that transcends merely making a profit.[42] The key argument is that people's labor should not be treated (as many economic theories do) merely as an anonymous input into a production function. Kant notes:

In the kingdom of ends everything has either a *price* or a *dignity*. Whatever has a price can be replaced by something else as its *equivalent*; on the other hand, whatever is above all price, and therefore admits of no equivalent, has a dignity.[43]

Because one's life cannot be reproduced with money, there is nonequivalence between the two concepts. It is immoral to buy or sell something that has intrinsic worth, meaning that there are moral limits to markets.

In Kant's day, rich people would buy healthy white teeth from indigents and have these implanted in their own mouths (as did George Washington, noted earlier). Kant condemned the practice, writing:

To deprive oneself of an integral part or organ (to maim oneself)—for example, to give away or sell a tooth to be transplanted into another's mouth, or to have oneself castrated in order to get an easier life as a singer, and so forth—are ways of partially murdering oneself.[44]

If selling a tooth is considered maiming—an adult human has thirty-two teeth—then selling a kidney or other organ would almost certainly be immoral to Kant on the same grounds: It would debase one's humanity. A poor person would simply become a collection of spare parts for sale to the rich, an idea that collides with each person's incalculable worth.

MARKETS AND DIGNITY

Supporters of markets note that private enterprise has played a role in promoting human dignity, freedom, equality, and other moral values in a community and across the globe. In *The Bourgeoise Virtues: Ethics for an Age of Commerce* (2006), Deirdre McCloskey shows how the rise of an exchange society in Europe promoted the development of moral virtues that previously were discouraged by feudal society.[45] Honesty, hard work, and thrift are encouraged by the incentives operating in competitive markets and are distinct from the incentives promoted by medieval religious orders and by mercantilism. Markets can intrinsically promote dignity by the absence of controls and instrumentally promote dignity through incentives that create higher income levels. A woman coerced by her bullying husband has an improved set of choices if markets allow her a means to increase her economic independence. Divorce rates rise with average income levels, suggesting that economic growth and access to financial resources liberates women (and men) from destructive relationships.

Although markets may sometimes destroy moral values, the policy of prohibiting market transactions creates its own set of problems and moral failures. One is that it politicizes activities by introducing the power of the state. The state may have stronger reach to destroy one's ideal of personhood through paternalism and an impersonal bureaucracy may be as corrosive to one's dignity as an impersonal market. Paternalism corrupts by robbing people of reasons for taking control of their own lives. Government regulators, moreover, may have less of an incentive to treat individuals well than would a market.[46] Finally, government prohibitions create black markets that typically have less reverence for intrinsic goods and concern for vulnerable persons. Herbert Spencer (1820–1903), the English philosopher, quipped, "The ultimate result of shielding men from the effects of folly, is to fill the world with fools."[47]

Another possible intrinsic benefit of the market is that exchange can be anonymous. A focus on money as the lubricant of provision—rather than special connections, skin color, or membership in a particular group—means that people can escape the narrow prisons of the social mores in which they may live. Although communities, families, and religious orders are sheltering institutions, they can also be smothering or repressive ones. A community approach to allocation can lead to gross inefficiencies.[48] A focus on individual rights is justified as a counterweight to those repressive forces. At the same time, the exclusive focus on individual liberty may be "seriously inadequate," according to libertarian Robert Nozick, who later in his life came to see that this short-changes important sources of joint symbolic meaning in the fabric of life.[49]Adam Smith likewise worried about the anonymity of big cities because the social restraints on behavior were eliminated: "[A man's] conduct is observed and attended to by nobody, and he is therefore very likely to neglect it himself, and to abandon himself to every sort of low profligacy and vice."[50]

LOOKING AHEAD

This chapter explores the notion that markets may fail to value something in an appropriate way. If so, this would create a type of market failure. For example, the goal of satisfying preferences may sometimes conflict with society's goals of preserving intrinsic moral values, protecting society's national defense, or shielding its vulnerable citizens. Society today prohibits the selling of votes, even though there are willing buyers and sellers. Society bans the selling of persons into slavery, even if the slave were to wish it. A house seller who prefers not to trade with an Asian American or Mexican American cannot in this day legally gratify that preference. The Constitution and related laws barring such discrimination reflect the "meta" preferences of society that outweigh individual preferences.

A premise of this book is that people approach choices pluralistically—sometimes considering virtue, sometimes considering duty, and sometimes considering outcomes. How people move between these realms depends on context and framing. Hence, monetary incentives that work to expand supply in some contexts become counterproductive in others, crowding out motivations of virtue and duty. Families, communities, and other social groups operate with implicit moral norms that leads to goods allocation using non-price mechanisms of lottery and rationing, especially during times of crisis.

A discussion of the moral limits of markets, as well as the moral virtues of markets, helps economists develop a better framework for evaluating institutions and public policies. Such evaluations are based not solely on consequentialist logic but also on an understanding of the moral sentiments that may underlie ethical duties and virtues. We turn now to Adam Smith's model of social interaction.

CHAPTER 8

The Science behind Adam Smith's Ethics

Experimental economists have discovered that people often act from a variety of motives, including self-interest, benevolence, and justice. Neuroscientists have discovered a mirror neuron network in the brain that mimics fellow feeling and the hormone oxytocin associated with emotional bonding. These discoveries provide evidence for Adam Smith's moral sentiments theory that postulates an explanation for trust in markets that goes beyond self-interest.

WHAT DOES SCIENCE TEACH US ABOUT ETHICS?

An outpouring of experimental research in the last three decades provides tantalizing clues about human nature and ethical conduct. These findings remain tentative because the results of laboratory experiments may not extrapolate perfectly into the outside world for reasons of selection bias and background effects that are difficult to model and control.

A common twentieth-century view that portrays economic actors as operating solely from ethical egoism seems out of place with the science of the twenty-first century. The narrowly self-interested, maximizing rational economic actor of textbooks has been replenished with a social nature, reviving Adam Smith's deep interest in sociability as the foundation for trade and morality. Vernon Smith, for example, argues:

> The most compelling feature of human nature is our sociality. It is our species' capacity for personal social exchange that first enabled task specialization and production above bare subsistence. . . . the rules for sharing and reciprocity run deep in our emotional psyches.[1]

Social exchange draws on both instinctual and emotional reactions that cannot be said to be based on the rational *calculation* of self-interest—even though such instincts may produce favorable outcomes. For example, the instinct to help another may, with reflection, be found to produce beneficial outcomes for oneself, including enhancing one's own status. But the *instinct* to help is often spontaneous, not part of the rationalization that follows. For this reason, the social perspective is difficult to squeeze into the standard economic model of self-interest. The key conclusions that behavioral economists, psychologists, experimental economists, neuro-economists, and others have reached in the last few decades is that:

1. People are not only self-interested but are also other regarding (demonstrating instinctual benevolence *and* malevolence toward others);
2. People care about motives and justice as well as outcomes;
3. People are not always rational calculators;
4. Economic behaviors can be altered by the autonomous release of hormones.

Researchers trying to understand the results of modern laboratory findings have turned to Adam Smith's social norms outlined in *The Theory of Moral Sentiments*.[2] The following section discusses this research before turning to an analysis of Smith's model.

LABORATORY EXPERIMENTS
The Ultimatum Game

A well-known experiment in economics called the **ultimatum game** demonstrates the nuanced role of social norms in decision making.[3] Two subjects, who play anonymously on computers, have no chance of bargaining or developing a reputation yet must agree on a one-time division of an economic payoff (for example, $10). The first player proposes the division, and the second player either accepts or declines but cannot negotiate. If the offer is declined, neither player receives any payment. In this zero-sum world, any gain to the first player is erased by a loss to the second. The standard neoclassical prediction is that the first player will propose an offer to the second player of a token minimum amount. Think about the reasoning behind this expectation: If you saw a $1 bill lying on the ground in a parking lot, wouldn't you bend over to pick it up? Wouldn't someone playing this game similarly want to get a free dollar, for no more effort than just clicking "accept" on the screen? Because the second player is assumed to want to maximize her economic return, any payment is better than no payment, and an offer of $1 would theoretically be sufficient to produce agreement.

This experiment has been repeated around the world in varying contexts and with large and small payout amounts. The results are surprisingly uniform: Proposers generally do *not* make the "rational" economic minimum offer of $1, nor do responders generally accept it if offered. Proposers almost always offer far more, with the most frequent offer being $5; and responders typically refuse offers below $2.50. What could explain these anomalous results? One explanation is that the proposers are simply being altruistic toward the responders. Another interpretation is that proposers are behaving strategically: They expect the responder to reject low offers, hence they offer higher ones.

But why would responders reject low offers in favor of receiving no money at all? In a classroom playing of this game students are quick to assert that a $1 offer is "greedy," "unfair," "unjust," or "shows a lack of respect" for the responder.[4] Responders care about motives and justice in addition to their own payouts and may refuse to participate if they think a transaction is unfair. These responders may be engaging in *altruistic punishment* to teach the proposer a lesson, even though it comes at personal expense. The basis for such altruism may not be benevolence (positive regard for others who later may play the game against this player) but rather malevolence (wishing bad outcomes for this transgressor).

In a related experiment called the **dictator game**, the proposer imposes the split of money on the responder, who is not allowed to reject the offer. In this situation the proposer's strategic considerations of trying to avoid a rejection disappear. Nevertheless, proposers continue to divide the funds evenly 76 percent of the time.[5] This would seem to be evidence for fairness as a strong motivator in human behavior. But the story gets more complex. Moral norms about the division of spoils likely arose very early in human hunting and gathering societies, preceding government. When the resources to be divided come from the experimenters like manna from heaven (random choice of who gets to be the proposer), a nearly equal division of spoils may be expected as the social norm. Social norms rely on language to frame the moral context, and researchers thus find that sharing is specific to cultural circumstances. The further removed the proposer is psychologically from the responder, the lower the offers. In particular, as the social isolation of participants is heightened through greater anonymity and lower potential for reciprocity, offers in dictator games fall.[6] In one variation, the proposer receives the right to suggest the division of money based on prior work effort and skill. With this different à priori condition, an equal division all but disappears: People prefer a division of reward that properly accounts for their contributions.[7]

The Trust Game

Background circumstances of motive and social relationships thus alter the dynamics of exchange and the social norms of conduct. These points are brought out more fully in an interesting variation called the **trust game**.[8] Two anonymous players must decide whether to trust and/or reciprocate. Player 1 starts the game by deciding whether to receive a sure payout of $20 for himself and Player 2 or of turning the decision over to Player 2. In the latter case Player 2 would then have the option of choosing $25 for each player or $30 for herself and only $15 for Player 1. A maximizing self-interested Player 2 would theoretically always take the $30 for herself in one-shot games because there are no strategic or reputation effects to worry about. Predicting that Player 2 will always defect in this way, Player 1 would always choose the $20 option, resulting in a trustless, suboptimal outcome.

What makes these trust experiments interesting is that subjects routinely defy the conventional prediction and customarily trust their anonymous partners, thereby earning more money. Almost two-thirds of the first movers trust Player 2s and pass the choice over to them. About two-thirds of Player 2s who receive the choice then reward Player 1's trust by opting for the even split of $25. Only one-third of second players chose to behave opportunistically by taking advantage of the first player's generosity. This is a fairly stunning refutation of the theory that most people are selfish and maximizing.

These results could be explained by arguing that people have a preference for altruism (Player 2 has benevolence is her utility function) or a preference for equality (Player 2 prefers more even splits). It turns out these explanations do not hold up under further investigation. In a followup **involuntary trust game**, Player 1 automatically transfers the choice on to Player 2. Because this handover is compulsory, the first mover cannot demonstrate his intention to trust the second player. If the preference for altruism or the preference for equality were the primary causes of cooperation, the results should be identical in this game as in the standard trust game. However, in this case Player 2's cooperation drops markedly from 65 percent to 33 percent when Player 1's choice is removed.

These results support the view that the moral context for decision making matters: Player 2 is twice as likely to cooperate when Player 1 is perceived to be motivated by trust. One theory for this is that Player 2's cooperative behavior reflects *gratitude*: Player 1's trustfulness generates appreciation, and Player 2 will respond with generosity. But there is another possible interpretation that also fits within Adam Smith's moral sentiments model. Player 2 may be acting not only from gratitude but also from *honor*. Player 2 may feel entrusted with something (a valuable choice). An ethical person would feel duty bound to behave honestly and to guard Player 1's property. Player 2 was given a fiduciary trust and strives to be worthy of that trust. Although we desire the approval of others, this game is played anonymously, so honesty derives in this case not from the expected praise or reward of others but from one's internal regard for being praiseworthy. Honor provides a complementary explanation to gratitude to explain these findings.

BIOLOGY AND COOPERATION
Oxytocin and Cooperation

Can socializing emotions be discovered in the laboratory? Neuroeconomist Paul Zak, building on Smith's idea of moral sentiments, developed a number of tests to see if autonomous hormones are at work in social interaction.[9] Zak discovered that, when engaged in trustful trade, the brain releases a dose of oxytocin, a powerful and pleasurable hormone also released during orgasm and breast-feeding. "Oxytocin," Zak notes, "is an evolutionarily ancient molecule that is an essential part of the mammalian attachment system."[10] By varying doses of this hormone in human subjects, Zak is able to alter the degree of empathy and fellow feeling and hence the degree of cooperation in monetary experiments.

Oxytocin does not last long in the blood stream (only about three minutes). But its impact on behavior is profound. Repeating the trust game, Zak drew blood from players before and after the game. First movers with initially higher levels of oxytocin were far more likely to trust Player 2. And Player 2s who had been trusted saw their oxytocin levels rise almost 50 percent higher than Player 2s who received money randomly (as in the involuntary trust game). These hormonal changes happen without purposeful control or even mindful awareness.

According to Zak, hormones and neural networks provide the biological scaffolding for sociability that underlies Adam Smith's conception of moral behavior. To activate the release of oxytocin, one gives a sign of trust. The person being trusted experiences a surge in oxytocin that makes her more likely to reciprocate, which generates a positive feedback loop—a virtue cycle. Zak has tested this theory around the world, demonstrating that group activities such as dancing, singing, or praying can also release oxytocin. Group activities can lead to intense bonding and caring that is not based on rational calculation of future gain but emotions spurred by hormones.

The experience of being trusted produces oxytocin and leads to the release of two other powerful chemicals, serotonin and dopamine, that make the incident both pleasurable and memorable. The tentative conclusion is that the emotional states of others are experienced physiologically within a subject's brain and that these stimuli affect the subject's later behavior because of the release of chemical messengers that enable emotional attachments. In roughly 98 percent of cases, Zak found that oxytocin was released in proportion to the degree of trust shown and produced a proportional behavioral response. Survival and reproduction are presumably enhanced when people develop networks built on deep layers of trust that go beyond rational self-interest.[11]

Although the physiological response is independent of conscious control, it can be affected by circumstances in the environment. Stress or fear, for example, can suppress other-regarding instincts. In a stressful situation our hearts pound and our palms become sweaty—physiological symptoms of a fearful emotion. One's awareness of this condition gives recognition to the feeling of being scared. Said differently, hormones cause the physical experience of emotions (for example, elevated heart rate), which in turn give rise to *feelings* about that experience.

Hormonal changes thus affect feelings of love and trust or hate and suspicion. In contrast to oxytocin, which allows people to feel safe and trusting of others, testosterone is another ancient molecule that is designed in part to protect us against others, especially those who would take advantage of us. Whereas oxytocin brings people closer together, testosterone pushes them apart. Oxytocin is cooperative, whereas testosterone is competitive. Both molecules likely exist for reasons of adaptation in natural selection: Someone who is always trusting is likely to be swindled or perhaps killed; someone who is always distrustful will have a hard time enjoying the benefits of specialized trade, as exemplified by the male–female reproductive roles. Both women and men release oxytocin and testosterone, although women on average have more of the former and men on average more of the latter. The bottom line is that behaviors observed in the laboratory and in the marketplace—self-interest, benevolence, and malevolence—are all part of the rich biological soup of evolutionary adaptation.

Mirror Neuron Networks

In addition to hormones that trigger bonding, humans may also have neural pathways for experiencing the pain and pleasure of others. A team of neurophysiologists in Italy accidentally discovered the existence of "mirror neurons" in the brains of monkeys (that presumably also exist in the brains of humans). When a human researcher picks up an object, neurons instantaneously fire in the brain of a monkey, just as if the monkey had picked up the same object.[12] Correspondingly, people watching a realistic horror movie may flinch and draw back, even though the monster is inflicting pain to others on the screen. This potentially demonstrates the neurological ability to use imagination to experience what we think others experience—in other words, it may reflect the aptitude for empathy or "fellow feeling." Like oxytocin, the mirror neuron response is automatic and preanalytical. The science of mirror neurons is controversial and rapidly changing. At least on the surface, this discovery is in line with Adam Smith's conjecture that "the pleasure and the pain [of fellow feeling] are always felt so instantaneously" so that mutual sympathy is not the result of a calculation of self-interest.[13] We turn now to develop Smith's theory.

ADAM SMITH'S PARENTING OF ECONOMICS

Adam Smith (1723–1790) is considered the founder of modern economics. In *The Wealth of Nations* (1776) he is concerned with prudence and financial gain. A desired goal of the commercial system is to produce economic growth—to enlarge the economic pie—to lift the poor out of poverty. Justice demands that every person be able to compete fairly for these economic gains. The policies to achieve this include freer trade, which would remove restraints that lead to monopolies owned by well-connected elites. It is no coincidence that Smith's treatise on trade appeared the same year as America's declaration of independence because one of Smith's peeves was the colonial trade. Smith's concern for justice was elaborated earlier in 1759, in *The Theory of Moral Sentiments* (TMS). In this book Smith attempts to explain and endorse the role that feelings play in the formation of trust and social norms. Caring and commitment, rather than calculation, are elaborated in Smith's theory.

Although much has been written about Smith's two books (including the allegation that they represent contradictory theories), a late-twentieth-century revival of scholarship on Smith shows that his writings reflect a consistent philosophical view.[14] Galileo and Newton in the sixteenth and seventeenth centuries popularized the notion that invisible forces (such as gravity) explained the working of the physical universe. Smith was one of the subsequent Scottish Enlightenment thinkers of the eighteenth century who attempted to model the invisible forces that held a society of persons together and enabled it to grow and prosper. To Smith, "The science which pretends to investigate and explain those connecting principles is what is properly called moral philosophy"—encompassing the fields we today call philosophy, psychology, sociology, economics, political science, and law.[15]

Human Nature, Institutions, and the Invisible Hand

The ultimatum, dictator, and trust experiments demonstrate that people in a lab trust others and cooperate much more than is predicted in the standard twentieth-century model of *Homo economicus*. If so, people expose themselves to the possible trickery and opportunism of others. Smith's *TMS*, which preceded Darwin's *Origin of the Species* (1859) by exactly 100 years, was the inspiration for Darwin's view of how humans come to cooperate in groups, despite the potential cost to those who trust.[16] Clearly, evolution would favor trust only if the gains to trust exceed the losses in terms of survival and procreation. Although Adam Smith did not know about evolution, his biological explanation begins with a deity that creates nature and its laws of survival: "Thus self-preservation, and the propagation of the species, are the great ends which Nature seems to have proposed in the formation of all animals."

Although nature embeds in all living things a desire for biological success, the mechanisms for achieving this are *instinctive* because human reasoning is "slow and uncertain":

But though we are in this manner endowed with a very strong desire of those ends [survival and propagation], it has not been intrusted to the slow and uncertain determinations of our reason, to find out the proper means of bringing them about. Nature has directed us to the greater part of these [ends] by original and immediate instincts. Hunger, thirst, the passion which unites the two sexes, the love of pleasure, and the dread of pain, prompt us to apply those means for their own sakes, and without any consideration of their tendency to those beneficent ends which the great Director of nature intended to produce by them.[17]

Not surprisingly, Smith is recognized today as one of the fathers of behavioral economics for his rejection of hyperrationality.[18] But society does not progress by instincts alone. Instincts can sometimes lead us to bad outcomes. Human taste buds crave fat and sugar, traits favorable for adaptive selection 30,000 years ago when these items were scarce in the diet. In today's world of caloric excess, the instinct for fat and sugar can produce diabetes and heart disease. Smith notes that the instincts that serve us need to be moderated by the rules or norms that arise out of social relations and that are transmitted across generations both as custom and law.

Thomas Hobbes, the philosopher who lived during the English Civil War of 1642–1651, also believed that mutually agreed institutions were needed for survival. In time of war, "every man is enemy to every man. . . . and the life of man [is] solitary, poor, nasty, brutish, and short."[19] To avoid bloodshed, people would rationally agree to form a government that would instill rules of order, even though people naturally prefer to live alone. This rationalistic account of the evolution of social institutions is rejected by Smith.

Rather than enlightened self-interest as the basis for social institutions, Smith argues that rules of cooperation are grounded in the natural instincts humans have to socialize and bond with others and are governed by emotional reactions. The social rules of human exchange create moral norms that can be either formal or informal and these change only slowly in response to a widening moral imagination and altered feelings about right and wrong.

For children or cultural newcomers, the socializing process is long and difficult. A baby just out of the womb bursts into a fit of crying that both clears the airway and draws attention to the baby's needs for care. Every healthy newborn behaves in this instinctively selfish manner. It is on this infantile nature that the *Homo economicus* model builds, forgetting that children undergo decades of training to forge them into a different kind of socially intelligent person. The process is not easy or seamless, which is why raising children is challenging and why many cultures involve grandparents and extended families in the process.

At some point in early childhood development, a healthy brain develops to the stage at which the infant is able to perceive differences between self and others. In addition to feeling their own emotions, infants begin to develop the capacity to experience the emotions of others. This instinctive ability is called "fellow feeling." When a child's emotions align with that of his parents, the child experiences pleasure; when they do not, he experiences discord. A child thus has a natural instinct to reach *emotional equilibrium* with others in his group. From experience and pain a child learns which behaviors are acceptable and which are not in the group. Eventually, a well-socialized child comes to adopt the rules internally.

Our emotional reactions depend on the circumstances, and virtue ethics cannot be reduced to a simple set of rules. Circumstances change, and so does the appropriate response. For example, if one's father dies, a normal reaction might be to grieve deeply. Others observing this behavior would feel in emotional equilibrium because it fits the situation. Suppose, however, you observe someone not grieving at all on losing a father: Such behavior would seem out of place and inappropriate. If we were to learn that the father had abandoned the family and had no interaction with them, the lack of emotional response would now make sense and be judged appropriate to the circumstance. No simple rule of behavior can cover the complexity of human experience, according to virtue ethics.

Although selfishness is a desirable and necessary instinct, two other instincts develop with age. One is the *pro*social instinct for benevolence: We desire to see good things happen to deserving people. Smith thinks this is an important enough disposition that he begins *TMS* with this line: "How selfish soever man may be supposed, there are evidently some principles in his nature, which interest him in the fortune of others, and render their happiness necessary to him, though he derives nothing from it except the pleasure of seeing it."[20] But altruism alone is not the basis for cooperation. A third and more powerful sentiment is malevolence: We desire to see bad things happen to bad people. Smith argues that this social instinct is the "main pillar" in the institution of justice, without which society would "crumble into atoms."[21] One can see this principle at work in the ultimatum game when players reject offers considered unfair, so as to punish perceived transgressors. People who are willing to incur a personal cost to uphold a socially beneficial norm are in some sense voluntarily contributing to a public good, even though they do not directly benefit in this case.[22]

The instincts *for* self, *for* others, and *against* others create internal conflicts. Socialization is the process by which adults sensitize offspring as to appropriate ways of balancing these impulses. Imagine this scenario: A loving parent smiles and jiggles some keys, causing a sympathetic emotional reaction in the child, who laughs and giggles. A few moments later the child turns and hits his younger sister with the keys. The parent's smile now turns to a frown, and the child's face that a moment ago was happy now looks unsure. The parent withholds mutual sympathy when the child is misbehaving. This forces the child to stretch his moral imagination, that is, his ability to see himself through the eyes of a parent. When the child gets older, he comes to develop the habit of understanding things as others see them and can recognize the pain caused to others. This compels the child's own selfishness to be naturally curtailed by a growing self-control.

The fellow feeling that provides the foundation for Smith's model of moral sentiments is genuine and not *calculated* to win favor with others (although it might have that effect). Smith writes:

But whatever may be the cause of sympathy, or however it may be excited, nothing pleases us more than to observe in other men a fellow-feeling with all the emotions of our own breast; nor are we ever so much shocked as by the appearance of the contrary. . . . But both the pleasure and the pain are always felt so instantaneously, and often upon such frivolous occasions, that it seems evident that neither of them can be derived from any such self-interested consideration.[23]

Over time, a socialized child begins to share fellow feeling not just with others but with an internal "spectator" who mindfully watches over conduct even when parents are away. In this way, a child begins to internalize appropriate norms of conduct as part of his or her identity. The ultimate standard is not the regard of *others* that our conduct is praiseworthy; it is the approval of *ourselves*. This is not a model of rational self-interest as the driver of human morals. Vernon Smith, one of the experimentalists mentioned above, reflects that "far from championing the individual's pursuit of self-love, [Adam] Smith saw the individual as not even defined except in a social context. There is no cognitive individual psychology except as it is born of a person's social circumstances, out of the 'social psychology' of his environs."[24]

The Creation and Evolution of Institutions

Adam Smith does not argue that morality is about changing human nature because that is fixed by nature. Nor does he argue that humans should simply follow their given instincts (such as the instinct for greed). Rather, a good society is created through the channeling and control of instincts through socially devised institutions. Institutions are the "rules of the game" that establish our duties with regard to others. Such institutions can be informal (norms about how to treat others) or legal (laws about how to treat others).

The reason Smith is skeptical of letting natural instincts run rampant is that our rash passions often mislead us. For example, in Shakespeare's *Romeo and Juliet*, the perception of family disrespect leads Tybalt to challenge Romeo to a duel that leads to multiple tragic deaths. Instinctual rage can lead people to kill. In the context of modern American society, killing another over such an insult would be considered a huge overreaction; fellow citizens would withhold their sympathy with the protagonist's feeling of being disrespected and instead sympathize with the victim and his family and friends. Justice in this case is on the side of the victim.

The rules of morality thus arise *initially* from the shared emotional reactions to experience, which when observed from a distant and rational perspective can be seen to produce desirable outcomes. The ban on murder produces better outcomes than without it. But Smith reiterates his differences with Hobbes: "But though reason is undoubtedly the source of the general rules of morality. . . . These first perceptions [of right and wrong] . . . cannot be the object of reason, but of immediate sense and feeling." Hence:

> The general maxims of morality are formed, like all other general maxims, from experience and induction. We observe in a great variety of particular cases what pleases or displeases our moral faculties, what these approve or disapprove of, and, by induction from this experience, we establish those general rules.[25]

The norms of justice reflect the sympathies of a particular culture at a particular point in time. In the Athens of Aristotle's era, parents could abandon an unwanted newborn on the roadside, exposing it to the elements and leaving its fate to the gods or passing strangers. Owning other humans as slaves was also a norm. Both of these practices are reviled today. Institutions evolve when enough people use their moral imaginations to sympathize in a new way, giving rise to updated norms of behavior.[26] The providentially given instinct for sociability as well as the humanly devised institutions of justice provide the context for understanding Smith's invisible hand.[27] This model is further elaborated in the following chapter.

This chapter connects the findings of modern science with the moral sentiments theory of Adam Smith. In contrast to the narrowly self-interested view of standard economic models, experiments demonstrate that people care about others in two senses: We are *pro*social in desiring good outcomes for family, friends, and others worthy of our benevolence, and we are *anti*social in craving bad outcomes for our enemies, particularly those who break the rules of justice. Paradoxically, the negative emotions of hatred and envy help to promote and enforce the social ends of species cooperation. We certainly want to know "What's in it for me?"—but we are never far from wanting to know what's in it for you, and others, and seeing that justice is meted out. A well-socialized person engages the community and can certainly be self-interested, ambitious, and striving. But those characteristics do not imply greed.

In a passage written a few months before his death, Smith clarifies his view that self-interest is not by itself sufficient to create a sustainable, desirable society. *All* the cardinal virtues are needed for that:

"Superior" prudence involves wise and judicious conduct directed to greater and nobler purposes than to the needs of the individual. It is the former prudence combined with greater and more splendid virtues: valour, extensive, strong benevolence, a sacred regard for rules of justice, and a proper degree of self-command. It necessarily supposes the utmost perfection of intellectual and moral virtues. It is the best head joined to the best heart.[28]

LOOKING AHEAD

Perfect prudence—"the best head joined to the best heart"—captures the essential critique that virtue ethicists make of other moral frameworks: These rely on virtuous persons, without which their systems would likely fail. Yet these alternative systems can provide no explanation or justification for how virtue arises and is sustained. To a virtue ethicist, good character is the invisible oxygen that supports society, even though it is often overlooked. The care and development of character is the essential obligation of one generation to the next. This is accomplished not by reading intellectual treatises but by studying examples—either in real persons or via the imagination (the world of stories and the arts). Garrison Keillor notes, "Stories give us the simple empathy that is the basis of the Golden Rule, which is the basis of civilized society."[29]

Smith's model is *not* about rational maximizing behavior leading to desirable outcomes (as the invisible hand is often incorrectly portrayed). In fact, Smith particularly notes that it is *irrational* behavior that plays a key role in human progress because people misperceive the connection between wealth and happiness. For Smith, the evolution of society toward greater progress is not the result of rational planning, but the consequence of a spontaneous order arising from seemingly disconnected actions of a crowd. Within this story, self-control is the preeminent moral virtue. During the deregulation of financial markets in the late twentieth century, however, the contrary view was adopted: that unrestrained greed and hyperrationality would correct market excesses, making institutional ethics and government regulations superfluous. We turn to these topics and the Great Recession of 2008 to see how Adam Smith's theories relate.

CHAPTER 9

Ethics and the Financial Crisis of 2008

This chapter explores ethical beliefs that contributed to financial
deregulation and the global financial crisis of 2008. Proponents of
laissez-faire markets argue that greed produces self-regulation and
sufficient safety, presumably based on Adam Smith's notion of an
invisible hand. This turns out to misrepresent Smith and his
ethical-economic model. To Smith, human instincts need to
be channeled through appropriate institutions; in his model,
regulations in financial markets are warranted.

INTRODUCTION

A financial panic originating on Wall Street led to a worldwide economic
downturn in 2008. Wealth in the United States shrank by $16 trillion,
about one-quarter of total wealth. More than 16 million households experienced a mortgage loan foreclosure between 2006 and 2012, and more
than 5 million households were evicted from their homes. Although the
crisis began in the United States, many other countries fared far worse.
The causes and consequences of this event are complex and controversial,
admitting of no single perspective.[1] The deregulation of financial markets
after 1980 played a part by creating a more fragile financial system. The
pooling of mortgage assets was intended to hedge risk but actually served
to amplify risks that were systemic and poorly understood. The rollback
of regulations had a strong moral and ideological premise that greed is
good and that greed leads to adequate self-regulation in the market. High
risk taking through financial innovation soon replaced the stodgy products and services mandated after the collapse of the Great Depression.

The Morality of Keynesian Economics

The Great Depression was a searing event in economic history. A quarter
of the labor force in the United States became unemployed in the dark
year of 1933. The suffering was recorded in Dorothea Lange's photojour-
nalism and in epic novels such as John Steinbeck's *The Grapes of Wrath*
(1939). What makes that episode so tragic is that many economists came

to see the severity of the depression as largely avoidable. Better policies and regulations by the monetary authorities at the Federal Reserve Board might have reduced runs on banks and prevented contagion effects, so that the downfall of one bank would not produce a systemwide collapse. Appropriate taxing and spending by the federal government could also have provided countercyclical balance in the macro economy. These latter ideas were the work of John Maynard Keynes and his converts.

Writing in 1936, British economist John Maynard Keynes argued in *The General Theory of Employment, Interest, and Money* that economic growth could be restored through appropriate economic policies. Keynes was not advocating deficit spending per se but rather *countercyclical* spending: Government should run deficits during recessions and surpluses during booms, so the long run effect would be a balanced budget. Keynesian economics overturned the conventional thinking that governments should "tighten their belts" during economic downturns and introduced a different ethical perspective—that helping the unemployed was a national obligation. In the preface to *The General Theory*, Keynes noted, "The ideas which are here expressed so laboriously are extremely simple and should be obvious. The difficulty lies, not in the new ideas, but in escaping from the old ones."[2]

The old ideas, called the classical school, viewed the economy as a self-righting machine. Jean Baptiste Say (1767–1832) was a French economist who popularized this view. In rough terms, **Say's law** states that "supply creates its own demand." There could never be a permanent oversupply of goods because producing commodities creates income and income generates demand for more commodities. This model is captured by the movie *Field of Dreams*: "If you build it, [they] will come!"

One complaint against Say's law is that workers may conserve income, rather than spend it. Say had a quick response: Savings put into investment *also* generates demand. A worker hired to build a new factory (an investment) is employed just as much as a worker hired to build a new television (a consumption good). But what if *all* workers decide to save at the same time? In that case the interest rate will drop, inducing some people to reduce their savings and other people to increase their borrowings for investment. Financial, labor, and real goods markets all reach equilibrium.

This sounds a little too idealistic, and in reality the classical model admitted to a normal cycle of booms and busts. Tides rush in and then rush out, just as markets expand and then contract. Things return to normal. The key point is that no government action is needed to restore equilibrium. The classical paradigm exerted a powerful impact on moral attitudes. Keynes wrote that "the ideas of economists and political philosophers, both when they are right and when they are wrong, are far more powerful than is commonly understood. Indeed the world is ruled by little else."[3] If the classical paradigm is correct that labor markets return to equilibrium on their own, then anyone who remains unemployed is *voluntarily* unemployed. It is morally repugnant to give a handout to an able-bodied person who simply chooses not to work. Doing so creates a **moral hazard** by offering an incentive for people to be lazy. Hence, the appropriate government policy in these circumstances is to let nature take its course. This is a powerful example of how a "positive" economic model (explaining the world) has profoundly "normative" implications (clarifying the ethical choices).

Keynes's theory, however, holds that labor markets do *not* adjust seamlessly to a downturn in demand. There could be significant wage and price rigidities that prevent markets from reaching equilibrium. In addition, Keynes believed that the interest rate might not fall far enough to produce full employment. If everyone tries to save at the same time, the interest rate will fall, but only to the point at which the return on bonds becomes less attractive relative to holding money (because money does not carry a default risk). If people at the margin prefer to hold money rather than bonds, such a "liquidity trap" prevents new savings from generating new investments needed to restart the economy. If these conditions persist, the economy could enter into prolonged depression.

In the Keynesian view, unemployment in these circumstances is not voluntary because the root problem is *systemic* (beyond any individual's control). Helping the unemployed becomes a moral obligation, and it is not appropriate to sit and wait for the market to self-correct in the long run:

... this *long run* is a misleading guide to current affairs. *In the long run* we are all dead. Economists set themselves too easy, too useless a task if in tempestuous seasons they can only tell us that when the storm is long past the ocean is flat again.[4]

In the decades after the Great Depression, most economists and politicians became "Keynesians," accepting the notion that collective action can mitigate the effect of recessions. And if collective action *can* do so, it *ought* to do so. In 1946 this view was formally adopted when Congress declared that "it is the continuing policy and responsibility of the Federal Government to use all practicable means . . . to promote maximum employment, production, and purchasing power."[5] The change in policy from "let nature take its course" to one of action and remedy had a remarkable effect on the economy. In the nineteenth century and up to the mid-twentieth century, economic downturns came often and persisted on average about twenty-one months. Under Keynesian policies the average recession lasted about half as long, only eleven months. Economic volatility has been substantially lower, and national income and employment higher, coincident with the change in fiscal and monetary policies.[6]

Nevertheless, Keynesianism became increasingly controversial in the 1970s when the economy entered a period of stagflation (simultaneously high inflation and unemployment). "New classical" theorists sought to develop the microfoundations for the macroeconomy. Assuming fully rational economic agents and perfectly flexible markets, Robert Lucas, who won the Nobel Prize for his work in 1995, argued that government policies failed because market participants could accurately predict and respond to them, offsetting the policy makers' intentions. Lucas' **rational expectations model** essentially reaches the same conclusions as the classical model: Public activism is ineffectual and, therefore, unwarranted. Others argue that recessions may not reflect a failure of markets to clear but a desirable response to changes in technology or other shocks. In this view, recessions and booms can be good things. If true, this changes the implications of countercyclical fiscal and monetary policies: Is it moral to interfere with the invisible hand?

THE RISE OF ETHICAL EGOISM

The virtue of greed was widely promulgated by some economists in the twentieth century. Kenneth J. Arrow and Frank Hahn, in their monumental work *General Competitive Analysis* (1971), assume that "greed" underpins economic efficiency. Walter Williams, an economist and columnist, writes, "Free markets, private property rights, voluntary exchange, and greed produce preferable outcomes most times and under most conditions." Allegedly it is Adam Smith who provides the "dignity to greed."[7] By the early 1980s, Smith's notion that institutions were needed to help *restrain* human excesses (discussed in Chapter 8) had been largely forgotten. In its place arose a focus on the individual as an autonomous and isolated consumer, with no duties or virtues to discern or develop. "Economic man" has no social preferences or identity to uphold, only an unrelenting quest to satisfy his own utility.

Ethical egoism had actually appeared much earlier in the twentieth century. One of the strongest advocates of this view was Ayn Rand (1905–1982), a Russian émigré who reacted vehemently against the rise of communism and communitarian ideals. She unabashedly celebrated the doctrine of ethical egoism in popular novels such as *The Fountainhead* (1943) and *Atlas Shrugged* (1957). Adherents of Rand's philosophy include Alan Greenspan (the former chairman of the Federal Reserve), Senator Rand Paul, and Congressman Paul Ryan (candidate for vice president in 2012). Ivan Boesky, a stock trader, echoed these sentiments when he told business school graduates in 1986 that "greed is healthy. You can be greedy and still feel good about yourself."[8] Shortly thereafter Boesky confessed to insider trading fraud and received three years in prison and a $100 million fine. In the popular movie *Wall Street* (1987), the main character Gordon Gekko gives an impassioned speech derived from Boesky in which he states, "Greed works. Greed clarifies, cuts through and captures the essence of the evolutionary spirit."

Ethical egoism can be justified on the theory that under the right circumstances market efficiency would produce the best possible outcomes for society at large (see the first fundamental welfare theorem, Chapter 5). This is called the "invisible hand theorem" even though we noted in

Chapter 8 that this is a misnomer; the idea that "greed is good" appears much earlier in the writing of Bernard Mandeville and is a doctrine that Adam Smith explicitly rejected.

Mandeville on Private Vices and Public Benefits

Bernard Mandeville (1670–1733) was a Dutch doctor and activist who moved to London and became a pamphleteer. In 1705 Mandeville published his famous poem, *The Grumbling Hive: or, Knaves Turn'd Honest*, reprinted in 1714 as *The Fable of the Bees, or: Private Vices, Publick Benefits*. The humorous verse describes a vice-filled beehive that flourishes because lust, vanity, and greed spur demand and create full employment. Vice feeds ingenuity and creates economic progress such that the "poor lived better than the rich before." In Mandeville's words, "Every part was full of vice / Yet the whole mass a Paradise." Virtue makes friends with vice for the "common good."[9]

But moralizers in the beehive are not content. They eventually ask their god to make society *honest*, and the wish is fulfilled. In an unexpected twist, the onset of virtue leads to economic depression and despair! Lacking profligate spending, aggregate demand collapses: "In half an Hour, the Nation round / Meat fell a Penny in the Pound," and Mandeville's conclusion is that "Fools only strive / To make a Great an honest Hive."[10] Mandeville thus anticipated Keynesian economics, by proposing that a drop in aggregate spending could cause lasting declines in employment and output. Mandeville's wider claim is about morality: that *vice* is *virtuous*.

Adam Smith devoted considerable attention to disputing Mandeville's attack on virtue and self-restraint. His doctrines, Smith wrote, are a "fallacy" and "wholly pernicious."[11] In the twentieth century Mandeville's doctrine reappeared, however, repackaged as "greed is good." It had a profound impact on financial deregulation.

Financial Deregulation and Moral Hazard

Financial industry proponents, in and out of government, chaffed under government regulations that had been imposed during the Great Depression. The Glass-Steagall Act prevented retail banks that accept deposits from speculating on stock markets, as do investment banks; interstate branching restrictions prevented size and contagion effects; government-permitted financial products were "plain vanilla" and highly regulated; and banks were required to keep high capital reserves. During the period from 1950 to 1970 the U.S. economy boomed within the constraints that forced financial firms to take low risks. This is not to imply that there were no bank failures. The debt crisis of 1982, for example, nearly brought down the global financial system when floating rate loans to Latin America imploded after the Federal Reserve raised interest rates.

But, after 1980, bankers perceived an opportunity to create more profits with ever-more-sophisticated and complex financial products. A revolving door of insiders from Wall Street went to work in the Treasury, the White House, and regulatory agencies, and they heavily lobbied Congress to liberalize financial markets. Deregulation began in the early 1980s and continued through 2006; over this period financial profits doubled from roughly 4 percent to 8 percent of GDP.[12]

Some of the new products included collateralized debt obligations (CDOs), which are bundles of liabilities, generally comprised of home mortgages of different locations and qualities. Houses provide the collateral for bonds sold to investors. These could be partitioned into tranches or levels that represent different stages of risk. Unfortunately, the financial market was rife with **moral hazard**—incentives for participants to take excessive risks that impose costs on third parties. Mortgage companies could earn higher profit by lending to riskier borrowers with subprime loans. These mortgages were sent to Wall Street for bundling with others into CDOs. Credit rating agencies earned high fees from the investment banks by grading CDOs as super-safe, on the theory that diversified housing markets would not all simultaneously burst. Financial institutions also hedged their risks by buying credit default swaps (CDSs) sold by large banks and by the insurance giant AIG. These provided protection against the risk of CDO default. However, AIG petitioned for a regulatory loophole that allowed it to keep zero reserves against any potential defaults.

Meanwhile, along the same lines, lobbyists employed by these financial firms worked to ensure that the vast market in financial derivatives would remain unregulated. Derivatives are bets on future prices that enable a company to hedge risky assets. But such derivatives can entail gambling when no underlying asset is owned. Major investment banks like Gold-man Sachs and Bear Stearns obtained exemptions from the rules so they too could boost profits by borrowing heavily to speculate on these assets, keeping little of their own equity at risk.[13] These banks also faced a moral hazard: They were now too large and interconnected to fail without creating an economic catastrophe, one that would bring down not only financial markets but also the "real" sector of manufacturers, farmers, and households. Hence, these megabanks could take on huge risks, relatively secure in the belief that the government would not let them fail.

The federal government played an important part in the real estate bubble through its implicit backing of Fannie Mae and Freddie Mac. These quasi-governmental organizations were formed decades earlier to promote home ownership by creating a secondary market in mortgages. Although these companies maintained rules for quality control that set industry standards, the standards became eroded when subprime mortgage originators like Countrywide bypassed them to sell directly to Wall Street. Fannie and Freddie lost market share and eventually lowered their own lending standards. Borrowers with questionable earnings and small (or no) down payments were able to get loans. Meanwhile, the Federal Reserve may have contributed to the severity of the recession by its see-saw policies, particularly in failing to lower interest rates in the summer of 2008.[14]

Collapse of the Efficient Market Hypothesis

The belief that financial markets can regulate themselves was critically tied to the "efficient market hypothesis"—the thesis that market prices rationally reflect all the available information and, therefore, that bubbles can never exist (a bubble is defined as an irrational price surge).[15] Greed would lead market participants to bet against overpriced securities, thereby popping any emerging bubbles. The invention of sophisticated new tools of analysis would enable firms to analyze product prices and evaluate risks appropriately. This perspective turned out to be shortsighted. Markets work well when incentives are appropriately aligned, not when widespread moral hazard exists due to asymmetric information and a "rigged" market with bailout guarantees.

Moreover, behavioral economics suggests that traders do not always operate on the basis of market fundamentals but may experience "animal spirits"—spontaneous swings in optimism or pessimism that result in unstable price gyrations. Keynes used the term in 1936 to describe his experiences as a stock trader and speculator.[16] Robert Shiller echoed the view of market imperfection when he published *Irrational Exuberance* in 2000, predicting a major correction in technology stocks (the "dot-com" bust). Over the fifteen months leading up to March 2000, the NASDAQ composite index of stocks skyrocketed 130 percent. Then it plummeted, losing three-fourths of its value by late 2002.

Investors quickly forgot about the fizzle in technology stocks and began creating new bubbles in housing and bond markets, buoyed by a flood of foreign capital into the United States from emerging markets.[17] The public (and government regulators) seemingly had failing memories about the Great Depression and the contagion effects that led to widespread banking failures. Arrogance and hubris—permanent features of the human psyche according to Adam Smith—led many to believe that markets would never fail again. Excessive risk taking and leveraging by the financial industry produced balance sheet problems that eventually precipitated a crisis. By 2006 housing prices had peaked, and the rate of mortgage defaults doubled the following year. Investors began to reconsider the risk of CDOs as losses mounted and banks scrambled to acquire liquidity (ready cash). In December 2007 the economy slid into recession.

In March 2008 the first bank to go under was Bear Stearns, which was absorbed into JPMorgan with the help of a large government subsidy. Six months later Lehman Brothers (the fourth largest U.S. investment bank) declared bankruptcy after a private merger failed. Government leaders balked at bailing it out because they feared creating a moral hazard or that they lacked legal authority. This was a short-lived policy because AIG, whose credit default insurance tentacles stretched around the world, collapsed the following week. It was too interconnected to fail without bringing down many other companies, and thus AIG was bailed out with massive injections of government capital, in exchange for partial nationalization. All the major banks (some under duress) absorbed large amounts of financing from the federal government, as did General Motors and others. The bailout fund known as the Troubled Asset Relief Program (TARP) eventually dispersed $430 billion, most of which was later repaid. The net cost to the government of the bailout was $32 billion.[18]

The massive experiment to see what would happen if greed were unleashed in financial markets came crashing down in 2008, causing a worldwide recession. Because Adam Smith's name was often invoked to support the deregulation of financial markets, it is instructive to examine what Smith wrote about these markets.

ADAM SMITH, GREED, AND FINANCIAL MARKETS

As noted in Chapter 8, twentieth-century economists wrongly caricatured Smith as a proponent of greed, based on a selective reading of his works. In support of this simplistic view is the frequently quoted passage in which Smith argues that striving merchants are motivated by an instinct for self-interest: "It is not from the benevolence of the butcher, the brewer, or the baker, that we expect our dinner, but from their regard to their own interest. We address ourselves, not to their humanity but to their self-love."[19] Later, in another famous passage, Smith analyzes whether government should impose constraints on the international flow of capital. Smith argues that no regulations are needed because businesspeople will naturally prefer to keep their capital close to home. Every entrepreneur intends only his own gain and strives to invest his capital in projects that earn the highest returns, and in doing so he is "led by an *invisible hand* to promote an end which was no part of his intention."[20] That unintended end is the betterment of society at large.

Smith thus made clear to his readers that self-interest plays an important and justifiable role in motivating behavior and creating a good society. Creating public policies on the false belief that benevolence is the only justifiable moral motive would be a mistake, because nature endows us with a strong and healthy instinct for self. Moreover, many people who claim to be acting out of benevolence are disguising their own selfish aims: "I have never known much good done by those who affect to trade for the public good," Smith wrote.[21] Common sense requires prudence and wisdom in economic affairs—a careful balancing of interests—including one's own interests to feed and clothe one's family. It is virtuous (in this narrow sense) to look after oneself, and it is a vice to rely on the handouts of others.

But it is a misreading of Smith to equate his self-interest with greed. Greedy individuals will generally lower the economic returns to society by conspiring to create monopolies, by rent seeking, and by free riding.[22] Smith shows that economic growth can be enhanced if institutional rules are in place—social and legal norms, regulations, and competitive markets—that keep greed in check. As to Mandeville's claim that greed inspires ingenuity, Smith notes that entrepreneurs are generally working for social rather than material rewards: "It is not ease or pleasure, but always honour, of one kind or another, though frequently an honour *very ill understood*, that the ambitious man really pursues."[23] The origin of exchange arises not from rational, goal-oriented profit seeking but from an instinct for sociability. Imagine two strangers passing on a lonely road. Their first instinct is to trade *ideas* and *feelings*. The desire to be believed, to persuade, and to share fellow feeling constitutes the social exchange that precedes the swapping of gifts.[24] When Smith talks about "self-love," it is not synonymous with greed because there is a social context of moral norms to which people would be expected to adhere. Smith's market examples usually rely on conversation, civility, and character. Hence, "to be laying a plot either to gain or to save a single shilling, would degrade the most vulgar tradesman in the opinion of all his neighbors."[25]

Even the wholesale merchant who deals in impersonal markets is alert to moral undercurrents. It is expensive to write and enforce contracts, hence Smith explains the paramount concern for *trust* when making investments: "He can know better the character and situation of the persons whom he trusts."[26] In Smith's view, a person of character is honest not because he has calculated the advantage of *appearing* trustworthy; a person of character loves virtue itself. Smith's commercial traders (the butcher, the brewer, and the baker) are embedded in a social web that motivates as well as constrains behavior through internal and external mechanisms.

Smith's version of self-interest thus means something different than the twentieth-century conception: It means paying appropriate attention to one's own interests within the wider context of one's duties to others. The ultimate result of the propensity to "truck, barter, and exchange" is a growing specialization of labor and a consequent improvement in labor productivity. The standard of living grows, but it is too simplistic to see this as rational calculation motivated mainly by greed.

The Invisible Hand and Public Policy

Adam Smith examined and explicitly rejected the notion that greed, unleashed without restraint, would automatically lead to socially desirable outcomes through the working of the invisible hand. Public policy needs to take account of human instincts and devise institutional rules that create incentives supportive of progress. It is a lesson that modern economists learned only painfully. After the 2008 crash, Alan Greenspan lamented, "Those of us who have looked to the self-interest of lending institutions to protect shareholders' equity, myself included, are in a state of shocked disbelief."[27] Simply letting instincts run rampant, even within a competitive market, may result in suboptimal outcomes. The public policy Smith proposed toward financial markets is thus quite different than many would suspect.

In Smith's model Divine Providence (meaning God's foresight and prudence) created the natural world within which humans live and act. That world is driven by human nature, biologically predetermined to strive for survival and procreation. Humans are not always aware of these ultimate goals and instead respond to proximate instincts (hunger, sexual appetite, and so on). Social institutions work with human nature and in the best circumstances produce progress for society (Figure 9.1).

FIGURE 9.1. Adam Smith's progress: Instincts and institutions.

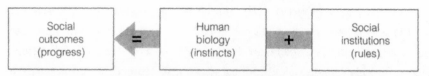

In Smith's model, the human instinct for betterment is a powerful force for progress that can overcome the obstacles of bad institutions. Instincts work best within the constraints of institutions that align personal interest with social interests (for example, a competitive market).

Social institutions are the rules, norms, and laws that guide behavior. Moral codes provide a check on selfishness, for example, by prohibiting actions that do not align with socially desirable outcomes. In medieval Europe, communities created property rights so as to place wealth and power in the hands of the oldest son and forbade the division of land. This practice, called primogeniture, enhanced security by insuring that communities could amass family power and wealth with clear lines of succession. The instinct for survival, along with the humanly devised institution of primogeniture, produced a beneficial outcome given the challenges to society at that time.

Institutions become outdated, however, and need periodic revision. Smith criticized primogeniture, for example, because that ghost institution survived long after the reasons for its existence had disappeared. Rules evolve slowly and only with much upheaval. The upshot is that human instincts and human institutions can often work together to produce good outcomes, like economic progress. The invisible hand does not guarantee success at any single point in time, but Smith is optimistic that the indomitable human spirit can overcome many of the obstructions that bad institutions produce.

When Smith argues that self-interest can produce beneficial results for society at large, it requires the coexistence of appropriate and fair institutions. In Smith's era, elites were granted monopoly privileges by the monarchy in a system called **mercantilism**. In this situation the instinct for self was paired with bad institutional rules and thereby thwarted society's desire for progress. In opposition to mercantilism, Smith supported fair rules via the restraining institutional force of competition, which he thought would channel self-interest in a socially productive way. Mandeville, by contrast, had argued that unfettered instincts, without any restraining institutions, would produce "Paradise." Smith had no such illusion, particularly in financial markets. Social and legal norms remind us of our obligations to others and prevent our rasher instincts from running wild.

Financial Market Regulations

In general, Smith supported the rights of individuals to use their talents in competitive exchange. But he had particular concerns about avarice in financial markets. He worried that the poor would gamble their life savings on risky speculation; hence, he advocated paternalism to restrict the products that banks could sell. Smith also worried that bank failures could have contagion effects that would hurt the wider economy.

Prudence means showing an appropriate regard for one's future well-being. In a world of weak regulations, however, a prudent banker competes against imprudent bankers, who in the short run can rack up larger profits by taking excessive risks. The risky banker **free rides** on others because the gains are *privatized* but the risks are *socialized* (through the implicit expectation of a bailout). For these reasons, Smith put his faith in appropriate rules that would restrict *all* bankers from taking excessive risks. This establishes procedural justice (Chapter 10) and creates a level playing field.

For the conditions of his day, Smith endorsed a regulation that he thought would prevent excessive risk taking—a **price ceiling** on the rate of interest. By limiting the interest that banks could charge, the policy deliberately generated a shortage of loans. In this circumstance bankers would prudently ration their funds to their most reliable borrowers, cutting out speculators and "prodigals." Smith noted that there would be a trade-off between market freedom and market safety, and he argued in favor of safety:

Such regulations may, no doubt, be considered as in some respects a violation of natural liberty. But those exertions of the natural liberty of a few individuals, which might endanger the security of the whole society, are, and ought to be, restrained by the laws of all governments.[28]

Thus, Smith is not an advocate of laissez-faire, which is a complete absence of government in economic affairs. Although a limited government is best, there are circumstances in which he thought institutional rules could produce better outcomes for society. Smith is a pragmatist who tries to devise reasonable policies for advancing economic growth.[29]

The analysis of this chapter makes us think more deeply about the interplay between human instincts and the social institutions that are meant to channel them in appropriate ways. The Great Recession of 2008 highlights an example of institutional failure. Although the causes and consequences of the crisis are beyond the scope of one chapter, several issues stand out with regard to ethics and economics. First, the rise of Keynesian economics changed the way society views and treats fellow citizens who are unemployed. Instead of seeing every case of joblessness as evidence of laziness, most economists by the mid-twentieth century came to accept the theory that forces beyond a person's control could cause involuntary unemployment during recessions or depressions. If correct, the moral responsibility to prevent or alleviate such suffering might lie with countercyclical government policies.

Second, changing these institutional rules introduces a moral hazard: The unemployed now getting assistance might become less diligent in searching for work and expansive fiscal policy might be hard to rein in once a recession is over, leading to ever-rising deficits. Paradoxically, by reducing the severity of recessions, the public may come to expect an era of stability in which riskier behavior is justified. A car that has an air bag is safer than one without, but that might spur the driver to become more reckless. Worst of all, the expectation of government bailouts creates a predominant moral hazard in which gains are privatized and losses socialized.

LOOKING AHEAD

Ethical egoism, proposed by Bernard Mandeville in the early eighteenth century and heralded by Ayn Rand and others in the twentieth century, was one of the intellectual edifices that contributed to the loosening of financial regulations after 1980. Adam Smith rejects the notion that greed alone can produce a prosperous society. In the context of the financial sector of his day, Smith endorses rules to constrain avarice by limiting risk taking and speculation.

The moral hazard created when the public bailed out the excessive risk takers on Wall Street will encourage more risk taking in the future, unless new institutions are forged to prevent it. Another major cost of the bailout is the widening perception that the capitalist system is rigged to favor wealthy and well-connected elites. Both the Tea Party and Occupy Wall Street movements fed off of this perception. Chapters 10 and 11 turn to the discussion of economic justice and rising inequality.

CHAPTER 10

Economic Justice: Process versus Outcomes

What is economic justice? This chapter and the following explore
conflicting frameworks and argue that a pluralistic understanding of justice
best captures the multidimensional approach to provide fairness of
process and equality of opportunity.

BIOLOGY AND FAIRNESS

Chapter 8 showed that humans have strong instincts for justice that appear to be a common attribute of the human experience. In repeated
experiments, humans reject offers considered unfair, even if the result
is less income for themselves. The expectation of fair treatment appears
to be deeply ingrained and can be inferred from the eye movements and
attention of fifteen-month-old infants.[1] However, the context for this behavior matters. If one subject has expended greater effort or shown more
ingenuity, the moral framework shifts and others are willing to accept
lower payouts.

Charles Darwin theorized that humans and animals share continuity
in evolutionary development with regard to such moral emotions. Like
humans, primates and some other mammals refuse to cooperate under
conditions considered unfair, such as when their social partners receive
higher rewards for equal activity.[2] If evolution proceeds at the level of the
group as well as of the individual, the mechanisms of solidarity would be
instinctively ingrained in social animals.[3] Franklin Roosevelt captures this
idea of multilevel selection in his second inaugural address:

In every land there are always at work forces that drive men apart and forces
that draw men together. In our personal ambitions we are individualists. But in
our seeking for economic and political progress as a nation, we all go up, or else
we all go down, as one people.[4]

Scarcity means that not all wants can be satisfied; when an economic
system generates very different outcomes, the fairness of these results
can be at issue. In his speech Roosevelt also argues, "The test of our

progress is not whether we add more to the abundance of those who have much; it is whether we provide enough for those who have too little." Ideology plays a role in shaping viewpoints about economic justice. What we see and how we interpret what we see are partly determined by our worldview, which is shaped from infancy by the environment interacting with our genes. Family and community morals typically emphasize sharing, particularly during times of crisis (see Chapter 7). Such behaviors, which evolved with small hunting clans tens of thousands of years ago, need not imply that the aggregate economy today should be motivated by the same customs.

For example, under the communist doctrines of Karl Marx, an economy would operate on the basis of a family ethic, "From each according to ability, to each according to need." The perversion of this code under authoritarian regimes led to the death by starvation and disease of perhaps 30 million people in China and 7 million people in the Soviet Union. The promulgation of communist equality led to horrific outcomes at both the aggregate and individual levels, revealing the fallacy of composition: the belief that a norm that works for the benefit of families would also be desirable for the macroeconomic system.[5] Inequality is an inevitable and in some views, a required outcome of normal economic evolution; no nation has perfect equality, and to achieve it would stifle ambition and freedom to an intolerable extent. Some inequality, after all, is simply the result of personal choices—of what career to pursue, how much vacation to take, whether to marry, and whether to have children.

Although biological forces create strong instincts for justice, Adam Smith was quick to insist that humanly devised institutions must work with those instincts to create good outcomes for society (Chapters 8 and 9). We turn now to that discussion.

ECONOMIC JUSTICE

In ethics, justice means the fair treatment of all persons. It is difficult to define what is just or fair in a way that all people would accept, yet there is widespread agreement in rich democracies that certain outcomes or practices are unfair today—child starvation or human slavery. Justice may be viewed in at least two different ways that reflect differences in underlying ethical viewpoints:[6]

1. Justice as a fair *process*; and
2. Justice as a fair *outcome*.

Justice as Fair Process (Procedural Justice)

The classical economics of Adam Smith is motivated by a deep concern for economic justice, using the metaphor of a footrace:

> In the race for wealth, and honours, and preferments, he may run as hard as he can, and strain every nerve and every muscle, in order to outstrip all his competitors. But if he should justle, or throw down any of them, the indulgence of the spectators is entirely at an end. It is a violation of fair play, which they cannot admit of.[7]

In *The Wealth of Nations* Adam Smith mainly promotes procedural or commutative justice—fair rules for trade through competitive markets. Government's role is to establish a system of impartial justice and allow effort and ingenuity to determine who wins the race. Like an impartial referee at a sporting event, government's aim should be to ensure procedural justice, not to determine which businesses win or lose. Smith vehemently opposed the mercantilist system of his time in which elites used governmental power to rig markets and fix prices, redistributing income from the poor to the rich:

> To hurt in any degree the interest of any one order of citizens, for no other purpose but to promote that of some other, is evidently contrary to that justice and equality of treatment which the sovereign owes to all the different orders of his subjects.[8]

Smith's main policy recommendation is to improve the earnings of the poor by removing the rigged process by which the rich exploit the poor through monopolies. Changing the rules of the game creates a level playing field—*a fair process*—by which the poor can raise themselves up once they get the boot of big government off their heads.

This approach emphasizes the *negative* rights of individuals—the right not to be harmed by others. Martin Luther King Jr. gave a celebrated speech in 1963 to commemorate the hundredth anniversary of the Emancipation Proclamation. In "I Have A Dream," King implores the nation to focus on the negative rights of African Americans to not be harmed based on their race. To King, freedom means being treated as an equal in the markets of exchange and in the voting booths of democracy. A fair process is urged. In future years, however, King led affirmative action boycotts to force open closed markets and lobbied for basic needs in housing and a guaranteed basic income. Progress in *outcomes* matters as well as in process.[9]

Justice as Fair Outcome (Distributive Justice)

Adam Smith also focuses on the actual outcomes of the poor and worries that some of the working poor will be left behind. Smith writes:

> No society can surely be flourishing and happy, of which the far greater part of the members are poor and miserable. It is but equity, besides, that they who feed, clothe, and lodge the whole body of the people, should have such a share of the produce of their own labour as to be themselves tolerably well fed, clothed and lodged.[10]

Smith's policies to achieve better outcomes include changing the rules (as already discussed) and in providing a subsidy for educating the poor. If outcomes are a suitable gauge for determining justice, a fair outcome in a family might be that every child is distributed an equitable portion of meat for dinner. Distributive justice would not require that each person receive an *equal* outcome, however, because consideration of equity might mean that some receive more than others for persuasive reasons. An underweight child might need more protein than others for healthy growth. A child who performed extra chores might receive an extra slice of pie for dessert. Likewise, soldiers in imminent danger receive a bonus of up to $225/month compared to their peers in safety.

From the perspective of distributive justice, the community can be said to have obligations to the individual to ensure a just distribution. Taxes could be imposed on the well-off to create a safety net of health, education, and retirement supplement for those at the bottom of the economic pyramid. Robin Hood, the legendary English outlaw, was interested in such distributive justice. Most socialist systems are in theory motivated to create fair outcomes in terms of basic needs. This approach emphasizes *positive* rights—the right of an individual to obtain benefits from others in certain circumstances.

When Franklin Roosevelt campaigned for president in 1932 he faced a collapsing economy and widespread unemployment. Roosevelt's populist campaign promised a "New Deal" if he was elected.[11] In the card game of life, some people had been dealt from a *stacked* deck: A new deal was needed to distribute economic gains more evenly. New Deal redistribution policies included Social Security (basic incomes for seniors), a minimum wage, financial market regulations, public employment programs, and stronger organizing power for unions. Subsequent Democratic presidents added a GI Bill for soldiers seeking higher education, the Great Society health programs of Medicaid (for the poor) and Medicare (for the elderly), the War on Poverty, and the Civil Rights Act. These programs contributed to narrowing the differences in economic outcomes in America over the decades from the 1930s to the 1960s, as commonly measured using the Gini coefficient.

The Gini index measures overall inequality on a scale from 0 to 1, with zero meaning households receive identical incomes and one indicating that one household receives all the income. The "Roaring 1920s" in America coincided with the rise of the Gini index to 0.45 or higher as markets surged with a stock boom. Then the Gini fell sharply with the Great Depression, Roosevelt's New Deal programs, and World War II. Several decades of relative stability followed even as the economy grew rapidly. These decades convinced many analysts that rising inequality was not a necessary condition for economic growth (as some economists had previously believed). This point was made more convincingly by the rapid rise in income and fall in Gini ratios in the newly industrializing countries of East Asia in the late twentieth century. While supporting growth of markets through export-led industrialization, governments

FIGURE 10.1. Gini index of U.S. inequality.

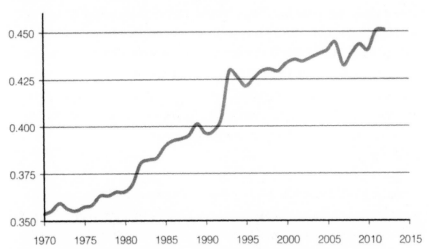

Income inequality among U.S. families has been rising steadily since 1970, measured by the Gini coefficient.

Source: Data from U.S. Census Bureau, Current Population Survey, Annual Social and Economic Supplements, Table F-4: Gini Ratios by Families, 2014.

redistributed education, health, and land to ensure that "shared growth" lifted all income groups, particularly the poor.[12]

America's income distribution did not remain constant. Figure 10.1 shows that over the roughly four decades between 1970 and 2012, the Gini coefficient for families grew from 0.35 to 0.45, an increase of 28 percent. Average wages stagnated during this period, after adjusting for inflation. Most of the income growth went to those in the top 1 percent—and more so in the top 1 percent of the top 1 percent. The United States now has the largest inequality of any industrial nation.

Some part of this change in inequality can be attributed to institutional changes. When President Ronald Reagan was elected in 1980 he sought to turn back the tide against the New Deal and distributive justice, arguing that taking from one citizen to give to another citizen was simply a form of theft. To many on the political right, this was a welcome move from an outcome-oriented view of justice to a procedural view. Welfare reform and tax and spending policies became somewhat more regressive:

Housing subsidies given to the richest 20 percent (through the mortgage interest deduction) are now four times larger than the housing subsidy provided to the poorest 20 percent of Americans.[13] Other economic and political forces are at work: the shifting of blue collar jobs overseas, the real minimum wage falling because of inflation, the rise of automation through technological innovation, and the deregulation of the financial sector, which allows for concentrated gains by those able to capture economic "rents"—payments in excess of opportunity cost.

Policy Implications

Virtually all societies justify using both distributive and procedural justice. That is, liberals and conservatives in the United States maintain that fair rules are important, but that some redistributions (for example, education and health care for children) are also necessary. However, people disagree quite strongly about the balance or mix of justice.

Those who favor distributive justice tend to support a more active role for government. In this view, government is needed to create a safety net for those at the bottom and a more equal starting point for all children. Although procedural justice can level the racetrack, distributive justice is needed to prepare children for the starting gate (discussed in Chapter 11). Poor children may show up to the classroom hungry and lacking the mental stimulation that promotes brain development. An active government would subsidize health and preschool opportunities so that children have more equal opportunities to start first grade ready to learn. Opportunities will never be identical because of important differences in parents' genes and environments; nevertheless, government and philanthropic programs can provide some measure of more equal prospects.

Those who favor limited government prefer to emphasize procedural justice. An active government may lead to dependency and moral decline; hence, the role of government should be constrained to providing and enforcing a framework of competition and property rights. The benefits of economic growth would "trickle down" to the poor. Those who emphasize process are more likely to approve the results of the market system—even if highly unequal—provided that individuals are given access to opportunity. Critics of trickle down theory point out that the rules themselves are set by an unfair process in which the rich and powerful sometimes rig the system (that was Adam Smith's critique of mercantilism). Proponents of limited government intervention point out that redistribution creates opportunities for the very regulatory capture and crony capitalism that results in a rigged system.[14]

NEOCLASSICAL ECONOMIC JUSTICE

Although modern economic views derive historically from classical utilitarianism, the implementation (and the end result) are quite different.[15] In the mainstream view of preference satisfaction it is perfectly acceptable to judge the goodness or badness of the economy's performance (that is, its efficiency) without any reference to the distribution of income and wealth. This weights the interests of persons unequally because, owing to their purchasing power, the preferences of the rich count more in the determination of efficiency than do those of the poor.

Efficiency in Historical Perspective

The historical byways through which the neoclassical model narrowed the scope of analysis to its present form are of interest. The classical approach to economics, exemplified by Adam Smith's *The Wealth of Nations* (1776), was an inquiry about the nature, sources, and distribution of wealth and included policy proposals for the general welfare. The interests of the poor figured prominently in Smith's analysis because they were by far the largest proportion of the population and had the greatest perceived needs. Smith's policy proposals favored rules that benefited workers. Throughout the nineteenth century and continuing into the early twentieth century, economic evaluations continued to emphasize distributional concerns using utilitarian arguments for maximizing happiness by considering each person's welfare equally.

Arthur Pigou, the British economist who standardized the approach to welfare analysis in the early twentieth century, held that utility was a measurable force (like gravity), and therefore changes in marginal utility could be compared between individuals. To Pigou and to his mentor Alfred Marshall, *interpersonal* comparisons of utility were both possible and desirable. Income distribution played an important part of this analysis. Under commonsense utilitarian assumptions, $100 taken from a rich person would cause less pain than the pleasure created by giving $100 to a poor person. Diminishing marginal utility of money means that redistribution through a progressive income tax could enhance the overall well being of society.

Vilfredo Pareto, in Switzerland, published an attack on such cardinal utility notions in 1906. As an engineer, Pareto asserted that no force such as utility could currently be measured, and hence economics based on utility theory was unscientific. If utility was not measurable, neither was the marginal utility that Pigou (and earlier Alfred Marshall) had relied on to undergird redistribution. Using mathematics, Pareto demonstrated that indifference curves (rather than utility curves) could be used to explain consumer choice without relying on cardinal utility. Pareto quite explicitly stated that his goal was to *understand*, not to make any judgments about welfare.[16]

In 1932, Lionel Robbins published a blistering critique of cardinal utility theory, calling attention to Pareto's groundbreaking work. In *An Essay on the Nature and Significance of Economic Science*, Robbins redefined economics as the study of *choice* in the face of scarcity.[17] Subsequent theorists recast the microeconomic framework without the use of measurable utility or the possibility of interpersonal comparisons of utility.[18] Banished from efficiency analysis is any explicit discussion of the distributional impacts of policies: An economist's tool kit is thus devoid of the means for analyzing fairness, as it is simply deemed outside the bounds of science.[19] Maximizing the capacity for preference satisfaction as a proxy for welfare stays in the domain of analysis, not without substantial difficulties (see Chapters 5 and 6).

Ian Little, in *A Critique of Welfare Theory* (1950), sharply criticized the turn away from distributional concerns.[20] Little proposes that for any policy change to be labeled as welfare enhancing, a necessary condition should be that it produce a "not-unfavorable" redistribution of income. E. J. Mishan, a leading proponent of cost–benefit analysis, takes a more modest approach, saying that if a proposed policy is believed to cause unambiguously regressive effects, economists have a "duty" to at least report it.[21] These proposals have had little impact.

Efficiency Implies Fairness

Neoclassical economics in the twentieth century moved toward studying the conditions for production and consumption efficiency and away from assessing the fairness of those outcomes. Efficiency, not equity, became the mantra of standard economics. Another reason for this apparent disinterest in studying income differences arises from the belief that *efficient* outcomes are also *fair* outcomes. This conviction, which often takes the form of an ideology, came from a famous theoretical deduction in the late nineteenth century by John Bates Clark and Philip Henry Wicksteed, that under assumptions of competitive markets and other ideal attributes, workers would naturally receive the value of the marginal product they produced. Clark, in *Distribution of Wealth* (1899), wrote that:

... the distribution of income to society is controlled by a natural law, and that this law, if it worked without friction, would give to every agent of production the amount of wealth which that agent creates.[22]

This hypothesis in positive economics became entangled in normative economics because the belief that workers *are* paid according to their marginal products gives rise to the belief that they *should* be so rewarded, according to natural law.

The neoclassical faith in fair distributions can be criticized, however, on the basis of market preferences, market structure, measurement, joint production, aggregation problems, and macroeconomic dislocations. We turn again to our well-meaning economist and a quizzical observer to flesh out these points:

Well-meaning economist: In a market system the profit motive provides an incentive for firms to employ and fairly compensate the most productive workers. In 1947 the Brooklyn Dodgers broke the color barrier by signing Jackie Robinson, whose proficient batting made him a better hire than any white player. Likewise, movie stars are rewarded for their box-office draws. Profit-seeking firms will, in this way, over time eradicate unfair discrimination based on race, gender, or ethnic background.

Observer: Isn't that perhaps too rosy a picture? Couldn't prejudice—as a type of "friction"—lead market forces to skew earnings and produce inequality through discrimination? If the majority of customers are racist or sexist, won't a business cater to those preferences? A hotel might refuse to serve African Americans if it expects to gain more business than it will lose. Likewise, a factory manager might refuse to hire a well-qualified woman if this upsets group harmony among the existing male workers. In one study, venture capitalists (who make loans to business start-ups) were more likely to support a project presented by a male—especially an attractive one!—than the *identical* project pitched by a female.[23] The profit motive cannot ensure that some people are not injured economically because of prejudices having nothing to do with individual productivity. The market can be "efficient" in satisfying racist or sexist preferences![24]

Economist: Okay, you are correct that the efficiency story is hard to endorse without assuming the background conditions of laws protecting basic human rights (as discussed in Chapter 5). Regulations barring discrimination set the constraints within which competitive markets work to ensure a fair return based on productivity.

Observer: But what if markets aren't competitive? Adam Smith worried about the *collusion* of employers to "sink the wages of labor."[25] The National Collegiate Athletic Association (NCAA), for example, monopolizes college athletics, rigging the rules to prevent student-athletes from being paid a competitive wage. The issue is more troublesome in developing countries where perverse incentives lead governments to endorse monopoly rather than competitive efficiency.[26] The notion that the invisible hand produces the best outcome under all circumstances is a misinterpretation (as discussed in Chapters 8 and 9).

Economist: Okay, we should always emphasize that *competitive* markets pay based on productivity but rigged markets do not.

Observer: You're not quite off the hook. The scoring output of a baseball slugger is relatively easy to determine (number of runs batted in). But how easy is it in general to translate individual performance into revenue gained when many workers contribute in diverse ways? Suppose a superb high school teacher inspires a student to pursue a brilliant career in medicine. The economic value of that teacher's contribution will appear only ten years in the future and is mingled with the contributions of many others in **joint production**. How can a market reward this teacher when the value of individual output is unknowable?

Economist: When it is difficult to identify individual achievement, the marginal productivity theory of distribution is obviously debatable. The transaction costs for making it work may be too high. So workers in some fields are paid in part on supply and demand and in part based on custom and negotiating power.

Observer: So if women historically were teachers, and if women historically have less negotiating power than males, then the tradition of paying women less than men could continue, even if it has nothing to do with productivity?

Economist: Point made. Are we done?

Observer: Not yet. The amount and quality of capital also affect labor productivity. Physical capital includes things like computers and trucks. But the most important input is *human* capital. This consists of cognitive capital (intelligence, education, training, and health); emotional capital (perseverance over obstacles, self-control); social capital (network of contacts); moral capital (shared beliefs about right and wrong); and even something as mysterious as spiritual capital (transpersonal beliefs and practices).[27] For the theory of distribution to have meaning, it must be possible to aggregate these different types of capital.

Economist: Sure. I buy that.

Observer: But there is an error in logic. The price of capital can be known only *after* the profit rate on capital is known! Thus, the amount of capital in production cannot be separated from its price and profit. This is circular reasoning.[28] Paul Samuelson, the Nobel laureate, admitted that the neoclassical model of distribution "cannot be universally valid." He concludes, "If all this causes headaches for those nostalgic for the old time parables of neoclassical writing, we must remind ourselves that scholars are not born to live an easy existence. We must respect, and appraise, the facts of life."[29]

Economist: Okay. Economists cannot prove that workers in competitive markets are paid the value of their productivity. But the facts of history speak for themselves. The rise of markets and the Industrial Revolution have made most people much better off.

Observer: That's certainly true in absolute terms. But the issue here is the *relative distribution* of the gains. From the 1950s to the early 1970s, increases in worker productivity led to equivalent increases in wages and benefits after adjusting for inflation. But after 1973, a great divergence appeared: Average worker productivity grew by 80 percent, but average compensation grew by *half* that amount.[30] Workers (on average) are much more productive, but markets are not rewarding that productivity."

This dialogue suggests that some markets at the microeconomic level may do an excellent job of rewarding productivity, but the overall results are mixed in terms of both theory and evidence. At the macroeconomic level, Keynesians believe that systemic forces beyond an individual's control can cause involuntary unemployment. Those out of work for extended periods will experience a permanent decrease in their lifetime earning capabilities. Circumstance, not moral turpitude, can explain some poverty.

LOOKING AHEAD

This chapter explains two initial approaches to grappling with economic justice: one based on outcomes, the other based on process. In the twentieth century neoclassical economics moved away from worrying about justice. One reason arises from the conclusion that because utility can never be measured in an absolute sense, interpersonal comparisons of utility are impossible. Hence, economists can make no scientific conclusions about the benefits of redistribution. A second reason arises from the ideological belief that markets generally reward workers based on their productivities; hence no attention to distribution is required. The difference with Adam Smith is that Smith was alert to market failures in labor markets and proactive in promoting a fair process (rather than simply assuming the process is fair).

The theory of marginal productivity was ultimately found to be questionable, both theoretically and empirically. The model does not need to be thrown out, however. Marginal productivity theory can still explain how inputs in production (like land, labor, and capital) are hired by profit-maximizing firms once their prices are known, but it cannot independently explain how wages, interest, and profit are determined within that system. Hence, it cannot explain the overall distribution of income. Despite these controversies, the ideology of the invisible hand of the market is more powerful than the science that seemingly refutes it. Stories of rags-to-riches entrepreneurs capture the imagination of society and provide anecdotal fuel for the idea that market distributions are fair, if not in every case, then in an overall sense. The next chapter turns to how societies create equal opportunities for all.

CHAPTER 11

Economic Justice: Equal Opportunity

A fair process may help ensure equal treatment of adults who compete on the basis of effort and skill in markets. Effort and skill both depend on the foundational capabilities developed early in life and on genetics. Economic justice might suggest, therefore, that equality of opportunity for children is a minimum right of citizenship. This approach raises further concerns about measuring progress and sustainability.

INTRODUCTION

Economic justice was a central concern to economists in the eighteenth and nineteenth centuries. Adam Smith, the founder of modern economics, was moved by the injustice of monopolies in writing *The Wealth of Nations*. The American Economic Association, the largest and most influential body of practitioners today, was cofounded in 1885 by Richard T. Ely in part to help discover the possible injustices of laissez-faire capitalism. As discussed in Chapter 8, laboratory experiments support the view that economic actors instinctively react to perceptions of injustice, because justice is an organic and irreducible part of the economic experience. Considerations of economic justice are thus central to the organization and functioning of an economic system.

THE INSPIRATION OF HORATIO ALGER

The previous chapter discussed why standard economics in the twentieth century generally moved away from concern over inequality. One reason arises from the belief in American *meritocracy*—the idea that in a competitive market the brightest and most talented workers (as measured by the market) will rise to the top. In this view people are rewarded for their productivity and the current distribution of income reflects *merit*.

Horatio Alger was a nineteenth-century novelist who championed the view that hard work, moral rectitude, and pluck were the virtues needed to lift destitute boys out of poverty. In *Ragged Dick; or, Street*

Life in New York with the Boot Blacks (1868), an orphaned boy comes of age shining shoes, and his industriousness and courage eventually lead to his advance into the middle class. Steve Jobs, the cofounder of Apple Computer, represents a genuine rags-to-riches orphan story. Born out of wedlock, Jobs was adopted into a working-class family in which neither parent had a college degree. After encountering and overcoming many obstacles, he came to define the Information Age with inventive products like the iPhone and iPad. According to the marginal productivity theory of distribution, Jobs deserved his enormous wealth because of his innovations, perseverance, and business acumen.

But such accounts should not be overly simplified. In Horatio Alger's stories, kindly benefactors and lucky breaks aid the boys. By luck, Jobs adoptive parents lived in Silicon Valley, an area south of San Francisco encompassing Stanford University. This region has more PhDs per capita than any other area on the planet, providing a rich intellectual environment for innovation and opportunity. Jobs's schoolmates were the children of successful pioneers in the microchip revolution. Jobs benefited from these friendships, such as with Steve Wozniak, who cofounded Apple and invented the first Apple computer. Jobs's adoptive parents made steep sacrifices to send him to an expensive private college. Although he quickly dropped out, that experience ultimately shaped his design philosophy at Apple.[1]

Cynics also note that Apple gained market share and profits through market rigging (which led to antitrust lawsuits by the Justice Department in the United States and by the European Union). In addition, the technology that made Apple successful was the result of research in basic sciences paid for by the U.S. government. Apple received financial backing from a government innovation fund, and the iPhone technology relies on a government-financed system of global positioning system (GPS) satellites and the Internet itself.[2] It is impossible to say how much of Jobs's success relates to his individual productivity and how much relates to the inputs of others when market prices are not used to allocate public education and research funds and information externalities are widespread.[3] What is clear is that Jobs was a leading innovator who enchanted consumers and enriched his shareholders using the laws and institutions of an advanced society.

EQUALITY OF OPPORTUNITY

Even if Steve Jobs's individual productivity alone were said to be the source of his wealth, one might ask, "*Why* is his productivity higher?" Is it simply the random accident of genes, or is there an important *interaction* between his genes and his environment? If the latter, how much of Steve's environment is due to factors that can be influenced by public policy? Adam Smith supported an egalitarian ethic, a belief that environmental circumstances created most of the observed variations in productivity between individuals: "The difference between the most dissimilar characters, between a philosopher and a common street porter, for example, seems to arise not so much from nature as from habit, custom, and education."[4]

If this belief in equality of underlying ability is broadly shared, societal goals may include "equal opportunity for all" as a basic right of citizenship. Equal opportunity involves two aspects; one is the negative right to not be injured due to exclusion from competing for the best jobs. Such **formal** equality of opportunity guarantees that jobs are allocated by merit and not by discrimination based on race, gender, nepotism, political connections, or other factors deemed irrelevant. Formal equality of opportunity involves considerations of procedural justice or fair rules of process under which market exchange takes place.

Formal equality may mean little, however, if workers are unable to compete on merit because of diminished circumstances beyond their control. One of the most important environmental factors determining an individual's economic success is the prior success, attitudes, health, and incomes of his parents. Inequality endures in large part because of the transmission through families of the various forms of capital: physical, financial, cognitive, emotional, social, and spiritual. According to Robert Fogel, who won the Nobel Prize in 1993, spiritual resources comprise the psychological tools to cope with disappointments and include "a sense of purpose, a sense of community, family and work ethics, and high self-esteem."[5] Although public policy can do little to effect many of these variables, communities can raise and redistribute funds so that education, health care, and other services can be allocated to children based on need, not the ability to pay. In starting the economic race it is not plausible to argue that "every child can compete" if poor children show up to the race barefoot and without adequate nutrition or training. Substantive equality of opportunity thus represents a positive right to certain basic goods necessary for starting the economic race.

Another factor beyond an individual's control is his or her sex. Being male confers advantages in many places. In South Asia, for example, about three-fourths of boys receive enough education to become literate; young girls are kept out of school to tend to fields and care for family members, so that only 50 percent of adult women are literate. In Sub-Saharan Africa, about two-thirds of adult men are literate compared to half of adult women.[6] Paradoxically, men in the United States receive a preference in college admissions so as to produce gender parity, because men on average are academically less qualified than women.[7]

Women have made progress economically in many countries, yet gender barriers remain. Eva Kittay notes, "A conception of society viewed as an association of equals masks inevitable dependencies, those of infancy and childhood, old age, illness and disability." As a result, women are "not well-positioned to enter a competition for the goods of social cooperation on equal terms."[8] Time out of the workforce to raise children may be a permanent career setback. Thus, women currently run only about 5 percent of Fortune 500 companies; on the other hand, women CEOs now lead multinational companies in previously male-dominated fields like computing, automobiles, and energy. The Great Recession of 2008 also markedly increased the share of stay-at-home fathers as caregivers.

The previous chapter showed that income inequality has been rising in the United States since the 1970s and is now the highest of any rich country. One of the consequences of this is that income mobility is also lower in the United States than many other developed nations. Figure 11.1 shows the relationship between income inequality (measured by the Gini coefficient discussed in Chapter 10) and the degree to which parents transmit this inequality to their children.

If the economic outcomes of parents had no impact on their children's adult incomes, the measure of intergenerational earnings elasticity on the

FIGURE 11.1. Cross-country comparisons of inequality and mobility.

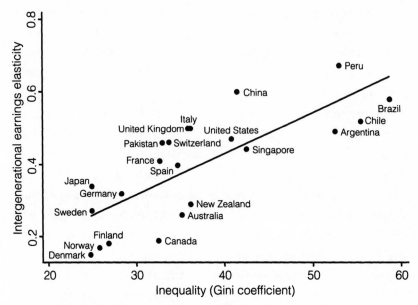

Countries in the bottom left of the chart have low levels of inequality and low levels of inequality transmission between generations.

Source: Miles Corak (2012) "The Economics of the Great Gatsby Curve," available at milescorak.com.

vertical axis would be zero. In the United States, an intergenerational earnings elasticity of about 0.50 means that 50 percent of a parent's income differential is transmitted to his or her adult offspring. Thus Logan, whose parents earned 80 percent more than the average income, can be expected to earn half that, or 40 percent more than the average income; Lucas, whose parents earned 30 percent less than the average income, can be expected to earn about 15 percent less than the average. A different study finds that a child growing up in the bottom fifth of the income distribution in the southern city of Atlanta has less than a 5 percent chance of making it to the top fifth, despite rapid economic growth in the region.[9]

Although a capitalist economy can lead to convergence in income and wealth through the spread of market skills, the opposite may be more likely according to some critics. Income and wealth gaps may grow because of the persistence of compound growth: As long as the return on capital exceeds the growth rate of income and output, the nonearned income derived from financial assets will outpace wages. Inheritance, not ingenuity, may explain part of growing inequality.[10]

The United States, which views itself as a meritocratic society, appears to offer less upward mobility than many European countries. A struggling average teenager depicted by Horatio Alger has a better chance of overcoming adverse background conditions if he grows up in Denmark than if he grows up in Detroit. This realization has led to a call for a concerted campaign to enhance the equality of opportunity. James Heckman, who won the Nobel Prize in 2000 for his work in labor economics, argues that many economic and social problems result from low levels of cognitive skills and social skills. Heckman's research shows that differences in parenting, particularly the extent of mental stimulation and emotional support, can alter children's future productivities. These differences become "locked in" due to brain development, which is path dependent. Thus, "about 50% of the variance in inequality in life-time earnings is determined by age 18."[11]

In adverse environments, the lack of cognitive and social learning at early ages is linked to poverty-creating behaviors such as criminality, teenage pregnancy, and dropping out of high school. No amount of money spent later has much impact on changing these behaviors because they are the result of brain underdevelopment. While respecting privacy and the primacy of the family unit, Heckman argues that social policy should focus on early interventions when childhood brains are still malleable. John Rawls, who was a philosopher at Harvard, points us in the direction to consider the "primary goods" that every citizen might reasonably expect.

JOHN RAWLS: JUSTICE AS FAIRNESS

A highly influential and controversial modern text that addresses distributive justice is by John Rawls (1921–2002). In *A Theory of Justice* (1971) Rawls takes aim at utilitarian ethics and the economic views that derive from it.[12] Rawls, who develops and extends a Kantian viewpoint, argues that differences in talent, gender, race, or social class into which one is born are not morally relevant differences. By themselves, they would not justify institutional arrangements in which people experience different life prospects.

Social contract theory models the moral relations between people, offering a device by which people can discover the forms of treatment that we can justify to others (and that others can justify to us). Rawls argues that a utilitarian ethic would never serve as a system of justice that could bind people together. The reason is simple: The extreme utilitarian (and economic) ethic examines only the *aggregate* welfare produced and has no concern for distribution or principles of justice. In a radical version of utilitarian ethics, it would be perfectly acceptable to kill Susan if it gives greater pleasure to Sam and Samantha.[13] Rawls asks, why would any rational, self-interested person agree to a system in which everyone works for the maximum good of the group and yet has no minimum assurance about personal interests? To Rawls, utility maximization fails because there are alternative approaches that would respect the distinctness of persons, and these alternatives would likely be selected in a fair bargaining scenario.

One problem in the world of actual policy making is that the currently powerful and successful individuals have greater bargaining power and can twist rules in their favor. The principles of social justice envisioned by Rawls require us to imagine an **original position** of equality from which the rules and institutions of society can be devised behind a **"veil of ignorance."** Rawls allows for general facts and assumptions about the world to enter into one's thinking behind the veil, but citizens do not know ahead of time what their own specific situations will turn out to be— whether they will be rich or poor, male or female, clever or dull, strong or disabled, and so on. Without specific background information, what principles of justice would people voluntarily agree to when they cannot tailor the answer to their own personal situations?

Starting from the original position is supposed to confer legitimacy on the society's basic institutions because people within the society could reasonably have chosen to live under those institutions. Only in this manner can people agree on rules that are fair to all. Behind the veil of ignorance, people are likely to be risk averse with regard to the "primary goods" that every person desires, including rights and liberties, opportunities, income and wealth, and social bases of self-respect. Rational individuals who are uncertain about their future status would never agree to bargain away certain safeguards. Rawls thus reaches two conclusions about the basic principles of justice to which he thinks people could agree, based on their own enlightened self-interests:

1. Each person would have an equal right to the most extensive basic liberty that is compatible with similar liberty for others; and
2. Social and economic inequality would be permitted and desirable, only to the extent that inequality (a) is attached to positions open to all based on equality of opportunity; and (b) is to the greatest benefit of the least advantaged.[14]

Item 2(b) is known as the **difference principle**, which allows for inequality only if it can be shown that those at the bottom are better off in *absolute* terms after inequality than they would be under pure equality. Morally arbitrary influences (such as a child's background circumstances) should not deprive someone of equal opportunity, nor should the random distribution of talent give excessive advantage to those who are especially gifted in the marketplace. According to Rawls, some redistribution of wealth and opportunity would likely be required to create fair opportunities for all. At the same time, perfect equality would be undesirable because it would impair the wealth-generating capacity of markets. Rewarding effort and ability with higher rewards creates incentives that make the economic pie larger, benefiting the least advantaged.

The Theory of Justice attracted many converts and many detractors. Robert Nozick, a libertarian and a Harvard colleague, took aim at Rawls in *Anarchy, State, and Utopia* (1974), arguing that the state has minimal central functions and redistribution is not one of these because of inherent conflicts with liberty. Imagine an ideal initial distribution of income and wealth that is deemed "just" according to Rawls's approach.[15] Suppose now that a million people are willing to pay a quarter each to see Wilt Chamberlain (a famous basketball player) dunk the ball. The subsequent distribution of income now greatly favors Chamberlain, yet was arrived in a perfectly just manner: The customers obtained their money through fair acquisition, and they parted with it through fair transfers. Nozick makes the point that any attempt to maintain an ideal distribution pattern will inevitably destroy freedom.

However, many people recognize that some policies involve conflicts between individual liberty and social welfare, and they are willing to trade some liberty for welfare at some rate. "Taxes are the price we pay for a civilized society," according to Oliver Wendell Holmes. Taxes are used for public goods that provide positive externalities such as national defense and a system of justice. Nozick would agree with these uses of public funds but object to redistribution and discretionary spending on substantive equality of opportunity. By contrast, Adam Smith supported government-subsidized education for the poor and progressive taxation.

To some critics, the social contract approach is inconsistent with the organic and historical ways in which social orders arise and evolve in path-dependent fashions. To Michael Walzer, this gives rise to "spheres" of justice as opposed to a single account of justice. If justice arises from pluralist perspectives, attempting to elicit a single set of primary goods across all social and historical worlds would render the exercise practically meaningless.[16] In the view of Friedrich Hayek, societies develop through a spontaneous order that cannot be manufactured or contrived from rational discourse. There is no reason, however, that social contract theory could not be used to offer guidance on how to shape the social order, consistent with other, nonrational, forces also shaping the social order. Human rationality can play an important part in the evolution of social institutions, even if previously such institutions sometimes arose spontaneously.

Another debatable issue is whether people behind the veil would automatically reject payouts that hurt the least well off. Suppose that in a society of 100 people, a set of rules (Institution A) would result in everyone earning income of $20,000/year. A different set of rules (Institution B) would result in ninety-nine people earning $40,000/year and one person earning $19,900/year. Given the option, and not knowing one's own status in advance, would most people vote for Institution B? Some individuals are gamblers who prefer a larger potential payout even if there is greater risk. Behavioral economics documents how people take excessive risks, overestimate their own capabilities, and otherwise hold irrational beliefs.

Rawls worries that people can act in shortsighted ways that are difficult to sustain, producing strains of commitment in the social contract. The principles of justice selected must be those that actual people can fully commit to over the course of an entire lifetime.

Rawls's lasting contributions may be his calling attention to the process by which individuals come to decide issues of justice and his caveat that preference maximization by itself is an inadequate means of organizing a good society. Amartya Sen built on Rawls's work even as he diverged in notable ways.

Negative freedom is the *absence* of restraints; it means being able to act without external interference. If you live in a society that upholds the right to a free press, you enjoy the negative freedom of reading or publishing what you want. Sen's capabilities approach asks us to consider a different problem: What if you cannot read? **Positive freedom** is the *presence* of something required for realizing one's goals, namely, the mastery of a skill needed to exercise one's right to read. These concepts are often rival: Negative freedom constrains government action; positive freedom could compel government action, such as through literacy programs.[17]

Amartya Sen observes that the major ethical theories are all deeply egalitarian along some particular dimension: Utilitarians value each unit of utility the same, economists value each dollar as equal to any other, Kantians value each human's rights identically, and most libertarians value each person's liberty as equal to any other. The key distinction is that they differ in their focus of what should be equalized.[18] Desiring equality along one dimension necessarily means forgoing equality along other dimensions.

The "equality of what" issue is complicated by the diversity of the human condition. The notion that "all men are created equal" suggests a degree of uniformity that is starkly missing from human reality. Humans are diverse in their external circumstances (economic class, culture, and environment) as well as their personal circumstances (gender, age, and cognitive, physical, and emotional abilities). In Sen's view, ignoring these differences can be deeply inegalitarian. **Substantive** equality is thus different from the notional equality explored by Rawls. Poverty is more than simply the lack of income.

In *Development as Freedom* (1999), Sen puts forth a new way of conceptualizing progress.[19] In this approach, freedom is both one of the means of development as well as its primary intrinsic goal. Poverty is reflected by the absence of substantive freedoms in various forms—political, economic, social, transparency, and security. To reach this conclusion Sen makes these distinctions:

- **Functioning** refers to what persons *actually* do and experience;
- **Capability** refers to having the *ability* to achieve a certain level of functioning.

Functions are what people choose to do with their *capabilities*. For example, suppose Mahira values the fact that she can read (a capability), even though she has a preference for listening to books on CD. Even though Mahira doesn't read much, her well-being depends on having the capability of reading. Reading is a part of basic education and provides intrinsic as well as extrinsic value. In a similar way, Mahira's biological fecundity is defined as her potential to bear children over a lifetime. In previous generations women often bore ten or more children. Mahira's fertility is the number of children she actually bears (for example, two). Mahira's capability is different from her functioning because she is capable of having more children than she freely chooses.

Sen argues that distribution policies should not be concerned with Mahira's functioning per se because so much of what people actually do is subject to personal choice (for example, how many children she has). Instead, Sen argues that social policy should focus on developing capabilities—the ability to achieve a level of functioning she desires. In this view, development is really about Mahira having the *freedom* to function as she chooses within a range of capabilities. Exactly what these capabilities should be is open to question, but most people could agree that education and health are likely components. In short, a substantive approach to well-being argues that poverty should be measured by the deprivation of capabilities across multiple dimensions; policies should focus on these dimension of inequality.

It is not enough, in Sen's view, to distribute primary goods without knowing whether people can effectively use those goods to pursue their own ends. People are highly diverse. With the same bundle of primary goods, a pregnant woman may have substantially less freedom than a single man. Primary goods, well-being, and freedom are interrelated but distinct concepts. Sen's critique of Rawls is that two individuals holding identical baskets of primary goods have the same *means* to achieve freedom but have two different experiences of the actual *extent* of that freedom enjoyed.[20]

Gender Inequality

Martha Nussbaum, a philosopher at the University of Chicago, developed the theory of capabilities and functioning in parallel with Sen. Her approach attempts to identify the characteristics of human flourishing in keeping with Aristotle's virtue ethics. In *Women and Human Development: The Capabilities Approach* (2000), Nussbaum calls attention to the widespread gender inequality that hampers the flourishing of women around the world:

Women in much of the world lack support for fundamental functions of a human life. They are less well nourished than men, less healthy, more vulnerable to physical violence and sexual abuse. They are much less likely than men to be literate, and still less likely to have preprofessional or technical education. . . . Similar obstacles often impede their effective participation in political life. In many nations women are not full equals under the law; they do not have the same property rights as men, the same rights to make a contract, the same rights of association, mobility, and religious liberty. . . . In all these ways, unequal social and political circumstances give women unequal human capabilities.[21]

Echoing Kant, Nussbaum argues that women need to be treated as ends in their own right and not simply as a means for others to achieve their ends. Sen and Nussbaum's work has been hugely influential in guiding economic development efforts around the world and in improving the equality of opportunity for women and the poor in general.

The Human Development Index

Over the past thirty years human outcomes worldwide have become more equal, not in monetary terms but in basic conditions of living. This is due to two interrelated factors: First, rapid growth in market economies raised the *absolute* living standards of many of the poorest people. As recently as 1990, 43 percent of the world population lived on less than $1.25 per day. By 2010, that number had fallen in half, after adjusting for inflation and purchasing power parity.[22]

Second, virtually every economic development agency now ascribes to the importance of addressing equality of opportunity as measured by capabilities.[23] Public and private resources have been redistributed to create these opportunities, contributing to a surge in literacy and life expectancy. In 1980, an average child born in the least developed part of the world could expect to live only about two-thirds as long as an average child born into the most developed part of the world. By 2010, that ratio increased to about three-fourths—even as rich country life expectancy expanded by 6.5 years. Although equal opportunity remains elusive for many, particularly for girls, substantial shifts in philosophy and practice have taken place.

Inspired by Sen's and Nussbaum's capabilities approach, the United Nations, under the direction of Pakistani economist Mahbub ul Haq, developed the **Human Development Index** (HDI) starting in 1990. Instead of focusing only on GDP per capita as a measure of development, the HDI includes several substantive measures of human welfare. Development is recorded when, for example, infant mortality rates fall (relative to benchmarks) and likewise when literacy rates rise (relative to benchmarks)—even if there is no change in money income. The HDI is comprised of three major indicators (and weights): education (one-third), health (one-third), and income (one-third). Two-thirds of the index thus reflects substantive measures of well-being; the last third reflects the indirect, preference satisfaction approach. The HDI thus creates a hybrid approach to measuring human well-being.

Comparing HDI with GDP can be an important exercise. South Africa is ranked seventy-eighth in the world based on its GDP per capita.

Once education and health outcomes are included, South Africa's rank in development drops to 110th, with an HDI score of about 0.60. Relative to the highest scoring country in each category, South Africa has reached only 60 percent of what is possible in terms of health, education, and income.[24] Per capita income is often a good proxy for conditions of living, but not in this case.

INTERGENERATIONAL JUSTICE

Distributions *within* generations can be seen in the wider context of distributions *between* generations. The individual choices and social policies made by the present generation determine, in part, the capabilities of future generations, and more so the very existence of those prospective peoples. This was vividly illustrated by Sen's analysis that China's "one-child" policy, introduced in 1978 to limit the number of births, led to gender-selective abortions and infanticide; as a consequence, up to 100 million girls are "missing" from the population.[25] These nonpersons have no choice in the matter and play no part in Rawls's social contract. In many ethical theories, nonpersons have no standing to complain. Derek Parfit in *Reasons and Persons* (1984) notes that future people cannot complain about the present generation's choices because without those choices these future persons might not have existed. The moral standing of future anonymous persons is thus in limbo.[26]

This section cannot provide an in-depth analysis of the rich literature that philosophers, environmentalists, and others have developed over the last decades. It does provide a taste for some of the ethical issues that touch upon economic analysis. We start with the question, "What are the obligations, if any, of the living generation to yet unborn generations?"

Economic Discounting

The economic welfare model maximizes the potential satisfaction of preferences based on spending power in the market. Because future persons are not part of the current market, their interests are not directly considered. However, the actions of current individuals can consider their interests in absentia. Grandparents who save and establish a fund for their yet-unborn grandchildren engage in intergenerational redistributions. Oil companies can stockpile oil in the ground in anticipation of future markets. Voluntary choices between the present and the future are captured by market behaviors and reflected in market rates of interest. The interest rate paid to a saver represents the reward for delaying gratification. With any positive rate of interest, the present value of money always exceeds the future value of that same amount.[27] Thus, future outcomes are given less weight than present outcomes.

Because of compounding, future interests disappear rapidly when compared to present interests. Suppose a rainforest in Malaysia contains valuable mahogany worth $1 billion on today's market. To harvest the mahogany requires cutting down sixty other trees for every mahogany tree, and the rainforest would be destroyed. Suppose also that the rainforest contains plants that in fifty years (if the rainforest still exists) could be used to treat cancer patients, providing a future value of $100 billion. However, after discounting (using an interest rate of 10 percent) the $100 billion in fifty years is worth only $850 million in today's dollars.[28] An economic resource that is more than 100 *times more valuable* to future generations is ignored by today's marketplace.

But market rates of interest may not be the appropriate discount rate for public policies. A "social" discount rate that is more future oriented might use a lower discount rate (say 5 percent). Under this scenario, $100 billion in fifty years is worth $9 billion in today's money, making it advantageous to preserve the rainforest.[29] Deciding what discount rate to use in public policy analyses is contentious. Although an individual can usefully consider discounting when planning current consumption to future consumption over his or her lifetime, public policies typically project over generations of different individuals. Choosing too high a discount rate could lead to the annihilation of the human species because colossal costs to future generations are essentially ignored by the present.

Along these lines the *Stern Review on the Economics of Climate Change* (2006) warned that inaction by the current generation could (in an extreme case) result in massive losses of up to 20 percent of GDP in future years.[30] The *Review* called on the present generation to bear the cost of immediate cuts in greenhouse gas emissions to mitigate these long-term costs. In reaching this conclusion the *Stern Review* applied a discount rate for future costs and benefits of only 1.4 percent, which includes a near zero pure rate of time preference of 0.1 percent. A zero rate of time preference means generational *neutrality*: All future generations enjoy the same weight on our decisions, as does the present. In a sense, the *Stern Review* asks us to decide climate change policy behind a veil of ignorance, *as if* we do not know which generation we will be born into.

The *Stern Review* was heavily criticized for this "radical" approach. William D. Nordhaus notes that if one were to build on Rawls, maximizing the well-being of the *least-well-off* generation would imply something quite different.[31] Too low a discount rate would lead the present generations to make draconian sacrifices for the future. This would be both paradoxical and unjust because future citizens are expected to be much wealthier than present citizens. Rather than *assuming* the parameters of a social discount rate, Nordhaus argues that an actual market interest rate of 6 percent better captures the true investment trade-offs between the present and future. Using a higher discount rate produces the finding that the costs of climate abatement to the present generation are great relative to the now highly discounted future benefits.

Many economists project that future generations will be richer than the present based on a belief that the productivity gains of the past two centuries will continue. These improvements imply that more, rather than fewer, natural resources will be available to future generations. For example, new technology for finding and drilling petroleum means that estimates of world petroleum reserves have actually increased by more than 100 percent over the past thirty years, despite record consumption of oil products.[32] If per capita productivity grows by 1.5 percent per year, real living standards on average will *double* in less than half a century, assuming no calamitous events like global climate change, wars, influenza pandemics, and so on.

Optimism is a feature of market ideology because humans have now learned how to innovate and societies have institutions for bringing new discoveries into fruition. Joseph Schumpeter wrote in 1942, "There is no reason to expect slackening of the rate of output through exhaustion of technological possibilities."[33]

Sustainability or Irreversibility

This optimism is under attack from within the economics profession as well as from environmentalists.[34] Environmentalists argue that it is arrogant to predict rosy economic futures when the planet is projected to increase from 7 billion to nearly 11 billion people by 2100.[35] Water table levels are plummeting from overirrigation, ocean fish stocks are dwindling from overtrawling, carbon levels and world temperatures are rising from atmospheric pollution—all problems stemming from a failure of markets to deal with common property resources. Markets cannot correctly price groundwater, wild fish, or the air we breathe because the profit motive will lead to overuse of resources that we share and that it would be difficult to privatize (the "tragedy of the commons").[36] Although market goods can be traded off for environmental quality at the margin, tipping points and path dependencies could lead to irreversible changes in outcomes.

Government taxes or regulations are two customary ways that economists would handle the problem of negative externalities. Recent work by Elinor Ostrom suggests that a decentralized third approach to preserving the commons can spring from local customs and community conventions.[37] The responsibility of humans to the environment is a long-standing tenet of many community and religious traditions. Early monotheistic texts extol the view that humans are only temporary stewards of a world created and owned by God. Ralph Waldo Emerson, the nineteenth-century founder of transcendentalism, promulgated the thesis that man and nature are inherently connected. Nature is the spirit that suffuses and connects all things: "The currents of the Universal Being circulate through me; I am part or particle of God."[38] If everything in nature is connected, breaking apart and commodifying a piece of it destroys the whole. Such transpersonal values inspired John Muir and other conservationists to push for the creation of national parks (such as Yellowstone and Yosemite) that preserve the landscape and its animals in a holistic, natural state.

With these spiritual beginnings, the environmental movement today is made up of disparate social, political, and economic groups. There are thousands of environmental sustainability and social justice organizations operating around the world with millions of members. No unifying moral philosophy binds these groups as might be envisioned by Rawls. Instead, they represent organic, spontaneously emerging, and evolving phenomena as envisioned by Hayek.

The global environment is *interdependent*, producing large-scale externalities. In this context, markets will fail to price goods appropriately because of a lack of property rights or high transaction costs to defend them. Public policy can address this through tax policy or regulations on tradable emissions permits or in local cases through community norms. A second principle is that survival of the human species requires the endurance of other species, such as bees to pollinate crops. The *complexity* of ecosystems creates uncertainty about which species are required for human survival. It is foolhardy to allow species extinction when we do not know how different parts work: "The first rule of intelligent tinkering is to save all the pieces."[39] A third principle is that no single blueprint for saving the environment exists because countries are *diverse* as to their constraints, and peoples differ as to their preferences.

The World Commission on Environment and Development (WCED) issued the influential Brundtland report, *Our Common Future* (1987), which proposes a *sustainability criterion* as the obligation of the present to the future. Sustainability means: "Meeting the needs of the present generation without compromising the needs of future generations."[40] At a minimum, future generations should be left no worse off than current generations.

One can visualize a relay team in which each generation passes on the baton of capital and resources to be used by the next generation, without dropping or diminishing it.[41] But is it realistic to think the baton should remain the same across generations? Future generations may face depleted oceans but enjoy overflowing electronic libraries. As some natural resources become scarcer, technology can leapfrog and reduce the need for those resources. Past generations confronted a crisis of basic needs—food, shelter, and health care. Present and future generations face different challenges of longer life expectancies, which combined with shorter years of work, create a crisis of leisure. Robert Fogel, in *The Fourth Great Awakening and the Future of Egalitarianism* (2000), shares the optimism of other neoclassical economists that future generations will be far wealthier and argues that we make a fundamental error to assume future generations will be struggling over material resources. Rather, self-actualization will become the new basic need:

The problem of self-realization . . . is the hallmark of our age and the greatest threat to the survival of our society. To achieve self-realization, each individual must have an understanding of life's opportunities, a sense of which of these opportunities are most attractive to him or her at each stage of life, and the requisite educational, material, and spiritual resources to pursue these opportunities. In the era that is unfolding, fair access to spiritual resources will be as much a touchstone of egalitarianism as access to material resources was in the past.[42]

In assessing what the baton of sustainability is or means, we must confront the difficult task of trying to count and combine incommensurable capital resources and assess the trade-offs between natural capital and human capital. The Brundtland Report reflects the moral intuition that we should not use resources in ways that harm others, including future people. Nevertheless, the relationship of human to natural resources has yet to be well understood. If human ingenuity can improve energy efficiency in machinery by 25 percent, a smaller natural resource base is needed to provide sustainability.

LOOKING AHEAD

Two approaches to inequality addressed in the previous chapter are the call for justice based on fair outcomes and the call for justice based on fair process or procedure. These concerns are interrelated in the present chapter when it comes to analyzing the equality of opportunity. It is not possible to have a fair economic contest unless all the children lining up to a race eat a morning breakfast, lace up similar running shoes, and received comparable physical education, cognition training, and emotional support. Basic capabilities are needed before the economic game can be played with equal opportunity. Although people may agree on the need for equal opportunity, there is widespread disagreement over its meaning and application. In the United States, where inequality is rising and economic mobility is low relative to other rich countries, two articles of faith remain: the belief that markets produce a meritocratic society and the conviction that technological advances will make future generations richer and better able to confront environmental challenges. The role of government in ensuring both these outcomes is a key question in the debate about economic justice.

A pluralistic approach would not attempt to decide between procedural justice and outcome justice but would see both approaches as offering valuable insights. In a world of uncertainty and complexity, the notion of maximizing a single value to the exclusion of all others seems shortsighted. Most countries have in practice adopted a pluralist approach to economic justice. The thesis of this book is that a pluralist approach to economics more generally offers insights for both positive and normative economics. The concluding chapter explores these issues in the theory and practice of economics.

CHAPTER 12

Ethical Pluralism in Economics

Pluralism is about having multiple frames of analysis. Understanding the diversity of moral theories and motivations strengthens the study of economic relationships and institutions. Economists, for example, rely in practice on more than one ethical framework for conducting their own investigations and for analyzing and evaluating market behaviors.

ETHICAL PLURALISM

One of the attractions of standard economic theory is that it doggedly pursues one method: It tries to understand how a rational economic actor with given and stable preferences would behave in order to maximize personal utility. Much useful work has been done within this model, and few people would disagree with its conclusions that expected outcomes influence choices and that incentives alter the behavior of economic actors. Proposed here is a complementary hypothesis, namely, that additional ethical models enlarge the understanding of some behaviors (a claim relevant to positive economics) and that multiple frames of ethical analysis are desirable for public policy analysis (a claim relevant to normative economics).

Pluralism is defined as some degree of acceptance of two or more valid values, or two or more valid principles, that pertain to the same or overlapping domains of reality and that cannot be reduced to a single value or principle.[1] Pluralism, as defined here, entails the recognition that multiple ethical frameworks can help explain the world and inform decision makers. To use the metaphor of Isaiah Berlin, a burrowing hedgehog knows only one big thing (for example, maximizing efficiency), whereas the pluralist fox knows lots of different things.[2] In Chapter 1 we introduced the pluralist 3-D thinking that highlights three ethical frameworks, oriented around outcomes, duties, or virtues. Pluralism in this context has two further aspects: the divergence of theories *across* domains (vertical pluralism) and the divergence of theories *within* domains (horizontal pluralism).[3]

FIGURE 12.1. Vertical ethical pluralism.

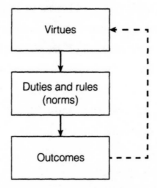

Virtuous habits like self-control are needed for carrying out duties and following rules without external rewards or punishments. Following duties and rules can lower transaction costs through greater trust, producing good outcomes in trade. Good outcomes like higher income can in turn spur moral development and the inculcation of virtuous habits, represented by the dotted line feedback loop.

Source: Jonathan B. Wight, "Economics within a Pluralist Ethical Tradition," *Review of Social Economy* 72(4)(December 2014).

Vertical Pluralism

Vertical pluralism is the recognition that multiple ethical frameworks are at work in market processes, linking virtue, duty, and outcomes. Figure 12.1 illustrates a model of *vertical* ethical pluralism.

In the messy world of life, the dimensions of virtues, duties/rules, and outcomes are interrelated and overlapping concepts to economic actors operating within social and economic institutions. The three frameworks may at times compete but also at times complete each other. In the work of Adam Smith, for example, moral sentiments give rise to institutions that provide the duties and rules for appropriate conduct. One might say that Smith is a rule consequentialist who sees good rules as producing good outcomes, but this shortchanges virtue ethics. If more people follow rules out of internal beliefs and commitments, external monitoring costs can be lower than otherwise. The interplay of values and principles is operative in Smith's pragmatic approach.

Consider this quandary: A minimum wage worker in a large dry cleaning company has just found $100 in a client's pants. Should she pocket the money, knowing there is no chance of getting caught? Or should she call the customer and return the money? People are often torn between instincts and principles. The first downward arrow in Figure 12.1 suggests that an economic agent who is honest by virtue of her character will adhere to rules and duties arising from habits of being trustworthy. She will make every effort to locate the rightful owner of the money because it is the right thing to do. The second downward arrow shows that adhering to the norms of honesty can produce beneficial outcomes, including company goodwill, a monetary reward, social recognition, or simply inner peace of mind that comes from doing the right thing. Recall that virtue ethics can produce desirable outcomes, but the calculation of outcomes is not the *motive* for virtuous behavior.

The upward dotted arrow in Figure 12.1 demonstrates the positive feedback between outcomes and virtues. Virtuous people who adhere to their duty to be honest will reduce the transactions costs in trade, resulting in more exchange and higher living standards. Higher living standards in turn can heighten moral imagination through travel and trade and generate an evolution of feelings about right and wrong (Chapter 8). Evidence suggests that participating in a well-developed market, for example, makes people more inclined toward positive, other-regarding behaviors. John Stuart Mill thus theorized that the "economical advantages of commerce are surpassed in importance by those of its effects which are intellectual and moral."[4] A virtue cycle results: Virtue produces good outcomes, and good outcomes generate more virtuous behaviors.

Horizontal Pluralism

Horizontal or *lateral* pluralism is the recognition that multiple modes of analysis exist within each different vertical framework (Figure 12.2).

Within the context of virtue ethics, one could derive the internal character of honesty from Adam Smith, Aristotle, Confucius, the Buddha, or others. Concepts of duty can likewise be based on God's Ten Commandments, on Kantian rationality, or on natural rights theory. In

FIGURE 12.2. Horizontal ethical pluralism.

Virtue ethics:

Adam Smith ←——→ Aristotle ←——→ Confucius ←——→ Buddha

Duty and rule ethics:

Divine command ←——→ Kantian ←——→ Natural rights

Outcome ethics:

Utilitarian ←——→ Neoclassical preference satisfaction ←——→ Multiple other outcomes

When economists explore how public policies affect multiple outcomes, they are engaged in horizontal ethical pluralism within an outcome-oriented ethical framework. One can likewise study duty and rule ethics, and virtue ethics, from within different traditions.

Source: Jonathan B. Wight, "Economics within a Pluralist Ethical Tradition," *Review of Social Economy* 72(4)(December 2014).

outcome-based ethics there are multiple ends to consider in evaluating pubic policies. Utilitarians focus on the total pleasure created, and neo-classical economists often focus on maximizing the preferences of current consumers (static efficiency). However, a multitude of other concerns or goals are often considered: saving lives, national security, freedom, fairness, and dynamic efficiency. For Smith, although economic growth was an important outcome, economic justice was an even greater concern. Can all of these outcomes be subsumed under the guise of a super value as suggested in the standard welfare model? If so, the goal of saving lives is important only because it is an *instrumental* good that leads to the *ultimate* good of satisfying preferences. Policy makers need not consider the issue of horizontal pluralism if one super value really exists.

But is such a claim of supremacy for a single value reasonable? Can everything "good" be captured by a single measure, such as "maximize preferences"? Humans have distinct and often irreducible goals, and achieving more of some goals at times requires sacrificing others (scarcity is a standard feature of economic life). Isaiah Berlin is well known for pointing out the basic clash between liberty and equality. Berlin, who as a youth witnessed mob actions during the Russian Revolution, recoiled at the notion that a single utopian value could overcome the moral conflicts intrinsic to human life. Berlin liked to quote Kant: "Out of the crooked timber of humanity, no straight thing was ever made," meaning that "no perfect solution is, not merely in practice, but in principle, possible in human affairs."[5]

How competing multiple goals can be analyzed alongside efficiency is the subject of an interesting workbook by Rendigs Fels and Stephen Buckles, *Casebook of Economic Problems and Policies: Practice in Thinking.* The authors take it for granted that critical thinking about public policy requires economists in each and every case to explore horizontal pluralism; ultimately, a qualitative normative account is needed to judge how the goal of efficiency stacks up alongside other worthy goals.[6]

This process makes some economists uncomfortable because it calls on them to step outside a comfort zone. Mark Twain has often been credited with saying, "To a man with a hammer, everything looks like a nail"; and to many economists, every problem looks like an efficiency problem. The pluralist account of how to do public policy does not lend itself to finding the "right" answer that can be arrived at by scientific method alone. Economic efficiency is one input into a deliberation about the right option; a policy solution is arrived at from considering multiple angles and through a rhetorical process of discovery.

Hence, rather than advocating preference satisfaction as the *only* indicator of welfare, economists may come to see preference satisfaction as *one* of various outcome measures that address human welfare (Chapter 7). The approach recommended here can help resolve the problem of Buridan's ass, the donkey that starved to death because it could not distinguish between two identical piles of wheat. Many economists claim that they cannot and should not make interpersonal comparisons of utility. Hence, they cannot distinguish between the extra money that a rich man would spend on an expensive bottle of wine and the same extra money a poor mother needs to buy medicine to save the life of her child.[7] Common sense would suggest otherwise, and economists already do something akin to interpersonal analysis when they support the goal of dynamic over static efficiency or when they support the concept of "life-years extended" instead of "lives saved" in public policy analysis.

The Narrowed Lens

Throughout history economic theorists adopted diverse and changing normative goals and guiding ethical frameworks. Adam Smith, the founder of economics, built a foundation to advance the overlapping concerns of economic justice, dynamic growth, and virtue ethics. In the late nineteenth century, however, the economic vision became constricted as economists attempted to create a physics of the social sciences. Both in method and content standard, economics became less amenable to address multiple ethical perspectives.

Pluralist approaches to both positive and normative economics—labeled *heterodoxy*—were marginalized in the mid-twentieth century, and textbook writers could argue that the mainstream consensus reflected scientific progress. Troubling, however, is the implication that some textbook writers knew that they were providing an artificial and false harmony but justified it by arguing that displays of doubt would undermine the profession in the eyes of the public.[8] Controversy was avoided to maintain the appearance of scientific unity, and this was done, in part, by reducing the scope of acceptable methodology. This excessively narrow focus led the American Economic Association in the late twentieth century to warn that graduate schools were turning out "*idiot savants*, skilled in technique but innocent of real economic issues."[9] Ronald Coase likewise worried, "It is suicidal for the field to slide into a hard science of choice, ignoring the influences of society, history, culture, and politics on the working of the economy. . . . knowledge will come only if economics can be reoriented to the study of man as he is and the economic system as it actually exists."[10]

In the twenty-first century this began to change as Nobel laureates like Amartya Sen and Vernon Smith popularized alternative approaches and as student activists demanded a more inclusive curricula. Graduate students in France, the United Kingdom, and the United States began campaigns after 2000 to expand the range of methods and content of economic analysis. This eventually gave rise to the *Real-World Economics Review*, an on-line journal of more than 20,000 subscribers from around the world.[11] Real economic issues are multifaceted and require complementary perspectives to enrich the analysis. This includes a pluralist account of human behavior and the history, institutions, and ethics of policy issues. Controversy can be the pedagogical tool by which students come to understand the nature of economic complexity.

The following section demonstrates that both vertical and horizontal pluralism are needed to understand how economists themselves conduct scientific research.[12]

THE ETHICAL ECONOMIST

Positive economics is the study of the world, as it currently exists. According to the standard textbook view, positive economics is value free. But a moment's reflection reveals the impossibility of this interpretation. Being impartial does not mean being value free, and ideology sometimes plays a role in shaping research agendas and methods.[13] Facts are defined, collected, and analyzed in a context in which values and ethical considerations play roles that cannot be avoided. Values are a necessary part of science and are fused with the knowledge obtained. Most economic data do not exist outside of the socially constructed context in which they were created. To be counted as "unemployed" in the United States, for example, a worker must actively seek work in the four weeks prior to the survey. The selection of four weeks instead of two or six weeks cannot be justified by science. It reflects a compromise between political and pragmatic judgments about what is acceptable so as to produce reliable and meaningful results.[14] There are also ethical issues involved in using human subjects in research; when surveying the unemployed in their homes, the Labor Department must use ethical standards of contact. A discouraged job seeker who answers the doorbell and confesses to the surveyor that he has *not* actively searched for work may be motivated to get up off the couch. Collecting the facts can change the facts, a phenomenon known in science as the Heisenberg principle.

Researchers also face budget constraints and must rank research projects by judging the expected importance to self or society. One typical value judgment by funding agencies is, "How much of a budget should we spend on *this* experiment to test behavioral economics, as opposed to *that* data collection needed to test labor migration theory?" Even when economists acknowledge they are stepping into normative territory, the underlying ethical framework is often obscure or unexamined.

The Consequentialist View

Standard economics posits that an economic actor can be adequately modeled using only an outcome-based behavioral framework. In particular, economic actors are said to strive to maximize the expected attainment of individual preferences. In this view, duty and virtue can enter the discussion only by way of satisfying preferences. One way to examine this theory is to ask: "Is this the way economists themselves actually act?"

Academic economists are involved in "selling" their scientific theories and research to other economists and the public. The market for science can be equated to other markets, and expected outcomes, particularly related to self-interest, can explain much activity, including some allegedly unethical behaviors. The movie *Inside Job* (2010) argues that economic practitioners have in recent years been "bought" by financial interests to deliver biased conclusions for hire. Charles Ferguson, who wrote and produced the film, charges:

Over the past 30 years, the economics discipline has been systematically subverted, in much the same way as American politics—by money, especially from the financial services industry. Many of the most prominent economists in America are now paid to testify in Congress, to serve on boards of directors, testify in antitrust cases and regulatory proceedings, and to give speeches to the companies and industries they study and write about with supposed objectivity.[15]

In one example, Frederic Mishkin, a renowned author of banking textbooks, was paid $124,000 by the Icelandic Chamber of Commerce to coauthor a study entitled, "Financial Stability in Iceland," which determined that "financial fragility is not high" and that the likelihood of a financial meltdown was "very low."[16] The Icelandic financial system crashed within two years.

The claim that Mishkin was dishonest rankles him and others because economists believe they operate within a system of implicit ethical norms.

Those violating these rules are ostracized from the club. Paul Samuelson, a Nobel laureate, notes that social status (more than monetary payoff) drives the profession: "In the long run, the economic scholar works for the only coin worth having—our own applause."[17] In the standard economic view, rational economic actors examine the costs and benefits of cheating and *enlightened self-interest* works to keep economic researchers honest: The cost of being caught means permanent exclusion from the club, including loss of income and status. Voluntary self-control—based on a consequentialist reckoning of self-interest—is relied on to maintain truth telling. In this view, trust arises from an instrumental calculation of enlightened self-interest.

Unlike law, accounting, medicine, architecture, psychology, and other professions, there is no external accreditation or licensing required for the practice of economics. The American Economic Association (AEA) is a voluntary organization that specifies no code of ethical conduct for continued membership, nor does it have any mechanism for punishing ethical transgressions. After the publicity of *Inside Job* and the publication of George DeMartino's *The Economist's Oath: On the Need for and Content of Professional Economic Ethics* (2011), however, the AEA did issue new requirements for financial disclosure and data transparency by authors in its journals.[18] Some "rules" in addition to self-regulation are currently in place.

Two problems arise in arguing that the academic market will police itself adequately using only outcome-based incentives. First, market failure in science arises because of **asymmetric information**. Researchers know more about their research methods than do customers (the journal readers). A **moral hazard** arises if the incentives in the system tilt in ways to encourage unethical behavior. Researchers in many situations have much to gain from fudging, falsifying, or even plagiarizing their findings. Many academic jobs are "publish or perish," meaning that successful publishing in academic journals is required in exchange for a lifetime of guaranteed employment through tenure.

The top journals in economics are usually associated with a nonprofit association or university and can attract high-quality editors and reviewers, who practice the virtues of competence, self-control, and honesty in evaluating evidence and not rewarding unethical behaviors. At the other extreme, for-profit journals are proliferating, and some reviews are perfunctory at best.[19] This is a case in which the principles of the market (the search for profit) collide with the principles of science (the search for truth). A **publication bias** also exists in which journals generally report only research with statistically significant findings. Investigators can nudge their results to produce statistically significant findings by omitting outliers, altering starting and ending dates, and changing model specifications. These actions can be legitimate and are justifiable if done for the right reasons, but they can also be done simply to produce publishable outputs.

Replicating a scientific paper constitutes a **public good** because the corroboration (or contradiction) of results provides external benefits to society. Replicators, however, are poorly rewarded because the task is time consuming and few of these papers are accepted for publication. This leads to the second potential market failure, the **free rider** problem: Others rely on reviewers and replicators, but the system does not provide ample incentives. As a result, little replication is attempted, even though these efforts occasionally result in stunning reversals of the original findings.[20]

For these reasons the *probability* of detecting deceitfulness in empirical work in economics is low.[21] Even if potential dishonesty is uncovered, fabricators can claim that errors were unintended and that duplicity was not the motive. When deliberate falsification can be proven, the penalty is often only a mild rebuke—the author will be forbidden from future publication in that particular journal. However, there are hundreds of other journals where that fraudulent paper can be sent. No licensing authority exists for publicly exposing misdeeds, and journal editors may remain mute to avoid libel suits. Even when a clear case of plagiarism is discovered, more than half the editors in prestigious journals said that they would refrain from reporting this to an author's department chair or dean.[22]

The consequentialist approach to truth telling and trust in economic research is predicated on the belief that the potential loss of one's reputation is strong enough to restrain most bad behaviors. The evidence, however, indicates that market failures exist, and in some contexts the expected benefits of cheating are large and the expected costs of cheating are small. Nevertheless, fraud in academic economic research appears to be limited to 5 percent or less of researchers.[23] This finding may be due to cases of malfeasance yet to be discovered or, alternatively, to the fact that economists are, as a group, generally truthful for intrinsic reasons: They consciously or unconsciously have adopted the principle of honesty and truth seeking in the presence of moral hazard. We turn now to a discussion of this possibility.

Norms of Virtue and Duty

The intuition that science advances using more than simply outcome-based ethics is a strong one. Market failures arising from moral hazard are well known, and society attempts to mitigate these problems using moral norms. The practice of medicine creates well-recognized problems of asymmetric information leading to a moral hazard. For thousands of years doctors have been asked to adhere to the Hippocratic duty to put patient interests ahead of personal interests. Certified public accountants likewise must profess an "unswerving commitment to honorable behavior, even at the sacrifice of personal advantage."[24] Similar injunctions apply in engineering, architecture, law, and many other professions. No one would suggest that these commands work all the time to restrain unethical behavior. But they do call attention to a very different standard for ethical choice, based not on consequences but on the consideration of duty and virtue for their own sakes.

Frank Knight, one of the founders of the celebrated "Chicago School" of economics, mentored a cadre of future Nobel laureates including Milton Friedman, George Stigler, James Buchanan, and Ronald Coase. Knight described the absolute moral code that should be religiously demanded of all practitioners:

Now scientific enquiry has, and rests upon, a moral code, or in sheer fact a "religion"; and it is supremely important that scientists recognize this fact. . . . The basic tenet of scientific research—truth or objectivity—is essentially a moral principle, in opposition to any form of self-interest.[25]

The economic scientist is called on to develop deep virtues of "integrity, competence, and humility." These qualities should be identified and nurtured, not only because they may lead to personal success but also because they are valued intrinsically as ideals to be upheld. Honesty is more than a preference in one's utility function that can be traded off against other goals in pursuit of personal gain; honesty is a solemn duty to others and constitutes a measure of one's character development.

The difference between a *consequentialist* ethic of honesty and a *virtue* ethics honesty is captured by this nineteenth-century maxim: "Honesty is the best policy, but he who is governed by that maxim is *not* an honest man." If your motive for being honest is driven by a desire for particular outcomes, you are simply being *opportunistic.* Hence, "if honesty is the best policy" then the best principle is to be honest from conviction, not from calculation.[26] For these reasons Amartya Sen argues, "Consequential analysis may be taken to be necessary, *but not sufficient,* for many moral decisions."[27]

Vertical pluralism demonstrates how more than one ethical framework can help address important public policy issues like the creation of trust. A *virtuous* scientist has the motive and the self-control to adhere to *duties* of honesty to others in the community, which will produce beneficial *outcomes* for that community and the wider society. But these good outcomes are produced in part from adhering to principles (or norms or virtues) that are not aimed at producing the best consequences. Economists, like many others, instinctively view dishonest behavior with disgust and repugnance. This moral sentiment provides a foundation for the behavioral norms in the "tribe" of economists. Ethical norms give rise to the recognition of duties and rules. From these flow desirable multiple outcomes for the benefit of science and society. Being an ethical role model is an important part of mentoring one's junior colleagues and impressionable students.

The science and art of economics thus advances using pluralist ethical institutions. Economists are truthful for complex reasons: Some ascribe to absolute moral rules of honesty based on divine command or Kantian conviction; some value honesty intrinsically for its own sake; some see their identity as virtuous persons and, though tempted, have developed a character of self-discipline; and some are deterred from cheating by incentives in which personal costs exceed personal benefits. A pluralist account of how and why scientists are honest recognizes and bolsters the institutions that promote trustworthiness. In thinking about what markets value or can degrade, Kenneth Arrow notes, "The multiplicity of control systems in the real world is probably no accident."[28]

By ignoring duty and virtue, or by attempting to shoehorn these concepts into enlightened self-interest, the standard economic model misses the role that nonconsequentialist ethics plays in economic life. Worse, it potentially degrades those frameworks in the minds of students, whose characters are amenable to manipulation. In a well-known study, researchers at Cornell discovered that exposing students to a course in standard economics reduced students' inclinations for cooperation and honesty, increased cynicism about these values, and increased free riding on others' contributions.[29] Trust is accomplished most cheaply when external constraints can be minimized because duty and virtue are upheld as norms by many in society. As the following section shows, this is true in business as well as in academics.[30]

MODELING A BUSINESS

Economic models often describe a simplified production function in which resource inputs magically convert into outputs of goods and services. The process of how this takes place is usually given little description or importance.

The Consequentialist View

In the standard model, economic agents—whether shareholders, managers, workers, or customers—are assumed to operate based on the model of individual preference satisfaction. This approach is useful for many purposes. As revealed in the preceding section, however, too narrow an ethical lens can lead to misunderstanding about how some social systems actually operate. One misunderstanding arises because the mathematics of a production function cannot capture the organic ways in which character and conscience matter to business. Chapter 1 discusses the famous debate initiated by Nobel laureate Milton Friedman that illustrates the issue. Friedman's *Capitalism and Freedom* contains a highly popular statement about the limited ethical obligations of corporations to the society in which they operate. Corporate executives, Friedman notes, have an ethical obligation to maximize profits for the benefit of shareholders.

Friedman's justification for profit maximization is based in part on a consequential analysis of outcomes. Profits are the instrument by which a free and competitive market signal the way resources ought to be used to best meet the preferences of consumers. The profit motive works automatically to generate outcomes that are efficient in the economic sense of satisfying preferences, assuming no externalities or other market failures. In Friedman's view, managers should not be asked to sidetrack the role of profit seeking by addressing social problems such as homelessness, unemployment, racial disparity, poverty, and environmental cleanup beyond the minimal required. These are not in the bailiwick of a business, nor is the manager's training likely to make him or her knowledgeable about these areas. Friedman notes, "If businessmen do have a social responsibility other than making maximum profits for stockholders, how are they to know what it is?"[31]

Norms of Virtue and Duty

As noted in Chapter 1, Friedman soon reverses himself. It turns out businesspeople *do* have a social responsibility to others, and it derives not only from outcomes but also from required duties. In attempting to maximize profits, Friedman says the manager must conform his or her actions to the "basic rules of the society, both those embodied in law and those embodied in ethical custom." The manager is duty bound to be honest, for example, because this is a bedrock ethical norm and not because it can be calculated in specific cases to increase profits. Friedman thus reveals himself to be, like Adam Smith, a pluralist—he needs more than one ethical framework to make his system work.

As in the conduct of economic research, the unbridled pursuit of one's own preferences is unacceptable if the actions taken to achieve it lie outside the mainstream of ethical norms and customs. Instead, Friedman enjoins managers to abide by Adam Smith's moral sentiments dictum to align actions with the basic "rules of justice." In Smith's view, people engaged in commercial activity can be virtuous because their habits of prudence, justice, and self-command are crucial to a well-functioning society. Virtuous people "religiously [uphold] the sacred rules of justice in spite both of the greatest interests which might tempt, and the greatest injuries which might provoke [them] to violate them."[32] For Smith, as for Friedman, self-interest is subsumed within a pluralist tradition of virtue and duty. Learning to exercise self-control in upholding one's duty to others is the preeminent moral virtue, from which "all the others virtues seem to derive their principal lustre."[33]

The importance of trust in business arises in many contexts, particularly considering the ubiquitous **principal-agent problem**. Because of asymmetric information, the manager knows more about the operation of a business than do the owner-shareholders. The incentives created by this knowledge discrepancy lead to a moral hazard: Managers can personally gain by running the business for their own benefit rather than the shareholders'. Shareholders can address the problem by using incentives to align the managers' interests with the long-run interests of the owners (for example, bonuses tied to measures of performance). One problem with the outcomes-based approach is that managers may quickly learn to manipulate earnings and growth so as to achieve bonuses, but at the expense of product quality, future innovation, or other objectives. A business operation is a holistic endeavor, and focusing on any particular performance outcome can be self-defeating.

A complementary approach is one implied in Friedman's article: to hire a manager who ascribes to duty and virtue ethics in their fiduciary obligations. A *virtuous* manager has the self-control needed to adhere to her *duty* to shareholders. This produces desirable *outcomes* for the shareholders and society at large. An interesting feature of this approach is that it casts new light on the role of stakeholders—the workers, suppliers, and customers to the corporation. If a manager is duty bound to adhere to moral rules of conduct toward shareholders, she will have basic moral duties to other stakeholders as well.[34]

In Adam Smith's account of the invisible hand (Chapters 8 and 9), the search for profit clearly guides behavior at one level. But considerations of character ground market behavior and lower the transactions costs needed for trade. As Adam Smith notes, a businessperson is attuned to "the character and situation of the persons whom he trusts."[35] Character arises from having the motive and discipline to advance honesty for the sake of honesty and not from the motive to be honest only if something can be gained. Sympathy or "fellow feeling" is critical to good management, for by it, "we place ourselves in [another's] situation, we conceive ourselves enduring all the same torments, we enter as it were into his body, and become in some measure the same person with him."[36] Sympathy forms the basis of moral imagination and enables managers to connect at an emotional level with employees, investors, suppliers, customers, and other stakeholders crucial to the success of commercial enterprises.[37] McCloskey notes that real economies overflow with real virtues—"love, justice, temperance, faith, hope and courage come tumbling out" in numerous experiments, providing the social and moral stew from which organizations and institutions operate to produce and allocate economic resources.[38]

A large literature demonstrates the ways in which profitability can be advanced by using Adam Smith's theory of moral sentiments and virtue ethics. Companies that exhibit concern for virtue are able to hire employees for substantially lower wages.[39] Stakeholders respond *emotionally* to company behavior that is perceived to be virtuous or heroic.[40] Companies exhibiting virtuousness have better performance relative to industry peers measured by customer retention, innovation, smaller labor turnover, greater flexibility, and profitability.[41]

MULTIPLE ETHICAL FRAMES

Milton Friedman's reasons for promoting markets and a limited government extend beyond simply supporting the instrumental role of profits in satisfying consumer preferences. More fundamentally, Friedman values the freedom that arises from a system of decentralized decision making. In evaluating markets, economists often switch their focus between different desirable outcomes or objectives. As reported in Chapter 6, for example, economists often advocate for efficiency that satisfies the preferences of existing consumers in the market. But many economists also support the awarding of monopoly patents that would stimulate innovation. Justifying this requires changing the consequentialist aim: *Dynamic* efficiency is now the goal, and it promotes the preference satisfaction of future consumers (present consumers will be hurt by paying higher monopoly prices). Similarly, in a public policy analysis of whether human organs should be sold in a market, a Nobel prize winning economist does not advocate for markets based on maximizing static efficiency, rather the defense of markets is all about saving lives.[42]

Although saving the most lives can sometimes be achieved through freer markets, that outcome is by no means certain. The vast sums of money spent on advertising Viagra (a drug for male sexual arousal) could likely save many more lives if allocated to other medical interventions. Market preferences may not lead to saving the most lives, and choosing "lives saved" as the primary goal of public policy changes the nature of the debate: Wealth maximization is suddenly off the table, and a different goal is advanced. Why should saving lives be the goal in this case but not the goal in all other cases? If switching goals (horizontal pluralism) is permitted, why not consider fairness as the major goal that economists should promote?

Economic policies generally produce outcomes that can be evaluated along many value dimensions. When one outcome can be traded off against other outcomes, the situation exhibits horizontal pluralism (Figure 12.2). We desire to make the nation safer, but not *so* safe that freedom is excessively encroached or that wealth creation through exchange is unduly impinged. Complex choice situations—which describe most important public policies—are rarely amenable to maximizing solutions, and more often may require choosing the *least worst* option from among the mix of outcomes, after considering the limitations imposed by rules, duties, and virtues.[43]

The notion of efficiency used in public policy analysis also relies on vertical pluralism because it involves some measure of compulsion or forced trade (see Kaldor-Hicks efficiency in Chapter 5). In this formulation it is claimed that the size of the economic surplus can ethically be increased through involuntary trade, as long as the winners gain more than the losers lose, and regardless of whether compensation is actually paid to losers. This normative claim cannot stand on its own: It requires other ethical frameworks and institutions outside the market to make it defensible. To see why, imagine that Mark owns a rare baseball card he values at $100, but Joe values it at $300. If Joe breaks into Mark's house and *steals* the card, the economic surplus rises by $200! The gain to Joe is $300 and the loss to Mark is $100, causing an increase in economic wealth of $200. In the Kaldor-Hicks version of efficiency, it is irrelevant that Mark was not compensated in this involuntary "trade." The theft reallocation enhances efficiency because the person who most values the product now has it.[44] This type of involuntary trade is essentially what happens when economists do cost–benefit calculations of efficiency as the basis for public policy: Some people will gain, and others will lose (and the losers are rarely compensated).

But wait, economists will shout: The standard welfare model *implicitly* assumes that there are basic human rights, including property rights and low transactions costs for defending property in court. But these constraints need to be stated explicitly rather than swept under the rug. Amartya Sen notes, "The violation or fulfillment of basic liberties or rights tends to be ignored in traditional utilitarian welfare economics. . . . no direct and basic importance is attached in the utilitarian framework to rights and liberties in the evaluation of states of affairs."[45]

Efficiency can be judged a good outcome only if there are in place complementary institutions that enforce process rules about not harming others. This requires a legal system and judges who will impartially uphold Mark's property rights. But in many countries judges are sometimes poorly paid civil servants, and a bribe from Joe could sway the ruling in his favor. Hence, it is not enough to have laws and courts; judges must be dutifully impartial. But *why* should judges uphold the law if they are self-interested consequentialists and determine that taking a bribe is in their own best interest? One answer is that society must socialize enough of its citizens to strive for virtuous and duty-bound conduct, despite the moral hazard. Kenneth Arrow thus postulates that for the price system to work well, a Kantian system is needed for balance: "The price system is not, and perhaps in some basic sense cannot be, universal. To the extent that it is incomplete, it must be supplemented by an implicit or explicit social contract. Thus one might loosely say that the *categorical imperative* and the price system are essential *complements*."[46]

Many Parts, Yet One Body

If the foot should say, "Because I am not a hand, I do not belong to the body," that would not make it any less a part of the body. . . . The eye cannot say to the hand, "I have no need of you," nor again the head to the feet, "I have no need of you." On the contrary, the parts of the body that seem to be weaker are indispensable.

—*First Letter of St. Paul to the Corinthians*

This quotation reminds us that any human institution is a holistic, organic entity. The attempt to make economics a purely reductionist science suffers from the realization that complex social interrelationships matter. Portraying economic actors as atomic units that form preferences and maximize utility in mental isolation provides many useful insights. But scores of laboratory and field experiments have shown that social motives and ethical considerations matter to positive processes and outcomes. Critical thinking requires a broader perspective that includes analysis from horizontal and vertical ethical pluralism. A practice of three-dimensional thinking examines consequences; it explores rules and duties; and it asks about virtue and character.

The standard economic viewpoint that focuses only on outcomes is highly useful if we are to solve many world problems. The concern expressed here is not with the economic way of thinking; it is with adopting this method to the exclusion of other systems of thought. This is *both* to understand how real people may actually behave and also to gain insights into normative issues. Economists should also worry that by emphasizing self-interested utility maximization, and ignoring the important functions of duty and virtue in economic life, they could unintentionally change the world for the worse.[47] Friedrich Hayek was likewise critical of the overly narrow approach to economic thinking. He wrote that "exclusive knowledge of a single sector of the social sciences is of little use. . . . if you know only economics and nothing else, you will be a bane to mankind, good, perhaps, for writing articles for other economists to read, but for nothing else."[48]

Robert Nozick, a philosopher curious about many areas of interest to economists, observed that it is problematical to think that an unfolding topic could or should be presented as a "finished, complete, and elegant whole." Rather, "There is room for words on subjects other than last words."[49] This book provides an introduction to the rich field of ethics in economics without providing the last word; the last word will be added by readers, in the ways they interact in the world with their new 3-D lenses.

Economists will continue to add tools to the standard tool kit as they address the messy problems of human development and public policy more broadly, and ethical questions will play a part: What do we mean by well-being? What are the moral limits to markets? To what extent should economic researchers be virtuous in their own conduct? Do businesses rely on duties and virtues nurtured in families, schools, religions, civic organizations, and other realms of life? Can the market flourish without such nonmarket institutions?

A 3-D approach may be necessary, in varying degrees, for institutions and relationships in society to perform well. As we learned, economic efficiency relies on the existence of human rights, without which the losers from public policies face unacceptable coercion. It also requires virtuous judges to enforce property rights and courageous journalists to expose abuses. Attempting to shoehorn all behaviors arising from duty and virtue into an outcome based utility maximization function is an exercise in defacement.[50] Moral frameworks are deeply interconnected but distinct, requiring reflection and judgment. This approach will not satisfy those who search for simple truths, and especially those who desire only quantifiable or mechanistic approaches to policy questions. To the 3-D pluralist, "a partial understanding of complex reality is better than the reassurance of false universal explanations."[51]

If consequences, duties, and virtues all play a role in sustaining and improving the economic landscape, how do we make final decisions when these ethical approaches occasionally collide—leading us in opposite directions? A pragmatic Smithian answer is that we muddle through, improvising, doing the best we can, and learning from our mistakes. The idea of achieving "perfection" in public policy is something Smith derided. For example, while Smith favored freer trade, he worried that moving in that direction too quickly would destroy the investments of those who had built factories under the old rules; economic growth *and* justice are both important in making policy, and there is no easy way to reach definitive answers on this trade-off between outcomes and duties except perhaps through trial and error and incremental reform.[52]

Ethical pluralism—in the sense used in this book—is not a lapse into relativism, or the notion that anything goes. Rather, it is the understanding of, and commitment to, principles and virtuous habits on which much economic activity relies. It is the further recognition that alternatives to the economic way of thinking provide insights needed for engaging in public policy debate. Scott Davis, a religious scholar and philosopher, notes, "The pluralism of the modern world is not likely to go away and engaging the actual commitments of those with whom we disagree, in all their complexity, is the best way to secure understanding."[53] Doing so is in the best tradition of economists as worldly philosophers.[54]

REFERENCE MATTER

Notes

PREFACE

1. Alfred Marshall, *Principles of Economics*, 8th edition (New York: Macmillan and Co., [1890] 1920), p. vi.

2. George Stigler, "The Economist and the State," *American Economic Review* 55(1/2) (1965): p. 2; emphasis added.

3. Ibid., p. 17.

4. See, for example, David C. Colander and KimMarie McGoldrick, eds., *Educating Economists: The Teagle Discussion on Re-evaluating the Undergraduate Economics Major* (Cheltenham, UK: Edward Elgar, 2009).

5. *Liberal* is used in its classical sense, not in a modern political meaning. See Jonathan B. Wight, "Moral Reasoning in Economics," in David C. Colander and KimMarie McGoldrick, op. cit.

6. Amartya Sen, *On Ethics and Economics* (Oxford, UK: Blackwell Publishing, 1988), p. 7.

7. Anthony B. Atkinson, "The Strange Disappearance of Welfare Economics," *Kyklos* 54(2/3)(2001): p. 204.

8. This quotation is from Frank Knight's presidential address in 1950 to the American Economic Association, "Principles in Economics and Politics," *American Economic Review* 41(1)(1951): p. 11.

9. Amartya Sen cited in Arjo Klamer, "A Conversation with Amartya Sen," *Journal of Economic Perspectives* 3(1)(1989): p. 141.

CHAPTER 1

1. A humorous cartoon on this event is by Oliphant, November 21, 2006; available at www.gocomics.com/patoliphant/2006/11/21/.

2. I use the terms *ethics* and *morals* interchangeably in this text. Some philosophers draw distinctions. *Ethics* derives from the Greek language and stresses personal character; *morals* derives from the Latin language and stresses choices or rules involving others. See Deirdre McCloskey, *The Bourgeois Virtues: Ethics for an Age of Commerce* (Chicago: University of Chicago, 2006), p. 63.

3. See David C. Rose, *The Moral Foundation of Economic Behavior* (Oxford, UK: Oxford University Press, 2011), p. 205.

4. Many of the revolutionaries ended their service to the country either killed or bankrupt. Virginia's patriots also had strong economic motives for desiring to break with British rule, in addition upholding the right of freedom. See Woody Holton, *Forced Founders: Indians, Debtors, Slaves and the Making of the American Revolution in Virginia* (Chapel Hill: University of North Carolina Press, 1999). The same observation that

economics plays an important, perhaps decisive role, in political affairs can be made about America's Civil War.

5. George Washington's letter to John Banister, April 21, 1778. In E .C. Stedman and E. M. Hutchinson, eds., *A Library of American Literature, Vol. III: Literature of the Revolutionary Period, 1765–1787* [1891], accessed at www.bartleby.com/400/prose/412.html.

6. See Herbert Gintis, Samuel Bowles, Robert Boyd, and Ernst Fehr, eds., *Moral Sentiments and Material Interests: The Foundations of Cooperation in Economic Life* (Cambridge, MA: The MIT Press, 2005).

7. Adam Smith, *An Inquiry into the Nature and Causes of the Wealth of Nations*, R. H. Campbell and A. S. Skinner, eds. Glasgow Editions (Indianapolis, IN: Liberty Press, [1776] 1981), pp. 26–27.

8. Adam Smith, *The Theory of Moral Sentiments,* D. D. Raphael and A. L. Macfie, eds. Glasgow Editions (Indianapolis, IN: Liberty Press, [1759] 1982).

9. Charles Darwin, *The Descent of Man* (New York: D. Appleton and Company, 1871). Accessed at http://books.google.com/books.

10. It can be seen at http://en.wikipedia.org/wiki/Freedom_from_Want_(painting).

11. Nancy Folbre, *Invisible Heart* (New York: New Press, 2001), p. vii.

12. See, for example, Julie A. Nelson, "For Love or Money: Current Issues in the Economics of Care," *Journal of Gender Studies* 14 (2011): pp. 1–20. See also Eva Feder Kittay, *Love's Labor: Essays on Women, Equality and Dependency* (New York: Routledge, 1998) and Elizabeth Frazer, Jennifer Hornsby, and Sabina Lovibond, eds., *Ethics: A Feminist Reader* (Oxford, UK: Blackwell, 1992).

13. Kenneth Boulding, "Economics as a Moral Science," *American Economic Review* 59(1) (1969): pp. 8–9.

14. Andrew Pollack, "$4.9 Billion Jury Verdict In G.M. Fuel Tank Case," *The New York Times*, July 10, 1999.

15. Milton Friedman defends this view in this interaction with students: www.youtube.com/watch?v=jltnBOrCB7I.

16. This is markedly different from how economists in administrative bodies (like the Environmental Protection Agency) determine the value of life. See Eric A. Posner and Cass R. Sunstein, "Dollars and Death," *The University of Chicago Law Review* 72(2) (Spring, 2005): pp. 537–598.

17. David W. Solomon, "Normative Ethical Theories," in Charles K. Wilber (ed.), *Economics, Ethics, and Public Policy* (Lanham, MD: Rowman & Littlefield, 1998), pp. 119–138.

18. This section draws on Martin Calkins and Jonathan B. Wight, "The Ethical Lacunae in Friedman's Concept of the Manager," *Journal of Markets & Morality* 11(2) (2008): pp. 221–238.

19. Milton Friedman, *Capitalism and Freedom* (Chicago: The University of Chicago Press, 1962), p. 133.

20. Milton Friedman, "The Social Responsibility of Business Is to Increase Its Profits," *New York Times Sunday Magazine*, September 13, 1970, p. 32.

21. Harvey S. James Jr. and Farhad Rassekh, "Smith, Friedman, and Self-Interest in Ethical Society," *Business Ethics Quarterly* 10(3): pp. 659–74. Friedman's response is found on p. 671, f2.

22. Jeff Bennett, "GM Knew of Ignition Flaws Earlier—Auto Maker Has Yet to Determine Complete Scope of Problem," *The Wall Street Journal*, March 13, 2014.

23. Evolutionary biologists might point out that improperly cooked meat can transmit bacteria, viruses, and parasites into human populations (for example, trichinosis). Hence, in the distant past some societies developed "rules of thumb" against eating pork. Over time the rules of thumb became habituated and strengthened in culture through religious law. Hence, what seems to be a religious duty may actually relate to the analysis of consequences. The essential point, however, is that some people today may obey on a commitment to religious principles in deciding whether to eat pork and not rely on an analysis of consequences.

24. Genesis 29 proscribes as follows: "Then God said, I give you every seed-bearing plant on the face of the whole earth and every tree that has fruit with seed in it. They will be yours for food."

25. Smith, *The Theory of Moral Sentiments*, op. cit., p. 14.

26. Amartya K. Sen, "Rational Fools: A Critique of the Behavioral Foundations of Economic Theory," *Philosophy and Public Affairs* 6(4) (1977): p. 332.

27. Ibid., p. 342.

28. Ibid., p. 336.

29. This is a paraphrase of John Philip Newell in reference to Judaism, Christianity, and Islam.

30. The Nobel Prize in economics is actually the Sveriges Riksbank (Bank of Sweden) Prize in Economic Sciences in Memory of Alfred Nobel. For simplicity it is referred to in this book as the Nobel Prize.

31. These are Joseph E. Stiglitz, Amartya Sen, Kenneth Arrow, James Heckman, and Daniel Kahneman. See Joseph E Stiglitz, Amartya Sen, and Jean-Paul Fitoussi, *Report by the Commission on the Measurement of Economic Performance and Social Progress*, 2009; available at www.stiglitz-sen-fitoussi.fr/en/index.htm.

32. David Zucchino, "With Unearthing of Infamous Jail, Richmond Confronts Its Slave Past," *Los Angeles Times* (December 18, 2008).

33. Jeremy Rifkin, *The Empathic Civilization: The Race to Global Consciousness in a World in Crisis* (New York: Penguin, 2009).

34. Lionel Robbins, "Mr. Hawtrey on the Scope of Economics," *Economica* 20 (1927): pp. 172–178. See also David Colander, "Searching for Keys under a Streetlight: Why Journalists Shouldn't Turn to Nobel Prize Winners for Expertise in Policy," paper presented to the Allied Social Science Associations Annual Meeting, San Diego, CA, January 4, 2013.

CHAPTER 2

1. This quote is often attributed to Vince Lombardi but may have originated with UCLA football coach Henry "Red" Sanders. See Steven J. Overman, "'Winning Isn't Everything. It's the Only Thing': The Origin, Attributions and Influence of a Famous Football Quote," *Football Studies* 2(2) (1999): pp. 77–99.

2. This would include pollution and other externalities.

3. This is also known as "commutative justice."

4. The Heritage Foundation offers an opposing view that political freedom and economic growth are mutually reinforcing goals. Its Index of Economic Freedom can be found at www.heritage.org/Index/.

5. Behavioral economists note that people disproportionately value what they already have.

6. Friedrich A. Hayek, *The Constitution of Liberty: The Definitive Edition* (Chicago, IL: The University of Chicago Press, [1960] 2011), p. 103.

7. See Benjamin M. Friedman, *The Moral Consequences of Economic Growth* (New York: Alfred A. Knopf, 2005).

8. An influential book that advocates a multiplicity of outcomes is by Herman E. Daly and John B. Cobb Jr., *For the Common Good: Redirecting the Economy toward Community, the Environment, and a Sustainable Future* (Boston: Beacon Press, 1989).

9. Jeremy Bentham, "Anarchical Fallacies: A Critical Examination of the Declaration of Rights," in *The Works of Jeremy Bentham*, vol. 2, 1838–1843; retrieved on August 8, 2013, from http://oll.libertyfund.org/title/1921/114230/2345508. .

10. Jeremy Bentham, *Introduction to the Principles of Morals and Legislation*, in J. H. Burns and H. L. A. Hart, eds., *The Collected Works of Jeremy Bentham* (Oxford, UK: Oxford University Press, 1996), pp. 11–12. A searchable text is available at www.econlib.org/library/Bentham/bnthPMLCover.html.

11. Ibid., p. 39.

12. Ibid., fn. p. 283.

13. Ibid., p. 12.

14. J. S. Mill, "Utilitarianism," in Alan Ryan, ed., *Utilitarianism and Other Essays* (London: Penguin Books, 1987), p. 278.

15. Ibid., p. 279.

16. Ibid., p. 281.

17. Cited in Frederick Rosen, *Mill* (Oxford, UK: Oxford University Press, 2013), p. 264.

18. A more nuanced account of rule utilitarianism could allow for unequal interests, if in following a rule that accords greater weight to one's own child one produced the greatest utility overall.

19. Peter Singer, *One World: The Ethics of Globalization*, 2nd edition (New Haven, CT: Yale University Press, 2002). Not all utilitarians would agree because total welfare might be enhanced if equal consideration were not given to all equally.

20. "Who We Are: Foundation Fact Sheet," Bill & Melinda Gates Foundation; retrieved on October 10, 2014 from www.gatesfoundation.org/Who-We-Are/General-Information/Foundation-Factsheet.

21. For an example of neuroeconomics, see Paul J. Zak, ed., *Moral Markets: The Critical Role of Values in the Economy* (Princeton, NJ: Princeton University Press, 2008).

22. Robert Nozick, "The Experience Machine," in Louis Pojman, ed., *Ethical Theory: Classical and Contemporary Readings*, 5th edition (Belmont, CA: Wadsworth, 2007), pp. 146–147. The article derives from Nozick's *Anarchy, State, and Utopia* (New York: Basic Books, 1974), pp. 42–43.

23. Cited by Richard Reeves, *John Stuart Mill: Victorian Firebrand* (London: Atlantic Books, 2007), p. 62.

24. I am indebted to Robison B. James for this analogy.

25. Rule utilitarians must still grapple with questions such as: What happens if people don't obey the rule that produces the greatest utility? Is it still the best rule?

26. Brad Hooker, "Rule Consequentialism," *The Blackwell Guide to Ethical Theory*, Hugh LaFollette, ed. (Oxford, UK: Blackwell, 2000), pp. 183–204, p. 187.

27. As noted earlier, certain caveats apply before economists would say that markets achieve efficient outcomes (there must be competitive markets, no asymmetric information, no externalities like pollution, and so on).

28. Adam Smith's support of freer trade derives from considerations of absolute advantage arising from specialization. Smith explicitly discounted the likelihood of capital outflows.

CHAPTER 3

1. Grant Rice, "Alumnus Football," *The Tumult and the Shouting: My Life in Sport* (New York: Barnes Publishing, 1954), p. 169.

2. For an overview see Gerald F. Gaus, "What Is Deontology? Part One: Orthodox Views," *Journal of Value Inquiry* 35(1) (2001): pp. 27–42 and "What Is Deontology? Part Two: Reasons to Act," *Journal of Value Inquiry* 35(2) (2001): pp. 179–193.

3. In practice some religious scholars do find exceptions to these rules by appealing to other divinely inspired writings or by reflection.

4. Deuteronomy 30:16.

5. See the Association of Christian Economists, the International Association for Islamic Economics, and scholars working on Judaic economics, Buddhist economics, and so on. The Ethics and Public Policy Center in Washington, D.C., is an institute dedicated to "applying the Judeo-Christian moral tradition" to critical issues of public policy. See also John P. Tiemstra, *Story Economists Tell: Studies in Christianity and Economics* (Eugene, OR: Wipf and Stock, 2012).

6. Kant makes this point in Chapter 1 of *Grounding for the Metaphysics of Morals*, translated by James W. Ellington (Indianapolis: Hackett, [1785] 1993, p. 8.

7. This assumes that no other parties besides the liar and the victims are affected. More important, rule utilitarians would argue that a general rule against lying produces more overall utility and hence supersedes the utility earned by any particular act of lying.

8. Kant, *Grounding for the Metaphysics of Morals*, op. cit., p. 14.

9. Ibid., p. 15.

10. Ibid., p. 30.

11. See Samuel Freeman, "Utilitarianism, Deontology, and the Priority of Right," *Philosophy & Public Affairs* 23(4) (1994): pp. 313–349.

12. Kant, op. cit., p. 36, emphasis added.

13. Jeremy Bentham, "Anarchical Fallacies," op. cit.

14. Smith, *The Wealth of Nations*, op. cit., p. 80.

15. Ibid., p. 372.

16. Ronald Dworkin, "Rights as Trumps," in Aileen Kavanagh and John Oberdiek, eds., *Arguing about Law* (New York: Routledge, 2009), pp. 335–344.

17. A rule utilitarian might argue that the creation of a doctrine of human rights could increase net happiness, and therefore she would be in favor of it—for a very different reason than natural rights theorists.

18. Cited in Lin Yutang, *The Importance of Living* (New York: Reynal & Hitchcock 1937), p. 94.

19. Cited in Sandra J. Peart, "We're All 'Persons' Now: Classical Economists and Their Opponents on Marriage, the Franchise, and Socialism," *Journal of the History of Economic Thought* 31(1) (March 2009): p. 17. Emphasis added.

20. John Stuart Mill, *Utilitarianism*, 2nd edition, George Sher, ed. (Indianapolis, IN: Hackett Publishing), p. 11.

21. Aristotle, *Nichomachean Ethics*, Book X, section 9, in Peter J. Steinberger, ed., *Readings in Classical Political Thought* (Indianapolis, IN: Hackett Publishing, 2000), p. 375.

22. G. Scott Davis, "Ethics and Religion," *Religion Compass* 2(6): pp. 1081–1101, p. 1086.

23. Smith, *The Theory of Moral Sentiments*, op. cit., p. 263.

24. Appropriate regard is not necessarily equal regard. One's duty to one's mother is greater than one's duty to a stranger.

25. See Deirdre McCloskey, *The Bourgeois Virtues*, op. cit. In a theological rendering, the spiritual virtues would be stated in reference to God's salvation.

26. Smith, *The Theory of Moral Sentiments*, op. cit., p. 287. Aristotle also notes that temperance should not be held to a mean.

27. See John B. Davis, *Individuals and Identity in Economics* (Cambridge, UK: Cambridge University Press, 2010) and George A. Akerlof and Rachel E. Kranton, *Identity Economics: How Our Identities Shape Our Work, Wages, and Well-Being* (Princeton, NJ: Princeton University Press, 2010).

28. The current association of *jihad* as "holy war" against the West is a twentieth-century reaction to imperialism. See Karen Armstrong, "Think Again—God," *Foreign Policy* (November 2009): p. 56.

29. See E. F. Schumacher, "Buddhist Economics," in *Small Is Beautiful: Economics as If People Mattered* (New York: Harper and Row, 1973), pp. 56–66.

30. See Irene van Staveren, *The Values of Economics: An Aristotelian Perspective* (New York: Routledge, 2001).

31. See Deirdre N. McCloskey, *The Bourgeois Virtues*, op. cit., and *Bourgeois Dignity: Why Economics Can't Explain the Modern World* (Chicago: University of Chicago Press, 2011).

32. Deirdre McCloskey, "Adam Smith, the Last of the Former Virtue Ethicists," *History of Political Economy* 40(1) (2008): pp. 43–71. James R. Otteson also makes this point in *Adam Smith's Marketplace of Life* (Cambridge, UK: Cambridge University Press, 2002).

33. Thomas Carlyle, "Occasional Discourse on the Negro Question," *Fraser's Magazine for Town and Country*, Vol. XL (1849), pp. 670–679; retrieved on October 10, 2014, from babel.hathitrust.org/cgi/pt?id=inu.30000080778727;view=1up;seq=690.

34. Ibid. See also David M. Levy, *How the Dismal Science Got Its Name: Classical Economics and the Ur-Text of Racial Politics* (Ann Arbor: University of Michigan Press, 2002).

35. Stanley Milgram, "Behavioral Study of Obedience," *Journal of Abnormal and Social Psychology* 67 (1963): pp. 371–378.

36. John M. Darley and C. Daniel Batson, "From Jerusalem to Jericho: A Study of Situational and Dispositional Variables in Helping Behavior," *Journal of Personality and Social Psychology* 27 (J) (1973): pp. 100–108.

37. Gilbert Harman, "No Character or Personality," *Business Ethics Quarterly* 13(1): pp. 87–94.

38. See, for example, Robert C. Solomon, "Victims of Circumstances? A Defense of Virtue Ethics in Business," *Business Ethics Quarterly* 13: pp. 43–62.

39. For the strongest defense of virtue ethics along these lines, see Maria Merritt, "Virtue Ethics and Situationist Personality Psychology," *Ethical Theory and Moral Practice* 3(4): pp. 365–383.

40. Ibid., p. 370.

41. For discussion and an alternative typology, see G. Scott Davis, op. cit.

42. Matthew 22:36–40.

43. Davis, "Ethics and Religion," op. cit.

44. Herbert Simon won the Nobel Prize in 1978 for his work on how managers in organizations make decisions. He coined the term satisficing to signify that in many, perhaps most, decisions, managers must achieve a blend of competing objectives—that is, they cannot maximize any one but have to achieve a satisfactory outcome on several. This concept is similar to virtue ethics in its approach to balancing different characteristics but may be different in that a virtue ethicist is striving for excellence, not simply getting by.

45. John Kay, "Angry Economics Students Are Naive—and Mostly Right," May 21, 2014; available at www.johnkay.com/2014/05/21/angry-economics-students-are-naive-and-mostly-right.

CHAPTER 4

1. Quoted in A. Barton Hinkle, "Open the State Checkbook to All Eyes," *Richmond Times-Dispatch*, January 29, 2008, p. A9.

2. For a further discussion of substantive outcomes, see Chapters 7 and 11.

3. Pigou's approach is still widely used today, although his microfoundations relying on measurable marginal utility were superseded by Pareto's choice approach (discussed in Chapter 5).

4. Arthur C. Pigou, *The Economics of Welfare*, 4th edition (London: Macmillan, 1962), p. 11. Note that the "economic way of thinking" is broader than simply a calculation of monetary costs and benefits. It can be used to understand divorce, crime, and other choices in life.

5. In practice, however, economists continue to use terms like *welfare* and *utility* as though they actually represent a particular mental state like happiness or pleasure. Technically, this attribution no longer applies.

6. Proper accounting is on the basis of opportunity costs. Proper accounting would include the social costs of pollution (a negative externality) and would include the social benefits of positive spillovers like vaccinations, schooling, and other public goods. Good information and competition are also essential if markets are to maximize net economic value.

7. Although invaluable goods don't have a price tag, the *"marginal* variations in commodity use are commensurable with each other and therefore with money," assuming that goods are perfectly divisible into infinitely small pieces and that the map of preference indifference is convex. See Kenneth J. Arrow, "Invaluable Goods," *Journal of Economic Literature* 35 (June 1997): p. 757.

8. Richard A. Posner, "Utilitarianism, Economics, and Legal Theory," 8 *Journal of Legal Studies* 103 (1979): pp. 119.

9. Adam Smith's famous example of the pin factory comes from the opening chapter of *The Wealth of Nations*, op. cit.

10. This analysis is a simplification because it uses only whole numbers.

11. Perfectly competitive markets have identical products and consumers have good information; therefore, producers have no power to make consumers pay a price higher than market equilibrium. The fact that many markets do exhibit price discrimination (for example, airline flights) signals that producers have some mechanism for getting consumers to pay a price closer to their demand price.

12. The area of the trapezoid under the demand curve is the average height times the base = ½ ($6 + $3) * 3 = $13.50.

13. Long-run supply curves for many agricultural and mineral productions slope upward because it is more costly to produce the last unit than the first unit. For example, some oil deposits lie close to the surface and can be easily extracted; gaining access to more oil requires drilling deeper, which is more costly. Supply curves can also be horizontal if opportunity costs are constant or even slope downward if opportunity costs fall as the industry expands (as in some manufacturing industries like computer chips).

14. As noted, perfectly competitive markets have identical products and producers have good information; therefore, consumers have no power to force producers to receive a price lower than market equilibrium.

15. The area of the trapezoid under the supply curve is the average height times the base = ½ ($1.50 + $3.00) * 3 = $6.75.

16. This is an approximation based on various assumptions, one being that a price change has no appreciable effect on consumers' real incomes. A rise in the price of chewing gum would cause no blip in most consumers' budgets and can be safely ignored; but a rise in the price of housing would be a contrary example, and the consumer surplus would diverge from that shown with the stationary demand curve previously discussed. In practice, the calculation of gains (and losses) may involve complicated estimation procedures. Adding up the consumer surpluses of individuals to reach an aggregate measure of surplus is also controversial because economists have previously said it is inappropriate to make interpersonal comparisons of ordinal preference rankings. Nevertheless, the use of consumer surplus in economic policy analysis is widespread.

17. Note that the justification of markets has become more ethically complex as we delve into the workings of resource markets (the factors of production). We must assume not only competition in labor markets but also basic rules of justice. This issue is further explored in later chapters.

18. In Figure 4.5, the deadweight loss would be the area of the triangle bounded by the equilibrium point and the letters M and N.

19. Qualifications are important: We assumed competitive markets, no externalities, perfect information, and no other market failures.

20. Leonard E. Read, "I, Pencil: My Family Tree as Told to Leonard E. Read," *The Freeman* (Irvington-on-Hudson, NY: The Foundation for Economic Education, 1958); retrieved on October 10, 2014, from http://www.econlib.org/library/Essays/rdPncl1.html.

21. Monopolistic completion means many buyers and sellers but differentiated products; oligopoly means just a few sellers; monopoly means only a single seller.

22. Government intervention raises its own set of problems, and hence market failures must be balanced against potential government failures.

CHAPTER 5

1. Vilfredo Pareto, *Manual of Political Economy*, translated by Ann S. Schwier, edited by Ann S. Schwier and Alfred N. Page (New York: Augustus M. Kelley, [1906] 1971), p. 261.

2. *Laissez-faire* literally means "allow to do." It was a doctrine promulgated by physiocratic reformers in France in the mid-eighteenth century. Although Adam Smith admired them, his own views were more pragmatic and favored some government intervention. In particular, Smith's view of the invisible hand would not support its use in this context, a subject we return to in Chapters 8 and 9.

3. The potential for government failure is covered in public choice theory. Ronald Coase notes that

NOTES TO CHAPTER 5

... whatever may be the characteristics of the ideal world, we have not yet discovered how to get to it from where we are. Contemplation of an optimal system may suggest ways of improving the system, it may provide techniques of analysis that would otherwise have been missed, and, in certain special cases, it may go far to providing a solution. But in general its influence has been pernicious. It has directed economists' attention away from the main question, which is how alternative arrangements will actually work in practice. It has led economists to derive conclusions for economic policy from a study of an abstract model of a market situation. It is no accident that in the literature ... we find a category "market failure" but no category "government failure." Until we realize that we are choosing between social arrangements which are all more or less failures, we are not likely to make much headway." Ronald H. Coase, "The Regulated Industries: Discussion," *The American Economic Review* 54(3) (1964): p. 195.

4. Vilfredo Pareto himself suggested that democracy was something of a sham: "In the fact, whether universal suffrage prevails or not, it is always an oligarchy that governs, finding ways to give to the 'will of the people' that expression which the few desire." *The Mind and Society*, translated by Andrew Bongiorno and Arthur Livingston, edited by Arthur Livingston, 4 volumes (Harcourt, Brace and Co., 1935), p. 1526. See also Benjamin I. Page, Larry M. Bartels, and Jason Seawright, "Democracy and the Policy Preferences of Wealthy Americans," *Perspectives on Politics* 11(1) (March 2013): pp. 51–73.

5. Kenneth J. Arrow, "Political and Economic Evaluation of Social Effects and Externalities," in *The Analysis of Public Output*, Julius Margolis, ed. (New York: Columbia University for the National Bureau of Economic Research, 1970), p. 4; retrieved on October 10, 2014, from http://www.nber.org/chapters/c3349.pdf.

6. Mark Blaug, *Economic Theory in Retrospect*, 5th edition (Cambridge, UK: Cambridge University Press, 1996): p. 700.

7. This is a *partial* analysis, because those who gain from trade include domestic wheat and corn farmers whose export markets would expand with freer trade. Foreign consumers also gain from cheaper prices of these products. Losers also include those domestic workers in dairy industry processing and foreign producers of wheat and corn subject to import competition. Calculating all these benefits and costs of trade would lead to a *general* equilibrium analysis. The salient issue of analysis remains the same whether we look at partial or general equilibrium.

8. This criterion is named for two British economists, Nicholas Kaldor and Sir John Hicks. Hicks was awarded the Nobel Prize in 1972.

9. A pioneering effort is by Abram Bergson, "A Reformulation of Certain Aspects of Welfare Economics," *The Quarterly Journal of Economics* 52(2) (1938): pp. 327–328.

10. Kenneth J. Arrow, *Social Choice and Individual Values*, 2nd ed. (New Haven, CT: Yale University Press, [1951] 1970). Arrow paradoxically named his theorem the "possibility" theorem, but its inversion is most cited. Arrow received the Nobel Prize in 1972 along with Hicks.

11. David G Luenberger, *Microeconomic Theory* (New York: McGraw-Hill, 1995), p. 363. One promising approach by Amartya Sen, discussed in the following chapter, offers a way out of Arrow's conundrum, but only by utilizing information regarding interpersonal comparisons.

12. Daniel M. Hausman and Michael S. McPherson, *Economic Analysis, Moral Philosophy, and Public Policy*, 2nd edition (Cambridge, UK: Cambridge University Press, 2006), p. 152.

13. James M. Buchanan, *Cost and Choice: An Inquiry in Economic Theory* (Indianapolis, IN: Liberty Fund, Inc., [1969] 1999), para. 6.3.12–13, emphasis added; available online at www.econlib.org/library/Buchanan/buchCv6.html.

14. Someone could have inherited the house from a parent on the promise to "never let it go out of the family." See Mark D. White, "Pareto, Consent, and Respect for Dignity: A Kantian Perspective," *Review of Social Economy* 67(1) (2009): pp. 49–70.

15. Nicole Neroulias, "In a Historical House, an Auction of Lincoln Memorabilia," *New York Times*, February 27, 2009; retrieved on February 27, 2011, from www.nytimes .com/2009/03/01/nyregion/westchester/01lincolnwe.html.

16. Kenneth J. Arrow, "Invaluable Goods," op. cit., p. 762.

17. Buchanan, op cit., para. 6.5.4.

18. Lionel Robbins, *An Essay on the Nature and Significance of Economic Science*, 2nd edition (London, UK: Macmillan and Co., [1932] 1945).

19. For this view of consent through voice, see Jean Jacques Rousseau, *The Social Contract* in *The Essential Writings of Rousseau*, translated by Peter Constantine and edited by Leo Damrosch (New York: Modern Library, [1762] 2013); and Albert O. Hirschman, *Exit, Voice, and Loyalty: Responses to Decline in Firms, Organizations, and States* (Cambridge, MA: Harvard University Press, 1970).

20. See Amartya Sen, "Rationality and Social Choice," *American Economic Review* 85(1) (1995): pp. 1–24.

21. Frank H. Knight, "Social Economic Policy," *The Canadian Journal of Economics and Political Science* 26(1) (1960): pp. 19–34.

22. John S. Rosenberg, "Toxic Memo," *Harvard Magazine*, May–June 2001. A Frontline video provides an example of what the Summers memo envisioned: www.pbs.org/ frontlineworld/stories/ghana804/.

23. As noted, cost–benefit analysis depends critically on whose harm is counted. In the pre–Civil War South, "If you harmed the slave, you violated the rights of the *owner*, not the slave, who had none." Cited in Steve Nash, "Oil and Water, Economics and Ecology in the Gulf of Mexico: Trying to Reckon What We've Destroyed," *BioScience* 61(4) (2011): pp. 259–263; emphasis added.

24. For additional discussion, see Amartya Sen, "Rationality and Social Choice," op. cit.

25. For a defense of cost–benefit analysis, see Donald C. Hubin, "The Moral Justification of Benefit/Cost Analysis," *Economics and Philosophy* 10(2) (1994): pp. 169–194; and Robert H. Frank, "The Status of Moral Emotions in Consequentialist Moral Reasoning," in Paul J. Zak, ed., *Moral Markets: The Critical Role of Values in the Economy*, op. cit., pp. 42–59.

26. David D. Friedman, *Price Theory* (Cincinnati, OH: South-Western, 1986), p. 347.

27. Lionel Robbins, op. cit., p. ix.

28. E. Reinhardt, "Health Care, Uncertainty and Morality," *Economix* (*New York Times*, August 13, 2010); retrieved from http://economix.blogs.nytimes.com/2010/08/13/ health-care-uncertainty-and-morality/.

29. Pareto, for example, to get away from using the word *utility* coined the term *ophelimity* to represent relative satisfaction; Pigou used the term *desiredness* "since it cannot be taken to have any ethical implication" (Pigou, op cit., p. 11).

30. Friedman, op. cit.

31. Kenneth J. Arrow, "Uncertainty and the Welfare Economics of Medical Care," *American Economic Review* 53(5) (1963): pp. 941–973, p. 942, cited by Uwe E. Reinhardt, "Can Efficiency in Health Care Be Left to the Market?" *Journal of Health Politics, Policy and Law* 26.5 (2001): pp. 967–992.

32. Abram Bergson, "A Reformulation of Certain Aspects of Welfare Economics," op. cit.

33. A partial list of Nobel economists (and year of award) who have written on the role of ethics in economic life would include Paul Samuelson (1970), Kenneth Arrow (1972), Gunner Myrdal (1974), F. A. Hayek (1974), Milton Friedman (1976), Herbert Simon (1978), James Buchanan (1986), Robert Solow (1987), Ronald Coase (1991), Robert Fogel (1993), Reinhardt Selten (1994), John C. Harsanyi (1994), Amartya Sen (1998), Daniel Kahneman (2002), and Elinor Ostrom (2009).

34. "The man whose whole life is spent in performing a few simple operations, of which the effects too are, perhaps, always the same, or very nearly the same, has no occasion to exert his understanding, or to exercise his invention. . . . He naturally loses, therefore, the habit of such exertion, and generally becomes as stupid and ignorant as it is possible for a human creature to become." Smith, *The Wealth of Nations*, op. cit., p. 506.

35. For discussion, see Amartya K. Sen, "Values and Choice," in *Collective Choice and Social Welfare* (San Francisco: Holden-Day, 1970), pp. 56–59; and I. M. D. Little, *A Critique of Welfare Economics*, 2nd edition (Oxford, UK: Clarendon Press, 2002), pp. v and 69.

36. Amartya Sen, *On Ethics and Economics* (Oxford, UK: Blackwell Publishing, 1988), p. 33.

CHAPTER 6

1. Franz Kafka, *The Castle*, translated by Mark Harman (New York: Schocken Books, 1998), p. 307.

2. A popular version of this tale is the poem by John Godfrey Saxe, "The Blind Men and the Elephant," available at www.constitution.org/col/blind_men.htm.

3. For overviews, see Hausman and McPherson, op cit., and Charles K. Wilber, ed., *Economics, Ethics and Public Policy* (Lanham, MD: Rowman & Littlefield, 1998).

4. Richard Thaler and Cass Sunstein, *Nudge: Improving Decisions about Health, Wealth, and Happiness* (New Haven, CT: Yale University Press, 2008). The fact that a teenager may not be capable of informed judgment does not require government intervention, however, if the teenager's parents act appropriately to restrain his foolish choices.

5. F. A. Hayek, "The Use of Knowledge in Society," *American Economic Review*, 35(4), pp. 519–530.

6. For a Kantian view on paternalism, see Mark D. White, *The Manipulation of Choice: Ethics and Libertarian Paternalism* (New York: Palgrave Macmillan, 2013).

7. Paraphrased from Brad DeLong, "$1.409 million," *Grasping Reality with Both Hands*; retrieved on August 20, 2011 from http://delong.typepad.com/sdj/2011/08/1049-million.html. For a discussion of integrating present and future selves, see John B. Davis, op. cit. For a discussion of procrastination, see Chrisoula Andreou and Mark White, eds., *The Thief of Time: Philosophical Essays on Procrastination* (Oxford, UK: Oxford University Press, 2010).

8. Kenneth Boulding, "Economics as a Moral Science," op. cit., p. 2.

9. Frank Knight, "The Ethics of Competition," in *The Ethics of Competition* (New Brunswick, NJ: Transaction Publishers, [1923] 1997), p. 38.

10. Boulding, op. cit., p. 2.

11. David George, *Preference Pollution: How Markets Create the Desires We Dislike* (Ann Arbor: University of Michigan Press, 2001).

12. For a discussion of the U.S. move toward prescription advertising, see Ishmeal Bradley, "Direct-to-Consumer Advertising of Prescription Drugs, Part 1," *Clinical Correlations* (July 30, 2010), retrieved on July 25, 2011, from www.clinicalcorrelations.org/?p=2867.

13. U.S. Supreme Court, *Virginia State Board of Pharmacy v. Virginia Citizens Consumer Council, 425 U. S. 748 (1976)*; retrieved on July 25, 2011, from http://supreme .justia.com/us/425/748/case.html; emphasis added.

14. Adam Smith developed a model for these issues (see Chapter 8).

15. This approach, dubbed a "negative income tax," was advocated by Milton Friedman in *Capitalism and Freedom*, op. cit.

16. In this case there are also negative externalities because Brian's presumed higher grade makes his resume more attractive than Susan's, potentially costing her lost job opportunities.

17. Markets *do* consider future consumers when products are nonperishable. For example, if oil companies expect future consumers to offer higher prices, and if the opportunity cost of waiting (the interest rate) is low, then firms can stockpile oil by simply leaving it in the ground for future generations. This is elaborated in Chapter 11.

18. Robert H. Frank and Ben S. Bernanke, *Principles of Micro-Economics*, 4th edition (Boston, MA: McGraw-Hill/Irwin, 2009), p. 179, emphasis added. This may be a semantic issue if the authors mean efficiency in its broad sense as a technique to achieve any end, but this then contradicts the previous statement that there are many goals in addition to efficiency.

19. For elaboration, see Amos Witztum, "Ethics and the Science of Economics: Robbins' Enduring Fallacy," *Journal of the History of Economic Thought* 33(4) (2011): pp. 467–486.

20. There are numerous assumptions that must be made before economists would say that market transactions produce the most efficient outcome. In this case we ignore the externalities of automobile and oil use.

21. For simplicity, assume all three patients are of the same blood type, age, and other characteristics.

22. See Mark Blaug, "Is Competition Such a Good Thing? Static Efficiency versus Dynamic Efficiency," *Review of Industrial Organization* 19 (2001): pp. 37–48.

23. A monopoly has an incentive to reduce output and raise price, thereby generating higher economic profit. A monopoly can do this because there are no close substitutes and the patent is a barrier to entry against competitors. Because the monopoly restricts output, it fails to provide the greatest potential preference satisfaction and results in a "deadweight" loss to today's society. (In the unlikely event the monopolist can charge each customer a unique price that captures all the consumer surplus, the monopoly will produce the same output as the competitive market and thus result in no inefficiency, only a redistribution of wealth.)

24. Joseph A. Schumpeter, *Capitalism, Socialism and Democracy* (New York: Harper, [1942] 1975), pp. 82–85, emphasis added. Retrieved from http://transcriptions.english .ucsb.edu/archive/courses/liu/english25/materials/schumpeter.html.

25. Sen, *Collective Choice and Social Welfare* op. cit., p. 22.

26. Sen, "Rationality and Social Choice," op. cit., p. 7.

27. Smith, *The Wealth of Nations*, op. cit., pp. 869–870.

28. See David P. Levine and S. Abu Rizvi, *Poverty, Work and Freedom: Political Economy and the Moral Order* (Cambridge, UK: Cambridge University Press, 2005).

29. Amartya Sen, "The Possibility of Social Choice," *American Economic Review* 89(3) (1999): pp. 349–378.

30. Forbes magazine, "The Chanel 'Diamond Forever' Classic Bag"; retrieved from www.forbes.com/2007/03/26/handbags-extravagant-expensive-forbeslife-cx_hp_0327handbags_slide_2.html.

31. Amartya Sen, *Rationality and Freedom* (Cambridge, MA: Harvard University Press, 2004), p. 82.

32. Ibid., pp. 82–83.

33. Gross Domestic Product (GDP) is not the same thing as the economic surplus. The two differ because consumer surplus is measured by the difference between what people would have been willing to pay but did not have to pay. The GDP measures only what people actually paid (and thus represents a smaller amount). Nevertheless, by providing a rough measure of economic activity, GDP is often used as an aggregate proxy for preferences satisfied. There are numerous problems with doing so, which are covered in a principles of macroeconomics course.

34. Hywel G. Jones, *An Introduction to Modern Theories of Economic Growth* (New York: McGraw Hill, 1976), p. 1.

35. Stiglitz, Sen, and Fitoussi. *Report by the Commission on the Measurement of Economic Performance and Social Progress*, op. cit.

36. Amartya Sen, "Real National Income," *Review of Economic Studies* 43(1) (1982), p. 32.

37. See Nancy Folbre, *Invisible Heart*, op. cit.

38. Sen, *On Ethics and Economics*, op. cit., p. 41.

39. Sen, "Rational Fools: A Critique of the Behavioral Foundations of Economics," op. cit., p. 329.

40. See, for example, Bruno S. Frey, *Happiness: A Revolution in Economics* (Cambridge, MA: MIT Press); and Bruno S. Frey and Alois Stutzer, *Happiness and Economics: How the Economy and Institutions Affect Well-Being* (Princeton, NJ: Princeton University Press, 2002). For a compendium of research, consult the World Database of Happiness research at Erasmus University, www1.eur.nl/fsw/happiness. For a critique of happiness, see Daniel M. Hausman, "Hedonism and Welfare Economics," *Economics and Philosophy* 26 (2010): 321–344.

41. A similar problem exists with other substantive measures of well-being like literacy. Being "literate" in one country could mean simply being able to read street signs; in another it could mean reading a newspaper.

42. Lionel Robbins, *An Essay on the Nature and Significance of Economic Science*, 2nd edition, op. cit., p. 16.

43. Gary Becker, *The Economic Approach to Human Behavior* (Chicago: University of Chicago Press, 1976).

44. See, for example, Marshall Sahlins, *Stone Age Economics* (New York: Routledge, 1972).

45. See Irene van Staveren, op. cit. One instinctual mechanism is the desire for *fairness*. Philosophers such as John Rawls have attempted to broaden discourse back to the question of income and wealth distribution, a topic we will pick up again in Chapter 11.

46. Two Nobel Prize winners give similar definitions involving social relations. Ronald Coase quotes Stigler as writing: "Economics is the study of the operation of economic organizations, and economic organizations are social (and rarely individual) arrangements to deal with the production and distribution of economic goods and services." Similarly, Coase writes: "What economists study is the working of the social institutions which bind together the economic system: farms, markets for goods and services, labor markets, capital markets, banking system, international trade, and so on." Ronald H. Coase, "Economics and Contiguous Disciplines," *Journal of Legal Studies* 7 (1978): pp. 201–212, pp. 206–207.

47. Sen, *On Ethics and Economics*, op. cit., p. 35.

48. Lin Yutang, *The Importance of Living* (New York: Harper Paperbacks, [1937] 1998), p. 3, cited in Denis Goulet, *Development Ethics: A Guide to Theory and Practice* (New York: The Apex Press, 1995), p. 200.

49. Daniel M. Hausman, "Hedonism and Welfare Economics," op. cit., p. 341, emphasis added.

50. One might still argue that the preferences of the *donors* to this philanthropy are being satisfied.

CHAPTER 7

Some of the arguments developed here were originally published in Jonathan B. Wight and John S. Morton, *Teaching the Ethical Foundations of Economics* (New York: The National Council on Economic Education, 2007); and Jonathan B. Wight, "Sociability and the Market," *Forum for Social Economics* 39(2/3) (2009): pp. 97–110.

1. For examples, see Michael Sandel, *What Money Can't Buy: The Moral Limits of Markets* (New York: Farrar, Straus and Giroux 2012); Elizabeth Anderson, "The Ethical Limitations of the Market," *Economics and Philosophy* 6 (2) (1990): pp. 179–205; and Kenneth J. Arrow, "Invaluable Goods," op. cit..

2. Paul Samuelson won the Nobel Prize in Economics in 1970. This quote comes from "Love," *Newsweek* (December 29, 1969), reprinted in Paul Samuelson, *Economics From the Heart: A Samuelson Sampler* (San Diego: Harcourt Brace Jovanovich, 1983), p. 11.

3. Vernon Smith, "Human Nature: An Economic Perspective," *Daedalus* 133(4) (2004): p. 76.

4. Alvin E. Roth, "Repugnance Is a Constraint on Markets," *Journal of Economic Perspectives* 21(3) (2007): pp. 37–58.

5. Horsemeat for human consumption is banned in California but considered perfectly acceptable on many European dinner tables. Despite the ban on eating cats and dogs, these animals are legally used in painful experiments.

6. Elisabeth M. Landes and Richard A. Posner, "The Economics of the Baby Shortage," *The Journal of Legal Studies* 7(2) (1978): pp. 323–348.

7. Jonathan Swift, "A Modest Proposal for Preventing the Children of Poor People in Ireland from Being a Burden to Their Parents or Country, and for Making Them Beneficial to the Public" (1729), reprinted by The Project Guttenberg, www.gutenberg.org/files/1080/1080-h/1080-h.htm; see also Sidney DeLong, "A Modest Proposal," *Journal of Legal Education* 42 (1992): 127–128.

8. Richard M. Titmuss, *The Gift Relationship: From Human Blood to Social Policy* (New York: Pantheon Books, 1971), p. 245.

9. For reviews of Titmuss, see Kenneth J. Arrow, "Gifts and Exchanges," *Philosophy & Public Affairs* 1(4) (1972): pp. 343–362; and Robert M. Solow, "Blood and Thunder," *The Yale Law Journal* 80(8) (1971): pp. 1696–1711.

10. Carl Mellström and Magnus Johannesson, "Crowding out in Blood Donation: Was Titmuss Right?" *Journal of the European Economic Association* 6(4) (2008): pp. 845–863.

11. Bruno S. Frey and Felix Oberholzer-Gee, "The Cost of Price Incentives: An Empirical Analysis of Motivation Crowding-Out," *American Economic Review* 87(4) (1997): pp. 746–755.

12. Ibid., p. 753.

13. Elinor Ostrom, "Policies That Crowd Out Reciprocity and Collection Action," in Herbert Gintis, Samuel Bowles, Robert Boyd, and Ernst Fehr, eds., *Moral Sentiments and Material Interests: The Foundations of Cooperation in Economic Life*, op. cit. p. 253.

14. Lorenz Goette and Alois Stutzer, "Blood Donations and Incentives: Evidence from a Field Experiment." Institute for the Study of Labor Working Paper No. 3580 (July 2008); available at SSRN: http://papers.ssrn.com/sol3/papers.cfm?abstract_id=1158977.

15. The sale of military medals and decorations is prohibited by 18 U.S. Code § 704, with fines and imprisonment of up to one year.

16. Paul Heyne, "Moral Criticisms of Markets," *The Senior Economist* 10(4)(April) (1995): 3–8.

17. Sandel, op. cit.

18. Ron Chernow, *Washington: A Life* (New York: Penguin Books, 2010).

19. In earlier times, executions were held publically to provide mass entertainment and to act as a deterrent.

20. Smith, *The Theory of Moral Sentiments*, op. cit., p. 85.

21. Samuelson, op. cit., p. 10, emphasis added. Samuelson credited Professor Lyle Owen of the University of Tulsa with this insight.

22. Kenneth J. Arrow, "Uncertainty and the Welfare Economics of Medical Care," op. cit., p. 967.

23. Heyne, op. cit.

24. Marcel Mauss, *The Gift: The Form and Reason for Exchange in Archaic Societies* (London: Routledge, [1923] 2001).

25. Vernon Smith, "Human Nature," op. cit., p. 76.

26. Scott C. Wiltermuth and Chip Heath, "Synchrony and Cooperation," *Psychological Science* 20(1) (2009): pp. 1–5.

27. See Paul J. Zak, *The Moral Molecule: The Source of Love and Prosperity* (New York: Dutton, 2012).

28. Some students are accepted to elite schools based on "legacy" relationship or other criteria than merit. And some students "buy" their way into college through their parents' donations. This latter situation is presumably rare, and many students would likely resent such market arrogance.

29. Ken Peterson, "Equity and Efficiency in a Game," *Classroom Expernomics*, 4(1) (1995): pp. 1–2.

30. The Columbia Law School source is Hayley Miller, "Americans Don't Know Their Constitution," Columbia Law School, available at www2.law.columbia.edu/news/surveys/surveyconstitution; the hot dog example is in M. K. Block, W. J. Boyes, J. S. Morton, "What

Young People in Arizona Know and Think about Market Economies," Arizona Council on Economic Education, working paper, 1999.

31. Debra Satz, *Why Some Things Should Not Be for Sale* (Oxford, UK: Oxford University Press, 2010).

32. Constance L. Hays, "Variable-Price Coke Machine Being Tested," *New York Times* (October 28, 1999).

33. Neil Irwin, "Uber's Surge Pricing Is Totally Logical and Fair. So Why Do People Hate It So Much?" *The Washington Post*, December 20, 2013.

34. Daniel Kahneman, Jack L. Knetsch, and Richard Thaler, "Fairness as a Constraint on Profit-Seeking: Entitlements in the Market," *The American Economic Review* 76(4) (1986): pp. 728–741.

35. *Theologia Moralis* 2-2, q. 77, art. 1.

36. Economists today have a more sophisticated view of cost. The seller's cost constitutes the "opportunity cost" of replacing the inventory, not the cost of buying the original item. Because it may be more expensive to replace inventory during a crisis, charging a higher price compensates for the higher replacement cost.

37. John Winthrop, *The History of New England from 1630 to 1649*, edited by James Kendall Hosmer (New York: Charles Scribner Sons, 1908): Volume 1, p. 317, available on Google ebooks.

38. Benjamin Blevins, Guadalupe Ramirez, and Jonathan B. Wight, "Ethics in the Mayan Marketplace," in Mark D. White, ed., *Accepting the Invisible Hand* (New York: Palgrave Macmillan, 2010), pp. 87–110.

39. See Benjamin Campbell, *Richmond's Unhealed History* (Richmond, VA: Brandylane Publishers, 2011).

40. Gary S. Becker, "The Economic Way of Looking at Behavior," *Journal of Political Economy* 101(3)(1993): pp. 385–409.

41. See Gary S. Becker, *The Economics of Discrimination* (Chicago: The University of Chicago Press, 1970); and Thomas Sowell, *Applied Economics: Thinking Beyond Stage One* (New York: Basic Books, 2004).

42. William M. Evan and R. Edward Freeman, "A Stakeholder Theory of the Modern Corporation: Kantian Capitalism," in T. Beauchamp and N. Bowie, eds., *Ethical Theory in Business*, 3rd ed. (Englewood Cliffs, NJ: Prentice Hall, 1988).

43. Kant, *Grounding*, op. cit., p. 40; emphasis added.

44. Immanuel Kant, *The Metaphysics of Morals* [1785], trans. and ed. by Mary J. Gregor (Cambridge, UK: Cambridge University Press, 1996), p. 177.

45. McCloskey, *The Bourgeois Virtues*, op. cit.

46. Arrow, "Invaluable Goods," op. cit., p. 764.

47. Herbert Spencer, *Essays: Scientific, Political, and Speculative* (London: Williams and Norgate, [1858] 1891). Retrieved on March 18, 2013, from http://oll.libertyfund.org/title/337/12303/599956.

48. In some African societies, for example, social norms require that wealth be shared with others via extravagant displays of communal consumption. Such community feasts are a mechanism of redistribution that provide prestige and, perhaps more important, enhanced security through diversification of relationships. On the negative side, wealth is dissipated through consumption rather than invested. Hence, some village leaders learn to make ostentatious displays of generosity while at the same time absconding with vast amounts of secret stocks outside the country. Social mechanisms for allocation thus offer

both solutions and drawbacks. See Mamadou Dia, "Development and Cultural Values in Sub-Saharan Africa," *Finance and Development* (December 1991): pp. 10–13.

49. Robert Nozick, *The Examined Life: Philosophical Meditations* (New York: Touchstone Books, 1989), pp. 286–287.

50. Smith, *Wealth of Nations*, op. cit., p. 795.

CHAPTER 8

1. Vernon L. Smith, "Some Economics and Politics of Globalization," Pope Lecture, North Carolina State University, March 2, 2005, pp. 4–5.

2. See, for example: Vernon Smith, "Human Nature," op. cit.; Gintis, Bowles, Boyd, and Fehr, eds., *Moral Sentiments and Material Interests: The Foundations of Cooperation in Economic Life*, op. cit.; and Paul A. Zak, "The Physiology of Moral Sentiments," *Journal of Economic Behavior and Organization* 77(1) (2011): pp. 53–65.

3. Werner Güth, Rolf Schmittberger, and Bernd Schwarze, "An Experimental Analysis of Ultimatum Bargaining," *Journal of Economic Behavior and Organization* 3 (4) (1982): pp. 367–388; and Daniel Kahneman, Jack L. Knetsch, and Richard Thaler, "Fairness as a Constraint on Profit-Seeking: Entitlements in the Market," *The American Economic Review* 76(4) (1986): pp. 728–741.

4. For a description of how to play this game in the classroom, see Jonathan B. Wight and John S. Morton, *Teaching the Ethical Foundations of Economics*, op. cit..

5. Daniel Kahneman, Jack L. Knetsch, and Richard H. Thaler, "Fairness and the Assumptions of Economics," *Journal of Business* 59(4-Pt.2) (1986): pp. S285–S300.

6. Elizabeth Hoffman, Kevin McCabe, and Vernon L. Smith, "Social Distance and Other-Regarding Behavior in Dictator Games," *American Economic Review* 86(3) (1996): pp. 653–660.

7. Todd L. Cherry, Peter Frykblom, and Jason F. Shogren, "Hardnose the Dictator," *The American Economic Review* 92(4) (2002): pp. 1218–1221.

8. Kevin A. McCabe, Mary L. Rigdon, and Vernon L. Smith, "Positive Reciprocity and Intentions in Trust Games," *Journal of Economic Behavior and Organization* 52(2) (2003): pp. 267–275.

9. Zak, *The Moral Molecule: The Source of Love and Prosperity*, op. cit.

10. Paul J. Zak, "The Physiology of Moral Sentiments," op. cit., p. 10.

11. Enlightened self-interest may make a person honest if the benefits of truth telling are high and the costs are low. But this type of honesty is weak because it is situational and can easily change with circumstances. Adam Smith outlines a stronger form of trust based on shared emotional connections (see the following discussion).

12. M. A. Umilta, E. Kohler, V. Gallese, L. Fogassi, L. Fadiga, C. Keysers, and G. Rizzolatti, "I Know What You Are Doing: A Neurophysiological Study," *Neuron* 31 (July 2001): pp. 155–165.

13. Smith, *The Theory of Moral Sentiments*, op. cit., p. 14.

14. One important clue in support of consistency is that Smith continued to edit both books throughout his life, completing the sixth edition of TMS a few months before his death. For additional views, see James R. Otteson, *Adam Smith's Marketplace of Life* (Cambridge, UK: Cambridge University Press, 2002).

15. Smith, *The Wealth of Nations*, op. cit., p. 769.

16. Darwin's theories about human evolution are contained in *The Descent of Man*, 2nd edition (London, UK: Penguin Classics, [1874] 2004). Darwin notes that ethical norms and

virtue are vital for group success: "A tribe including many members who, from possessing in a high degree the spirit of patriotism, fidelity, obedience, courage, and sympathy, were always ready to aid one another, and to sacrifice themselves for the common good, would be victorious over most other tribes; and this would be natural selection" (pp. 157–158).

17. Smith, *The Theory of Moral Sentiments*, op. cit., pp. 77–78.

18. Nava Ashraf, Colin F. Camerer, and George Loewenstein, "Adam Smith, Behavioral Economist," *Journal of Economic Perspectives* 19(3) (2005): pp. 131–145.

19. Thomas Hobbes, *The Leviathan*, "Chapter XIII: Of the Natural Condition of Mankind As Concerning Their Felicity, and Misery," The On-Line Library of Liberty, Liberty Fund. Retrieved on July 3, 2013, from http://oll.libertyfund.org/title/585/89842/2025613.

20. Smith, *The Theory of Moral Sentiments*, op. cit., p. 9.

21. Ibid., p. 86.

22. For elaboration, see Samuel Bowles and Herbert Gintis, *A Cooperative Species: Human Reciprocity and Its Evolution* (Princeton, NJ: Princeton University Press, 2011).

23. Smith, *The Theory of Moral Sentiments*, op. cit., p. 13.

24. Vernon Smith, "Adam Smith: From Propriety and Sentiments to Property and Wealth," *Forum for Social Economics* 42(4) (2013): p. 288.

25. Smith, *The Theory of Moral Sentiments*, op. cit., p. 319.

26. Such norms may be tied to economic development because higher incomes allow for travel and expanded moral imagination. See Friedman, *The Moral Consequences of Economic Growth*, op. cit..

27. For elaboration, see Jonathan B. Wight, "The Treatment of Smith's Invisible Hand," *The Journal of Economic Education* 39(3) (2007): pp. 341–358.

28. Smith, *The Theory of Moral Sentiments*, op. cit., p. 216.

29. Garrison Keillor, "Eulogy for the Winnebago," *Funny Times* (August 2008): p. 3.

CHAPTER 9

1. To compare the range of perspectives, see Andrew W. Lo, "Reading about the Financial Crisis: A 21-Book Review," *Journal of Economic Literature* 50(1) (2012): pp. 151–178; and the *Financial Crisis Inquiry Commission Report* (2011) found at http://fcic-static.law.stanford.edu/cdn_media/fcic-reports/fcic_final_report_full.pdf.

2. John Maynard Keynes, *The General Theory of Employment, Interest and Money* (New York: Harcourt, Brace & World, 1936), p. viii.

3. Ibid., p. 383.

4. John Maynard Keynes, *A Tract on Monetary Reform* (New York: Prometheus Books, [1923] 2000), p. 80; emphasis in original.

5. The Employment Act of 1946; available at http://fraser.stlouisfed.org/docs/historical/congressional/employment-act-1946.pdf.

6. Recessions are dated by the National Bureau of Economic Research; see "US Business Cycle Expansions and Contractions"; retrieved on October 22, 2014, from www.nber.org/cycles/cyclesmain.html. From the 1950s to the present, the U.S. economy experienced ten recessions. Most of these were relatively brief, and some were engineered by the Federal Reserve Board to reduce inflation.

7. The first source is Kenneth J. Arrow and F. H. Hahn, *General Competitive Analysis* (San Francisco, Holden-Day, 1971), p. vii; the second is Walter Williams, "The Virtue of Greed in Promoting Public Good," *Richmond Times-Dispatch*, October 6, 1999, p. A15;

the third is Max Lerner in his introduction to *The Wealth of Nations*, Edwin Canaan, ed. (New York: Modern Library Edition, 1937), p. ix.

8. Ivan Boesky, commencement address, School of Business, University of California, Berkeley, May 18, 1986.

9. Bernard Mandeville, *The Fable of the Bees*, edited by Irwin Primer (New York: Capricorn Books, [1714] 1962), p. 31.

10. Ibid., pp. 33 and 38.

11. Smith, *The Theory of Moral Sentiments*, op. cit., pp. 312–313.

12. For an in-depth analysis, see Alan S. Blinder, *After the Music Stopped: The Financial Crisis, The Response, and the Work Ahead* (New York: The Penguin Press, 2013).

13. "Leverage" is the ratio of assets to equity. This number rose to 40 to 1 in some cases for investment banks. This indicates that for every $40 of assets acquired, $39 comes from borrowing and only $1 from capital at risk. This makes for larger profits when the market is rising, but a drop in asset value of only 2.5 percent could wipe out all shareholder equity. Fannie Mae and Freddie Mac had far higher leverage ratios, up to 75 to 1.

14. Robert L. Hetzel, *The Great Recession: Market Failure or Policy Failure?* (Cambridge, UK: Cambridge University Press, 2012), p. 204. In Hetzel's view, the market did not fail; monetary policy did.

15. Paul Volker, "Financial Reform: Unfinished Business," *The New York Review of Books*, November 24, 2011.

16. See chapter 12 in Keynes, *The General Theory*, op. cit..

17. A "global savings glut" resulted from developing countries exporting more than they were importing. Much of the surplus earning was invested in the United States, pushing down interest rates and pushing up stock prices. The Federal Reserve was well aware of the issue. See Ben S. Bernanke, "Global Imbalances: Recent Developments and Prospects," September 11, 2007; retrieved from www.federalreserve.gov/newsevents/speech/bernanke20070911a.htm.

18. Blinder, op. cit., p. 205.

19. Smith, *The Wealth of Nations*, op. cit., pp. 26–27.

20. Ibid., p. 456; emphasis added.

21. Ibid. Here Smith derides those who lobby for special favors from government, claiming that they are doing so for a public purpose.

22. Monopolies lower output and employment to increase prices and profits. Such behavior destroys potential value in the economy unless there is a valid concern for economics of scale or patent innovation. "Rent seeking" refers to using resources to gain unearned income, such as monopoly rights. "Free riders" are those who refuse to pay into a social fund (for example, for road building and repair) but nevertheless use those investments.

23. Smith, *The Theory of Moral Sentiments*, op. cit., p. 65; emphasis added.

24. Smith notes that "if any one has a talent for making bows and arrows better than his neighbors he will at first make presents of them, and in return get presents of their game. . . . different genius is not the foundation of this disposition to barter. . . . The real foundation of it is that principle to persuade which so much prevails in human nature." *Lectures on Jurisprudence.* R. L. Meek, D. D. Raphael, and P. G. Stein, eds. Glasgow edition (Indianapolis, IN: Liberty Fund, 1982), p. 493.

25. Smith, *The Theory of Moral Sentiments*, op. cit., p. 173.

26. Smith, *The Wealth of Nations*, op. cit., p. 454.

27. Cited in Edmund L. Andrews, "Greenspan Concedes Error on Regulation," *New York Times*, October 24, 2008.

28. Smith, *The Wealth of Nations*, op. cit., p. 324.

29. See Jacob Viner, "Adam Smith and Laissez Faire," in J. M. Clark et al., *Adam Smith, 1776–1926* (Chicago: University of Chicago Press, 1928).

CHAPTER 10

1. Marco F. H. Schmidt and Jessica A. Summerville, "Fairness Expectations and Altruistic Sharing in 15-Month Old Human Infants," *Public Library of Science Journal* (October 7, 2011); available at www.plosone.org/article/info%3Adoi%2F10.1371%2Fjournal.pone.0023223

2. Sarah F. Brosnan, "An Evolutionary Perspective on Morality," *Journal of Economic Behavior & Organization* 77(1) (2011): pp. 23–30.

3. For a biological presentation, see David Sloan Wilson and Edward O. Wilson, "Rethinking the Theoretical Foundations of Sociobiology," *The Quarterly Review of Biology* 82(4) (2007): pp. 327–348.

4. Franklin D. Roosevelt, Second inaugural address, January 1937. Retrieved from www.bartleby.com/124/pres50.html.

5. Communist systems are also rife with corruption and hypocrisy, as captured by George Orwell's *Animal Farm* (New York: Signet Classics, [1945] 1996), p. 118: "All animals are equal, but some animals are more equal than others."

6. A third concept is "general justice," which deals with the obligations of an individual to the community. President John F. Kennedy extoled this form in his inauguration speech on January 20, 1961: "Ask not what your country has done for you, ask what you have done for your country." Retrieved from www.bartleby.com/124/pres56.html.

7. Smith, *The Wealth of Nations*, op. cit., p. 83.

8. In this passage Smith attacks woolen manufacturers, who want to establish a monopoly in finished products by outlawing imports, as well as a monopoly in inputs by outlawing exports of raw wool. *The Wealth of Nations*, op. cit., p. 654.

9. See one of King's last addresses, "Where Do We Go From Here?" (1968); available at http://mlk-kpp01.stanford.edu/index.php/kingpapers/article/where_do_we_go_from_here/.

10. Smith, *The Wealth of Nations*, op. cit., p. 96.

11. His cousin, President Theodore Roosevelt, had previously campaigned on the populist creed of a "Square Deal."

12. The World Bank, *The East Asia Miracle* (Washington, DC, 1993). China is a notable exception, with rising inequality with growth.

13. *The Economist*, October 13, 2012, p. 13.

14. This is also the complaint of Thomas Jefferson, who in the Declaration of Independence argued for a new set of rules. Jefferson's stance was incongruous: America's independence would eliminate Britain's trade monopoly and raise prices received by Virginia's tobacco exporters; at the same time, slaves would continue to produce the tobacco under the laws of bondage.

15. See Richard A. Posner, "Utilitarianism, Economics, and Legal Theory," op. cit.

16. Vilfredo Pareto, *Manual of Political Economy*, op. cit., particularly his introduction and p. 261. For the development of Pareto's ideas, see Luigino Bruni and Francesco Guala, "Vilfredo Pareto and the Epistemological Foundations of Choice Theory," *History of Political Economy* 33(1)(2001): pp. 21–49.

17. Robbins, *An Essay on the Nature and Significance of Economic Science*, op. cit.

18. In addition to Pareto, the formal model was elucidated by John Hicks and R. G. D. Allen, "A Reconsideration of the Theory of Value," *Economica* 1(1) (1934): pp. 52–76.

19. Arnold Harberger demonstrated that distributional weights could be used in standard policy analyses, but he was ultimately unsatisfied with this prospect. Arnold C. Harberger, "On the Use of Distributional Weights in Social Cost-Benefit Analysis," *The Journal of Political Economy* 86(2) (Part 2, April 1978): pp. S87–S120.

20. I. M. D. Little, *A Critique of Welfare Theory* (Oxford, UK: Oxford University Press, [1950] 2003).

21. E. J. Mishan, *Cost–Benefit Analysis: An Informal Introduction* (London: Unwin Hyman, 1988), p. 170.

22. John Bates Clark, *The Distribution of Wealth: A Theory of Wages, Interest and Profits* (New York: The Macmillan Company, [1899] 1908), p. 1; retrieved from the Library of Economics and Liberty, www.econlib.org/library/Clark/clkDWo.html. This conclusion is mathematically possible only under "constant returns to scale," a special circumstance in which, as the productive inputs of labor, capital, and land grow by some proportion, the output produced also grows by that exact proportion. If there are decreasing or increasing returns to scale, however, the payments to factors of production exceed or fall short of the total output, respectively, and the marginal productivity theory of distribution cannot be binding.

23. Alison Wood Brooks, Laura Huang, Sarah Wood Kearney, and Fiona E. Murray, "Investors Prefer Entrepreneurial Ventures Pitched By Attractive Men," *Proceedings of the National Academy of Sciences of the United States of America*, PNAS 2014: 13212021111VI-201321202 (2014).

24. For an analysis of the economic effects of racial discrimination against African Americans in the modern U.S. South, see Gavin Wright's, *Sharing the Prize: The Economics of the Civil Rights Revolution in the American South* (Cambridge, MA: Belknap Press, 2013).

25. Smith, *The Wealth of Nations*, op. cit., p. 84; edited for American spelling.

26. Daron Acemoglu and James A. Robinson, "Economics versus Politics: Pitfalls of Policy Advice," *Journal of Economic Perspectives* 27(2) (2013): pp. 173–192.

27. Nicholas N. Capaldi and Theodore Roosevelt Malloch, *America's Spiritual Capital* (South Bend, IN: St. Augustine's Press, 2012).

28. The value of capital can either be measured by production costs (which have a time horizon of construction) or by the present value of the future output created (which assumes a rate of interest). One cannot determine the value of capital without preknowing the interest rate, which is the return on capital. This is known as the "Cambridge capital controversy" of the late 1950s and 1960s. See Avi J. Cohen and G. C. Harcourt, "Whatever Happened to the Cambridge Capital Theory Controversies?" *Journal of Economic Perspectives* 17(1) (2003): pp. 199–214.

29. A. Samuelson, "A Summing Up," *The Quarterly Journal of Economics* 80(4) (1966): pp. 568–583.

30. The figures are even more striking for the median male worker, whose compensation remains essentially stagnant at its 1973 level. "Median" means that half the workers are above and half are below this reference point. Data are from Lawrence Mishel, "The

Wedges between Productivity and Median Compensation Growth," Economic Policy Institute, April 26, 2012; available at www.epi.org/publication/ib330-productivity-vs-compensation/.

CHAPTER 11

1. See Walter Isaacson, *Steve Jobs* (New York: Simon & Schuster, 2011).

2. See Mariana Mazzucato, *The Entrepreneurial State: Debunking Public vs. Private Sector Myths* (New York: Anthem Press, 2013).

3. Information externalities exist when knowledge is transferred without price, such as when an academic researcher presents a conference paper that shares data and methods of discovery. The audience receives a benefit that was not paid for (a positive externality). Computer software firms cluster in Silicon Valley to maximize knowledge spillovers.

4. Smith, *Wealth of Nations*, op. cit., pp. 28–29.

5. Robert W. Fogel, *The Fourth Great Awakening and the Future of Egalitarianism* (Chicago: The University of Chicago Press, 2000), p. 178.

6. The World Bank Development Indicators on-line, data for 2011; retrieved from http://databank.worldbank.org/data/.

7. Richard D. Kahlenberg, "Are Admissions Preferences for Men OK?" *Chronicle of Higher Education*, March 17, 2011.

8. Eva Kittay, *Love's Labor: Essays on Women, Equality and Dependency* (New York: Routledge, 1998), p. xi.

9. Raj Chetty, Nathaniel Hendren, Patrick Kline, and Emmanuel Saez, "Where Is the Land of Opportunity? The Geography of Intergenerational Mobility in the United States," The Equality of Opportunity Project working paper; retrieved on October 24, 2014, from www.equality-of-opportunity.org/.

10. This is the claim by Thomas Piketty in, *Capital in the Twenty-First Century*, translated by Arthur Goldhammer (Cambridge, MA: Harvard University Press, 2014).

11. James J. Heckman, "Schools, Skills, and Synapses," *Economic Inquiry* 46(3) (2008): p. 314.

12. John Rawls, *A Theory of Justice*, revised edition (Cambridge, MA: Harvard University Press, [1971] 1999).

13. As noted in Chapter 2, the act utilitarian framework is open to such charges; the rule utilitarian ethic would not permit murder.

14. Adapted from Rawls, *A Theory of Justice*, op. cit., p. 266.

15. Nozick, *Anarchy, State, and Utopia*, op. cit.

16. Michael Walzer, *Spheres of Justice: A Defense of Pluralism and Equality* (New York: Basic Books, 1983), p. 8.

17. The terms *freedom* and *liberty* are used interchangeably in this text. See Isaiah Berlin, "Two Concepts of Liberty," in *Four Essays on Liberty* (New York: Oxford University Press, 1970); and "Positive and Negative Liberty," *Stanford Encyclopedia of Philosophy*; available at http://plato.stanford.edu/entries/liberty-positive-negative/.

18. Amartya Sen, *Inequality Reexamined* (Cambridge, MA: Harvard University Press, 1992).

19. Amartya Sen, *Development as Freedom* (New York: Alfred A. Knopf, 1999).

20. Once a society has achieved basic capabilities for all citizens, the issue of distribution beyond that point would still need to be solved.

21. Martha Nussbaum, *Women and Human Development: The Capabilities Approach* (Cambridge, UK: Cambridge University Press, 2000), p. 1.

22. The World Bank, *World Development Report 2013* (Washington, DC: The World Bank, 2012). Data are in constant dollars for 2005. A drop in Chinese poverty was a key factor in this decline.

23. See: *World Development Report 2006: Equity and Development* (Washington, DC: The World Bank, 2005).

24. See United Nations Development Programme; retrieved on July 27, 2011, from http://hdr.undp.org/en/data/build.

25. Amartya Sen, "More Than 100 Million Women Are Missing," *New York Review of Books* 37(20) (December 20, 1990).

26. Derek Parfit, *Reasons and Persons* (Oxford, UK: Oxford University Press, 1984).

27. For example, consider this choice: Would you prefer to receive $100 today or $100 in one year? With an interest rate (r) of 10 percent, the $100 invested today would be worth $110 a year from now. By contrast, $100 received in one year is only worth $90.90 in today's money (because $90.90 could be invested at 10 percent and produce $100 in one year). The present value (PV) formula discounts the value of future money payouts (FV_t) when compared to the present: $PV = FV_t / (1 + r)^t$, where t is the number of time periods in the future.

28. $PV = FV_t / (1 + r)^t = \$100b / (1.1)^{50} = \$852$ million. Said differently, $850 million invested today could buy $100 billion worth of cancer treatment in fifty years.

29. $PV = FV_t / (1 + r)^t = \$100b / (1.05)^{50} = \$8.7$ billion. As discussed in Chapters 5 and 6, there are other important considerations to policy making in addition to cost–benefit calculations.

30. Nicholas Stern, *The Economics of Climate Change* (Cambridge, UK: Cambridge University Press, [2006] 2007). This is also available from the British HM Treasury website at http://web.archive.org/web/20081211182219/http://www.hm-treasury.gov.uk/stern_review_final_report.htm.

31. William D. Nordhaus, "A Review of the *Stern Review on the Economics of Climate Change*," *Journal of Economic Literature* 45(3) (2007): pp. 686–702.

32. Oil reserves estimate the amount that can be brought to the surface given current technology and economic conditions. See Index Mundi, "World Crude Oil Reserves by Year," retrieved from www.indexmundi.com/energy.aspx?product=oil&graph=reserves.

33. Joseph A. Schumpeter, *Capitalism, Socialism, and Democracy,*, op. cit., p. 118.

34. Robert J. Gordon, "Is U.S. Economic Growth Over? Faltering Innovation Confronts the Six Headwinds," NBER Working Paper No. 18315 (August 2012); and Tyler Cowen, *Average Is Over: Powering America Beyond the Age of the Great Stagnation* (New York: Dutton, 2013).

35. United Nations, *World Population Prospects: The 2012 Revision* (New York: United Nations, 2013); available at http://esa.un.org/unpd/wpp/index.htm.

36. Garrett Hardin, "The Tragedy of the Commons," *Science*, 162 (1968): pp. 1243–1248.

37. Ostrom, a political scientist, won the 2009 Nobel Memorial Prize in Economics for her work on local governance in the commons. See Elinor Ostrom, "Collective Action and the Evolution of Social Norms," *Journal of Economic Perspectives* 14(3) (2000): pp. 137–158.

38. Ralph Waldo Emerson, Essay on *Nature* (1836); available at http://oregonstate.edu/instruct/phl302/texts/emerson/nature-contents.html.

39. This is a paraphrase of Aldo Leopold: "To keep every cog and wheel is the first precaution of intelligent tinkering." Cited in Luna B. Leopold (ed.), "Conservation," *Round River* (Oxford, UK: Oxford University Press, 1966), pp. 146–147.

40. The United Nations World Commission on Environment and Development, *Our Common Future* (New York: Oxford University Press, 1987), p. 43.

41. Nordhaus, op. cit., p. 693.

42. Fogel, *The Fourth Great Awakening*, op. cit., p. 178.

CHAPTER 12

Some of the ideas in this chapter were outlined in "Economics within a Pluralist Ethical Tradition," Presidential address to the Association for Social Economics, Philadelphia, January 2014, available in the *Review of Social Economy* 72(4)(December 2014): pp. 417–435.

1. Adapted from Edward Fullbrook, "To Observe or Not to Observe: Complementary Pluralism in Physics and Economics," *Real World Economics Review* 62 (2012).

2. Isaiah Berlin, *The Hedgehog and the Fox: An Essay on Tolstoy's View of History*, 2nd edition (Princeton, NJ: Princeton University Press, 2013 [1953] 2013).

3. This treatment uses simplified terminology compared to what philosophers might use. See "Value Pluralism" in the *Stanford Encyclopedia of Philosophy*; available at http://plato.stanford.edu/entries/value-pluralism/.

4. John Stuart Mill, *The Principles of Political Economy with Some of Their Applications to Social Philosophy* (New York: D. Appleton and Co., 1895), p. 135. For a similar argument, see Friedman, *The Moral Consequences of Economic Growth*, op. cit.; and Gintis, Bowles, Boyd, and Fehr, eds., *Moral Sentiments and Material Interests*, op. cit.

5. Isaiah Berlin, *The Crooked Timber of Humanity: Chapters in the History of Ideas*, 2nd edition, Henry Hardy, ed. (Princeton, NJ: Princeton University Press, 2013), p. 50.

6. Rendigs Fels and Stephen Buckles, *Casebook of Economic Problems and Policies: Practice in Thinking*, 5th edition (St. Paul, MN: West Publishing, 1981). A similar approach is that of "prudent pragmatism," found in William Bluhm and Robert Heineman, *Ethics and Public Policy: Methods and Cases* (Upper Saddle River, NJ: Prentice-Hall, 2007).

7. Peter J. Hammond, "Ethics, Distribution, Incentives, Efficiency and Markets," *Social and Ethical Aspects of Economics*, 2nd edition (Vatican City: Pontifical Council for Justice and Peace, 2011), p. 80.

8. Robert F. Garnett Jr., "Rethinking the Pluralist Agenda in Economics Education," *International Review of Economics Education* 8(2) (2009): pp. 58–71; and Andy Denis, "Pluralism in Economics Education," *International Review of Economics Education* 8(2) (2009): pp. 6–22.

9. William J. Barber, "Reconfigurations in American Academic Economics: A General Practitioner's Perspective," *Daedelus* (Winter 1997): p. 98.

10. Ronald Coase, "Saving Economics From Economists," *Harvard Business Review*, December 2012.

11. Edward Fullbrook, ed., *Real-World Economics Review*, available at: www.paecon.net/PAEReview/.

12. For a more in-depth analysis, see Jonathan B. Wight, "The Ethical Economist: Duty and Virtue in the Scientific Process," in *The Handbook of Professional Economic Ethics*, George DeMartino and Deirdre McCloskey, eds. (Oxford, UK: Oxford University Press, forthcoming), on which this section is based.

13. For discussion see Joseph A. Schumpeter, *History of Economic Analysis* (New York: Oxford University Press, 1954); and Hilary Putnam and Vivian Walsh (eds.), *The End of Value-Free Economics* (London: Routledge 2011).

14. This includes an analysis of Type I (false positive) and Type II (false negative) errors.

15. Charles Ferguson, "The Director of 'Inside Job' Replies," *Economists' Forum*, October 14, 2010; retrieved on March 23, 2012, from http://blogs.ft.com/economistsforum/2010/10/the-director-of-inside-job-replies/#axzz1UJ5C49lj.

16. F. S. Mishkin and T. T. Herbertsson, *Financial Stability in Iceland* (Reykjavik: Iceland Chamber of Commerce, May 2006); retrieved on March 23, 2012, from www.economicdisasterarea.com/wp-content/uploads/2010/08/Tryggvi-Herbertsson-Friedrich-Mishkin-Financial-Stability-in-Iceland.pdf.

17. Cited in Ronald Coase, *Essays on Economics and Economists* (Chicago: University of Chicago Press, 1994), p. 31.

18. George F. DeMartino, *The Economist's Oath: On the Need for and Content of Professional Economic Ethics* (New York: Oxford University Press, 2011).

19. To demonstrate this, a *Science* reporter sent an obviously fake research paper on a cancer "wonder drug" to 304 journals. Despite obvious flaws in methodology and interpretation, more than half the journals agreed to publish it, often for a hefty fee. See John Bohannon, "Who's Afraid of Peer Review?" *Science* 4 (October 2013)(342)(6154): pp. 60–65.

20. In 2013, a graduate student attempted to reproduce a famous paper by Reinhart and Rogoff that purported to show how high debt levels constrain growth. Numerous methodological errors were uncovered. See Thomas Herndon, Michael Ash, and Robert Pollin, "Does High Public Debt Consistently Stifle Economic Growth? A Critique of Reinhart and Rogoff," *Political Economy Research Institute—Working Paper Series*, No. 322 (April 15, 2013). The original paper is by Carmen M. Reinhart and Kenneth S. Rogoff, "Growth in a Time of Debt," *American Economic Review* 100 (2) (2010): pp. 573–578.

21. As late as 2004, top journals in the field did not require authors to submit their raw data and the program code employed in testing the model. Even after a data disclosure rule was instituted, many journal editors have not enforced it.

22. W. Enders and G. A. Hoover, "Whose Line Is It? Plagiarism in Economics," *Journal of Economic Literature* 42(3) (2004): pp. 487–493.

23. J. A. List et al., "Academic Economists Behaving Badly? A Survey on Three Areas of Unethical Behavior," *Economic Inquiry* 39(1) (2001): pp. 162–170. Academic dishonesty may be proliferating, however, because of the profits to be made in "plagiarism, invented research and fake journals" that in 2013 was estimated to be worth $150 million ("Looks Good on Paper," *The Economist*, September 28, 2013).

24. American Institute of Certified Public Accountants, "Code of Professional Conduct"; retrieved on April 5, 2012, from www.aicpa.org/Research/Standards/Code ofConduct/Pages/et_50.aspx.

25. Frank Knight, *Freedom and Reform* (New York: Harper and Brothers, 1947), p. 244.

26. The first quote is from Richard Whately, a nineteenth-century theologian. The second quote is from John Kay. Both are cited in John Kay, "Being Ethical in Business Is Not as Simple as 'Doing the Right Thing,'" *Financial Times*, November 6, 2013.

27. Sen, *On Ethics and Economics*, op. cit., p. 76; emphasis added.

28. Arrow, "Invaluable Goods," op. cit., p. 765.

29. Robert H. Frank, Thomas Gilovich, and Dennis T. Regan, "Does Studying Economics Inhibit Cooperation?" *Journal of Economic Perspectives* 7 (Spring 1993):

pp. 159–171. See also Julie A. Nelson, "Poisoning the Well, or How Economic Theory Damages," *The Handbook of Professional Economic Ethics*, George DeMartino and Deirdre McCloskey, eds. (Oxford, UK: Oxford University Press, forthcoming).

30. The following section draws on Martin Calkins and Jonathan B. Wight, "The Ethical Lacunae in Friedman's Concept of the Manager," op. cit.

31. Milton Friedman, "The Social Responsibility of Business Is To Increase Its Profits," *New York Times Sunday Magazine*, September 12, 1970, p. 32.

32. Smith, *The Theory of Moral Sentiments*, op. cit., p. 241.

33. Ibid.

34. For a more elaborate defense of stakeholder theory, see Robert Phillips, *Stakeholder Theory and Organizational Ethics* (San Francisco: Berrett-Koehler Publishers, 2003).

35. Smith, *The Wealth of Nations*, op. cit., p. 454.

36. Smith, *The Theory of Moral Sentiments*, op. cit., p. 9.

37. Patricia H. Werhane, *Moral Imagination and Management Decision Making*, The Ruffin Series in Business Ethics (New York: Oxford University Press, 1999).

38. McCloskey, *The Bourgeois Virtues*, op. cit., p. 128.

39. Robert Frank, *What Price the Moral High Ground? Ethical Dilemmas in Competitive Environments* (Princeton, NJ: Princeton University Press, 2004).

40. The mechanism for this could be the release of oxytocin (Chapter 8).

41. See, for example, Kim Cameron, David Bright, and Arran Caza, "Exploring the Relationships between Organizational Virtuousness and Performance," *American Behavioral Scientist* 47(6) (2004): pp. 1–24; read also the use of moral sentiments by the founder of Whole Foods, John Mackay, "Rethinking the Social Responsibility of Business: Putting Customers Ahead of Investors," *Reason* 37(5) (October 2005): pp. 28–32. Some industries may not be as good candidates for a virtue ethics approach (for example, some aspects of finance).

42. Gary S. Becker and Julio Jorge Elías, "Introducing Incentives in the Market for Live and Cadavderic Organ Donations," *Journal of Economic Perspectives* 21(3) (2007): pp. 3–24. Becker won the Nobel Prize in 1992.

43. For elaboration, see Laslo Zolnai, *Responsible Decision Making* (New Brunswick, NJ: Transaction Publishers, 2008).

44. Judge Richard Posner would object to this line of argument, noting that the thief has not *demonstrated* the hypothetical value through bidding in the market. But Posner's objection seems contrived: Joe could indeed be *willing and able* to pay $300,000 if he had to, but if an opportune moment arises to steal it, Joe maximizes his consumer surplus by getting it for free. Posner himself allows for this when he imagines someone of financial means facing starvation in the woods who breaks into an unoccupied cabin to steal food. The thief, in this case the rich person, has wealth and willingness to pay but the transaction costs for locating the cabin's owner are high, and Posner argues that efficiency is enhanced in this situation when food is stolen. See Richard A. Posner, "Utilitarianism, Economics, and Legal Theory," *The Journal of Legal Studies* 8(1)(1979): pp. 103–140.

45. Amartya Sen, "Rationality and Social Choice," op. cit. p. 12.

46. Kenneth J. Arrow, "Gifts and Exchanges," op. cit., p. 347; emphasis added.

47. Robert H. Frank, Thomas Gilovich, and Dennis T. Regan, "Does Studying Economics Inhibit Cooperation?" op. cit.

48. F. A. Hayek, *The Trend of Economic Thinking: Essays on Political Economists and Economic History, vol. II, The Collected Works of F. A. Hayek*, W. W. Bartley III and

S. Kresge, eds. (Chicago, IL: University of Chicago, 1991), p. 42. George Stigler, another Nobel economist, wryly (and perhaps unintentionally) promoted the value of pluralism when he quipped, "If we only know one model, we confuse it with the truth." Quote attributed to Stigler by his student, David M. Levy. Personal correspondence, August 1, 2011.

49. Robert Nozick, *Anarchy, State and Utopia* (New York: Basic Books, 1974), p. xii. I am indebted to Jason Brennan for bringing this quote to my attention.

50. See, for example, James Halteman and Edd Noell, *Reckoning with Markets: Moral Reflection in Economics* (New York: Oxford University Press, 2012).

51. John Kay, *Culture and Prosperity: The Truth about Markets—Why Some Nations Are Rich but Most Remain Poor* (New York: HarperBusiness, 2004), p. 355.

52. In *The Wealth of Nations* (op. cit., p. 303) Smith notes: "The undertaker of a great manufacture who, by the home markets being suddenly laid open to the competition of foreigners, should be obliged to abandon his trade, would no doubt suffer very considerably. . . . The equitable regard, therefore, to his interest requires that changes of this kind should never be introduced suddenly, but slowly, gradually, and after a very long warning."

53. Davis, "Ethics and Religion," op. cit., p. 1098.

54. Robert L. Heilbroner, *The Worldly Philosophers: The Lives, Times and Ideas of the Great Economic Thinkers*, 7th edition (New York: Touchstone Books, [1953] 1999).

Index

84–88, 89–91, 92, 96, 97, 100–101, 226–27; ethical assumptions in, 77, 89–91, 92, 93, 96; in ignition-switch case, 14–15; and Kaldor-Hicks criterion, 21, 82, 84, 88, 96–97, 226–27; and nonpecuniary costs and benefits, 84–88; and Pareto test, 81–82, 96; and public policies, 76, 77, 78, 81–82, 84–93, 96, 226–27, 241n7, 255n29. *See also* external costs

Countrywide, 168

courage, 49–50, 51, 54, 104, 129, 159, 225

credit default swaps (CDSs), 167, 169

credit rating agencies, 167

culture, 25–26

Daly, Herman E.: *For the Common Good*, 236n8

Darley, John, 53

Darwin, Charles: on cooperation, 154, 176; *The Descent of Man*, 6, 249n16; on ethical norms, 249n16; on moral capabilities, 6; on natural selection, 249n16; *Origin of Species*, 154

Davis, Scott: on pluralism, 230

deadweight loss, 73, 75, 95, 240n18, 244n23

death penalty, 132

debt crisis of 1982, 167

demand: demand curves, 63, 64, 65–66, 69, 70–71, 111, 239n12, 240n16; lack of effective demand, 62, 63; law of, 65; and marginal benefit of consumption, 63–65

DeMartino, George: *The Economist's Oath*, 218

deontology, 38, 55

derivatives, financial, 167–68

dictator game, 148–49, 153–54

distributive justice, 24, 34, 179–82

dopamine, 151

dot-com bust, 169

due process, 89–90, 92

duty, 3, 4, 8, 116, 123, 150, 211, 217, 224, 238n24; Kant on, 13, 15, 36,

38, 40–44, 123, 142–43, 213, 221, 227–28; and motivational crowding out, 127–28; relationship to rights, 43–46, 89; relationship to social groups, 134, 136, 137; unwritten duties in sports, 37–38

duty- and rule-based ethics, 12–14, 38–46, 78; as absolutist, 36, 38, 43–44; and business operation, 223–25, 229; and cost-benefit analysis, 89, 91; criticisms of, 41–42, 43–44, 45, 48, 51; and ethical pluralism, 18, 21–22, 145, 210, 211, 212, 213, 226, 228; and freedom, 25; and markets, 132–33; motivation in, 3, 40, 42, 126; and natural rights, 43–46; vs. outcome-based ethics, 15–16, 34, 38, 39–41, 42, 47, 54–55, 56; religious rules and duties/divine command theory, 12, 13, 14, 15, 38–40, 44, 45, 54, 123, 132–33, 221, 235nn23,24, 237n3; and research in economics, 220–22; unwritten duties in sports, 37–38; vs. virtue-based ethics, 15–16, 37, 38, 40, 43, 48, 51, 55, 56. *See also* Kant, Immanuel

econometrics, 20, 52, 88

economic agents, 6, 7, 11, 83, 106–7, 128, 164, 212, 222–23, 228; as *Homo economicus*, 4, 19, 154, 155, 165, 210

economic efficiency, 3, 56, 59–60, 74–75, 98–99, 106, 118, 183–84, 210, 225, 229, 236n27; as conflicting with other goals, 25, 99, 107–10, 141, 214, 244n18; dynamic vs. static, 109–10, 213, 214–15, 225–26; efficient market hypothesis, 168–70; as ethical concept, 93–95, 96, 119; Kaldor-Hicks criterion of, 21, 82, 84, 88, 96–97, 226–27, 241n8; as maximization of economic surplus/value, 11, 18, 20, 35, 60, 69–71, 74, 75–76, 80, 81, 86, 89–91, 99–100, 108–9, 110, 116, 138–39, 213, 223;

economic efficiency (*continued*)
  vs. medical efficiency, 108–9; Pareto
    test of, 21, 77–80, 79, 81–82, 86, 92,
    96, 100, 110, 141; and public
    policies, 214; relationship to fairness,
    185–88; relationship to greed, 165
economic growth, 26, 61, 109, 112–13,
    144, 162, 180–81, 194–95, 257n20;
    and absolute living standards, 202; in
    China, 25, 252n12; and freedom,
    24–25, 235n4; Smith on, 153, 171,
    174, 213, 215, 230; trickle down
    theory, 182–83
economic justice, 24, 175, 176–88; as
    equality of opportunity, 176, 179,
    182–83, 189, 190, 192–203, 197,
    208–9; as fair outcome, 24, 178,
    179–82, 188, 208, 209; as fair
    process, 24, 174, 178–79, 181–82,
    188, 192, 208, 209, 227; just price
    theory, 140–41; pluralistic approach
    to, 209
economics: defined, 60, 115–16, 184,
    246n46; research in, 216–22, 229,
    257n23, 257nn20,21
economic surplus/value, 72–73, 227; vs.
    gross domestic product (GDP),
    245n33; maximization of, 11, 18, 20,
    23–24, 50, 51, 60, 62, 69–71, 74,
    75–76, 80, 81, 86, 89–91, 99–100,
    108–9, 110, 116, 138–39, 213, 223;
    quantitative measurement of, 94–95,
    110–11; vs. total economic benefit,
    65–66, 239n12
ecosystems, 207
education, 202–3
efficient market hypothesis, 168–70
Ely, Richard T., 190
Emerson, Ralph Waldo: on consistency,
    22; on man and nature, 206
eminent domain, 86–88, 89, 97
emotional bonding, 146
emotional commitment, 7
emotional equilibrium, 155–56
empathy, 152–53
Enlightenment, 40, 44–45, 51, 153
entrepreneurship, 71

environmental economists, 88
environmental outcomes, 27, 35, 204–5,
    206–8, 209
Environmental Protection Agency,
    234n16
Epicureanism, 30
equality, 143, 177, 178, 236n19; and
    freedom, 214; moral equality, 29,
    31–32, 33–34; of opportunity, 176,
    179, 182–83, 189, 190, 192–203, 197,
    208–9; preference for, 149–50; in
    social groups, 136; substantive
    equality, 192–93, 199–201. *See also*
    inequality
equilibrium in markets, 65, 68–74, 77,
    78–79, 80, 96, 130, 162–64
ethical egoism, 13, 54, 146; in
    corporations, 11; defined, 5; as greed,
    148, 157, 159, 160, 161, 165–66, 168,
    170, 171, 172; Rand on, 165, 175;
    and Smith, 6, 157
ethical pluralism, 17–19, 21–22, 37,
    54–56, 145, 209; and business
    operation, 223, 224; definition of
    pluralism, 210; and economic
    research, 216–22; horizontal
    pluralism, 55, 210, 212–14, 216, 226,
    228; role in analysis of public
    policies, 210, 213, 214, 221, 225–50;
    vertical pluralism, 54–55, 210,
    211–12, 216, 221, 228
ethical role models, 221
Ethics and Public Policy Center, The,
    237n5
ethics defined, 4
experimental economics, 20, 88, 146,
    147–50, 190
exports, 180–81, 251n17
external costs, 130, 132, 202, 206, 207,
    240n19, 244n16, 244n20; pollution,
    12, 62, 75, 100, 235n2, 236n27,
    239n6

fairness, 134, 142, 148, 156, 184, 213;
    and biology, 176–77; of distribution,
    79–80, 136–37; instinctual desire for,
    246n45; just price theory, 140–41; of

needs vs. wants, 111–12
neoclassical economics, 50, 61–69, 88,
    93, 94, 98, 207–8, 213; economic
    justice in, 183–88; and government
    intervention, 75, 96; marginal
    productivity theory of distribution,
    185–89; and Pareto test, 78; value of
    lives in, 118
neuroscience, 146, 147, 150–52
Newell, John Philip, 235n29
Newton, Isaac, 153
Nike suppliers case, 19
Nordhaus, William D., 205
normative economics, 11–12, 63, 75;
    defined, 9; as instrumental theory
    of well-being, 99–101; vs. positive
    economics, 8–9, 20, 59, 163, 185,
    209, 210, 215
normative ethics: defined, 8; relationship
    to economics, 9
North, Douglass: on institutions, 18
Nozick, Robert: *Anarchy, State, and
    Utopia*, 45, 197–98; on individual
    liberty, 144, 197–98; on last words,
    228; on pleasure and pain, 32; on
    Rawls, 197–98
nuclear waste depositories, 127–28
Nussbaum, Martha: on capability,
    201, 202; *Women and Human
    Development*, 201

Occam's razor, 34–35
Occupy Wall Street, 175
oil reserves, 205, 255n32
oligopoly, 75, 240n21
opportunism, 221
opportunity costs of production, 67, 68,
    70, 126, 135, 182, 239n6, 240n13,
    244n17, 246n36; and profit, 71, 72
Orwell's *Animal Farm*, 252n5
Ostrom, Elinor, 128, 206, 243n33,
    255n37
Otteson, James R.: *Adam Smith's
    Marketplace of Life*, 238n32
outcome-based ethics (consequentialism),
    11–12, 23–26, 76, 123; criticisms of,
    30, 31–33, 36, 40–41, 48, 51, 91,

195–96; decision making based on
    outcomes, 26, 27; vs. duty- and
    rule-based ethics, 15–16, 34, 38,
    39–41, 42, 47, 54–55, 56; and
    economic outcomes, 23–24, 27, 59;
    and ethical pluralism, 17–18, 21–22,
    145, 210, 211, 212, 213, 228; and
    general good, 27; and modeling a
    business, 222–25; and political
    outcomes, 24–25, 27, 35–36; possible
    outcomes, 23–26, 27, 55, 59–60; and
    research in economics, 217–20; vs.
    virtue-based ethics, 14, 40, 48, 50,
    51, 56, 221. *See also* utilitarianism
outsourcing of jobs, 26, 35, 141
overproduction, 73
oxytocin, 146, 150–52, 258n40

Pareto, Vilfredo, 94, 239n3, 253n18; on
    democracy, 241n4; *The Mind and
    Society*, 241n4; on *ophelimity*,
    242n29; Pareto efficiency test, 21,
    77–80, 79, 81–82, 86, 92, 96, 100,
    110, 141; on utility, 184
Parfit, Derek: *Reasons and Persons*,
    203
patents, 109, 225–26, 244n23
paternalism, 102–3, 105, 117, 118, 144,
    174, 243n4
path dependency, 195, 198, 206
Paul, Rand, 165
Paul, St., 228
peak-load pricing, 138–39
pharmaceutical advertising, 105
Pigou, Arthur, 94, 239n3; on *desiredness*,
    242n29; on economic welfare, 61,
    239n4; on interpersonal comparisons
    of utility, 183–84; *The Economics of
    Welfare*, 61
Piketty, Thomas: *Capital in the Twenty-
    First Century*, 253n10; on
    inheritance, 253n10
plagiarism, 219
pleasure and pain, 14, 25, 40–41, 184,
    213, 239n5; Bentham on, 12, 28–30,
    114; measure of, 28–29, 32; Mill on,
    30–31, 32–33, 48, 55, 114; Nozick

Science, 257n19

Scientific Revolution, 40

self-control, 211, 218–19; Smith on, 157, 159, 160, 224; in virtue-based ethics, 14, 36, 47, 49, 53, 104, 160, 221

self-interest, 7, 149, 152, 153, 216, 227, 228; as enlightened, 5–6, 8, 19, 49, 117–18, 146–47, 197, 218, 222, 249n11; vs. greed, 159, 171, 172; vs. selfishness, 5; Smith on, 5–6, 8, 16, 146, 157, 159, 170, 171–72, 173; vs. truth seeking, 220

selfishness, 6, 8, 156–57; vs. self-interest, 5. *See also* ethical egoism

Selten, Reinhardt, 243n33

Sen, Amartya, 215, 235n31, 243n33; on agency vs. well-being, 113–14; on capability, 199–201, 202, 203; on consequential analysis, 221; *Development as Freedom*, 200; on economic efficiency, 110; on equality, 199–200; on freedom, 200, 201; on functioning, 200; on Human Development Index (HDI), 95, 113; on interpersonal comparisons of utility, 111–12, 241n11; on Kaldor-Hicks criterion, 97; on needs vs. wants, 111–12; *On Ethics and Economics*, 110; on Pareto efficiency, 110; "The Possibility of Social Choice," 111–12; on poverty, 200; *Report by the Commission on the Measurement of Economic Performance and Social Progress*, 235n31; on rights and liberties, 227; on utility maximization, 16–17; on welfare indicators, 113

sensitivity analysis, 88

serotonin, 151

sex, 193

Shakespeare, William: *Hamlet*, 134; *Romeo and Juliet*, 158

Sharia law, 133

Shiller, Robert: *Irrational Exuberance*, 169

Silicon Valley, 253n3

Simon, Herbert, 243n33; on satisficing, 239n44

Simpson, O. J.: *If I Did It*, 3, 4

Singer, Peter: on global obligations, 32

slavery, 18–19, 29, 33, 52, 126, 145, 158, 178, 242n23, 252n14

Smith, Adam: on anonymity of big cities, 144; on arrogance, 169; on benevolence, 134, 159, 170; on collusion of employers, 186; on distributive justice, 179; on division of labor, 142; on economic growth, 153, 171, 174, 213, 215, 230; on economies of scale, 63; egalitarian ethic of, 192; on environmental circumstances, 192; on fellow feeling/sympathy, 155, 156–57, 158, 225; on financial markets, 173–74, 175; on free trade, 153, 230, 237n28, 259n52; on greed, 157, 166, 171, 172, 173–74, 175; vs. Hobbes, 155, 158; on honor, 171; on instincts, 154–59, 170, 172–73, 177; on institutions, 157–59, 165, 171, 172–73, 177, 211; on the invisible hand, 159, 160, 161, 170, 172–73, 186, 224, 240n2; on justice, 153, 156, 158, 159, 178, 179, 188, 213, 215, 223–24, 230; *Letters on Jurisprudence*, 251n24; on malevolence, 156, 159; on Mandeville, 166; on mercantilism, 173, 178, 183; and modern research, 146, 147–54, 159; on monopolies, 45, 153, 173, 178, 190, 252n8; on moral norms, 154–55, 157, 158, 171, 173, 211; on moral sentiments, 6, 8, 16, 17, 20, 48, 134, 146, 150, 151, 152–53, 155–56, 158, 211, 223–25; on natural rights, 44–45; on needs vs. wants, 111; on persuasion, 171, 251n24; on pin factory, 239n9; on pleasure and pain, 152–53, 157; on procedural justice, 178–79, 188; on progress, 160, 172–73; on property and labor, 44–45; on public policies, 170, 172, 174, 178, 179, 183, 198, 240n2, 251n21; on reason, 158;

CPSIA information can be obtained
at www.ICGtesting.com
Printed in the USA
LVOW07s1456120717
541113LV00001B/29/P